Revolting Prostitutes

Revolting Prostitutes

The Fight for Sex Workers' Rights

Molly Smith
and
Juno Mac

VERSO
London • New York

This edition published by Verso 2020
First published by Verso 2018
© Molly Smith and Juno Mac 2018, 2020

1 3 5 7 9 10 8 6 4 2

Verso
UK: 6 Meard Street, London W1F 0EG
US: 20 Jay Street, Suite 1010, Brooklyn, NY 11201
versobooks.com

Verso is the imprint of New Left Books

ISBN-13: 978–1–78663–361–3
ISBN-13: 978–1–78663–362–0 (UK EBK)
ISBN-13: 978–1–78663–363–7 (US EBK)

British Library Cataloguing in Publication Data
A catalogue record for this book is available from the British Library

Library of Congress Cataloging-in-Publication Data

Names: Smith, Molly, author. | Mac, Juno, author.
Title: Revolting prostitutes : the fight for sex workers' rights / Molly
  Smith and Juno Mac.
Description: London ; Brooklyn, NY : Verso, [2018] | Includes index.
Identifiers: LCCN 2018032847| ISBN 9781786633606 | ISBN 9781786633637
(ebook)
Subjects: LCSH: Prostitutes—Civil rights. | Prostitution—Government policy.
Classification: LCC HQ118 .S65 2018 | DDC 306.74—dc23
LC record available at https://lccn.loc.gov/2018032847

Typeset in Sabon by MJ & N Gavan, Truro, Cornwall
Printed in the UK by CPI Group

For Sharmus, Paula, Mariana, Daria, Jessica, Luciana, Tania, Gemma, Anneli, Annette, Romina, Emma, Rivka, Lenuta, Jasmine, Xiao Mei, Bonnie, Shirley

The women who are really being emulated and obsessed over in our culture now – strippers, porn stars, pinups – aren't even people. They are merely sexual personae, erotic dollies from the land of make-believe. In their performances, which is the only capacity in which we see these women we so fetishize, they don't even speak. As far as we know, they have no ideas, no feelings, no political beliefs, no relation-ships, no past, no future, no humanity.

– Ariel Levy

When you consider how expansive something like prostitution really is, it should be alarming that we rarely hear the actual voices of people who have firsthand experience in this industry. When I think about the relevance of prostitution in social movements as well as its stark exclusion from them, I cannot help but wonder about the com-pelling opportunity for linkage, about the aspects of radical social justice movements that parallel the prostitution rights movement, that of visibility, autonomy and equanimity from the ground up.

– Pluma Sumaq

Contents

Introduction

Sex workers are everywhere.[*] We are your neighbours. We brush past you on the street. Our kids go to the same schools as yours. We're behind you at the self-service checkout, with baby food and a bottle of Pinot Grigio. People who sell sex are in your staff cafeteria, your political party, your after-school club committee, your doctor's waiting room, your place of worship. Sex workers are incarcerated inside immigration detention centres, and sex workers are protesting outside them.

Although we are everywhere, most people know little about the reality of our lives. Sex workers are subject to a lot of curiosity and discussion in popular culture, journalism, and policy. When we are visible as workers – on the street, in signposted brothels, in digital spaces – our presence provokes disquiet. We are increasingly visible as workers in political spaces, and here too our presence provokes disquiet. Many people want to stop us from selling sex, or just ensure

---

[*] The term *sex work* was coined in 1978 by sex worker and activist Carol Leigh. The term *sex workers* refers to people who sell or trade their own sexual labour in exchange for a resource, which is often money but can also be drugs, alcohol, or shelter. Although the term *sex work* covers, by design, many different kinds of sexual labour – stripping and peepshows, porn work and camming, phone-sex chatlines and BDSM work – we primarily use it in this book to refer to activities traditionally understood as prostitution. Where another kind of sex work is meant, we will make that clear.

The sex workers' rights movement does not consider managers or bosses to be sex workers, and our usage is consistent with that understanding, which we share.

Sex worker is a political term, and therefore not all people in the sex trade may use it to openly identify themselves. When it is used, it generally indicates that the speaker thinks that selling sex is or can be work. It is therefore rejected by those who think that selling sex is not work.

they don't have to look at us. But we are notoriously hard to get rid of, at least through criminal law.

Prostitution is heavy with meaning and brings up deeply felt emotions. This is especially the case for people who have not sold sex, and who think of it in symbolic terms. The *idea* of prostitution serves as a lightning rod for questions about work, masculinity, class, bodies; about archetypal villainy and punishment; about who 'deserves' what; about what it means to live in a community; and about what it means to push some people outside that community's boundaries. Attitudes towards prostitution have always been strongly tied to questions of race, borders, migration, and national identity in ways which are sometimes overt but often hidden. Sex work is the vault in which society stores some of its keenest fears and anxieties.

Perhaps the most difficult questions raised by prostitution involve what it means to be a woman in a patriarchal society. Feminist writer Kate Millett notes feminist rhetoric suggesting 'that all women are prostitutes, that marriage is prostitution'.[1] Sex workers have long noted with ambivalence the interplay between prostitution as a site of metaphor and as an actual *workplace*. In 1977, the sex worker led collective PROS – Programme for Reform of the Law on Soliciting – wrote (in the iconic UK feminist magazine *Spare Rib*) that it wanted the women's liberation movement 'to think about the whole thing [prostitution] and discuss it, but not just *use* it', explaining that the women's movement has 'used the word *prostitute* in a really nasty way – about housewives, to sum up their idea of the exploited situation of women'.[2] They noted that this interest in the metaphorical uses of *prostitute* was not accompanied by much practical support for sex workers' efforts to tackle criminalisation.

In some ways, little has changed. Contemporary feminists' disapproval of prostitution remains unmoored from pragmatism. More political energy goes to obstructing sex work than to what is really needed, such as helping sex workers avoid prosecution, or ensuring viable alternative livelihoods that are more than respectable drudgery. As trans sex worker community leader Ceyenne Doroshow has said: 'If you don't want sex workers doing the work, sweetie, employ them! Employ them, have a solution!'[3]

Our concern is for the safety and the survival of people who sell sex. Like Doroshow and PROS before us, we are ultimately focused on the practical and material rather than the symbolic or metaphorical. Approaching sex work from this perspective provokes certain questions. What conditions best enable someone who wants to quit sex work to do so? What conditions lead people to sell sex, or make sex work their only opportunity for survival? What gives a sex worker more power in negotiating with an employer, and what reduces their power? All over the world, sex workers use strategies to stay safe: working with a friend in the next room, or in a small group on the street; visibly noting down a client's car number plate or asking for his ID, to show him that he is not anonymous. Can a sex worker call a colleague in as back-up if a client refuses to use a condom? What are the consequences of calling the police – or of being visible to them as a gaggle on the street? What does it mean for a sex worker when their client or manager is afraid of the police? Who is at risk of deportation and homelessness, and why? These are the kinds of questions – questions about people's material conditions – that concern us, as authors and as sex workers.

This Is Not a Memoir

This book – and the perspective of the contemporary left sex worker movement – is not about enjoying sex work. This book will not argue that sex work is 'empowerment'. We are not interested in making an argument around sexual freedom or the supposed capacity of the sex industry to facilitate sexual self-actualisation for workers or for clients. Despite the expectation that sex workers will 'tell our stories', this is not a memoir and we will not be sharing any sexy escapades. (Although, as the founders of sex worker magazine *$pread* told a journalist at the launch of their first issue, 'It's not intended to arouse – but people are turned on by all kinds of things, so maybe someone will be turned on by sex workers fighting for social justice.')[4] We are not interested in forming a movement with men who buy sex. We are not here to uplift the figure of the 'sympathetic' client, nor the idea that any client has a 'right' to sex. We are not here to prioritise discussion on whether the sex industry, or even sex itself, is intrinsically good or bad.* Nor – as we will unpack over the course of this book – are we uncritical of what *work* means in a context of insatiable global capitalism and looming environmental catastrophe.

Sometimes people who support sex workers' rights attempt to show their support by arguing that the sex industry is not actually a site of sexism and misogyny – an argument that is, in our view, misplaced. The sex industry is both sexist and misogynist. We do not argue that nobody experiences harms within sex work, or that these harms are minimal and should be disregarded. On the contrary, the harms that people experience in sex work – such as assault, exploitation, arrest, incarceration, eviction, and deportation – are the *focus* of this book.

We are feminists. Women, both transgender and cisgender, are at the centre of our politics, and, as a result, at the centre of this book. People of all genders sell sex: transgender and cisgender men, non-binary people, and those with indigenous or non-western genders such as hijra, fa'afafine and two-spirit people. It is important to acknowledge this because peoples' gender shapes their route into sex work, their experiences while selling sex, and their lives beyond. Equally, however, it is important not to lose sight of the fact that the sex industry *is* gendered: the majority of those who sell sex are women, and the vast majority of those who pay for sex are men. In this book we often refer to sex workers as 'she', and to clients as 'he'. We are not under the mistaken impression that this is literally true in every single instance, but nor is it an error, or something we have neglected to consider. It is a deliberate choice because in our view it reflects the gendered reality of the sex trade, as well as our own feminist politics and priorities.

---

* In the sense that we wish to see an end to all work, particularly the gendered and exploitative nature of prostitution, many sex worker activists are in fact 'sex industry abolitionists'. As the English Collective of Prostitutes have said, 'Ultimately we are organising for an end to prostitution … When women are able to claim back the wealth we helped produce, the economic conditions which have forced millions of people everywhere to sell their mind, body, time and skills in order the survive or improve their standard of living, prostitution will no longer be there.' See 'English Collective of Prostitutes', *Screaming Violet*, 1 May 2015, wewantawomensmag.wordpress.com.

You may be expecting statistics and numerical data 'proving' that prostitution is one thing or another. Many existing books make the case for, or against, decriminalising the sex industry with these kinds of arguments. Of course, data is useful: crucial, even, in many contexts. When the World Health Organisation wants to think about how to reduce HIV transmission among sex workers, it needs numbers. Sometimes, however, heavy reliance on statistics risks becoming a form of 'argument by authority': someone cites a study saying one thing, others cite a study saying another, and the argument is 'won' on the basis of whose numbers are more memorable or whose study was published in the more prestigious journal. Some research can be poor in quality, or misused by commentators, and much time is given to arguing about its credibility, instead of using simple logic and empathy. The dependence on statistics in the prostitution debate is often a result of our invisibility, and our illegitimacy as commentators. Sex workers perhaps seem alien and mysterious, and the questions we raise too political; but numbers are reassuring, seemingly apolitical, and knowable.

We *use* numerical data – in our writing and in our activism – but it is not central to our approach. Instead of using a few key figures that 'prove' sex workers' rights arguments, we want readers to *think empathetically* about how changes in criminal law change the incentives and behaviours of people who sell sex, along with clients, police, managers, and landlords. If you understand *how* those behaviours change and *why*, then you will have a much deeper understanding of how changes in the criminal law make people who sell sex more – or less – safe.

'It Takes about Two Minutes to Politicise a Hooker'

Sex workers are the original feminists. Often seen as merely subject to others' whims, in fact, sex workers have shaped and contributed to social movements across the world. In medieval Europe, brothel workers formed guilds and occasionally engaged in strikes or street protests in response to crackdowns, workplace closures, or unacceptable working conditions.[5] Fifteenth-century prostitutes, arraigned before city councils in Bavaria, asserted that their activities constituted work rather than a sin.[6] One prostitute (under the pseudonym Another Unfortunate) wrote to the *The Times of London* in 1859 to state, 'I conduct myself prudently, and defy you and your policemen too. Why stand you there mouthing with sleek face about morality? What is morality?'[7] In 1917, 200 prostitutes marched in San Francisco – in what has been called the 'original Women's March' – to demand an end to brothel closures. A speaker at the march declared, 'Nearly every one of these women is a mother or has someone depending on her. They are driven into this life by economic conditions ... You don't do any good by attacking us. Why don't you attack those conditions?'[8]

Caring for each other is political work. During the second-wave feminist movement, many pioneering radicals raised their children collectively and cared for each other beyond the boundaries of the biological family unit. Much less known, and missing from the usual tellings of feminist history, are the similar and preceding efforts of sex workers. For example, in nineteenth-century Great Britain and Ireland, prostitutes created communities of mutual aid, sharing income and childcare. A journalist observed at the time that 'the ruling principle here is to share each other's fortunes ... In hard times one family readily helps another, or several help one ... What each company get is thrown into a common purse, and the nest is provisioned out of it.'[9]

Likewise, *watembezi* [street based] women in colonial-era Nairobi formed financial ties to one another, paying each other's fines or bequeathing assets to one another when they died.[10] Although largely invisible to outsiders, this sharing of resources – including money, workspaces, and even clients – persists as a significant form of sex worker activism today.

Workers often collectively pitch in to prevent an eviction or to offer emergency housing. This kind of community resource-sharing is often the only safety net sex workers have if they're robbed at work or if an assault means they need time off to heal.

Mutual defence, too, is a site of collective action. When eight sex workers were murdered in the small city of Thika, Kenya, in 2010, others from around the country flocked to support them. Phelister Abdalla, an organiser with the Kenya Sex Workers Alliance, writes that 'hundreds of sex workers, from different parts of Kenya went to protest in Thika … our fellow sisters had been killed, and enough was enough'.[11] They endured harassment and beatings from the police even as they marched the streets, demanding an end to the violence.

The bravery and resilience of sex workers has played a part in many liberation struggles. In the 1950s, prostitutes were part of the Mau Mau uprising that led to Kenya's liberation from British colonial rule.[12] In the 1960s and 1970s they were part of the riots at Compton's Cafeteria in San Francisco and the Stonewall Inn in New York that kickstarted the LGBTQ liberation movement in the United States.[13] In times of rapid social change, working class sex workers are often at the heart of the action. As sex worker activist Margo St. James has put it, 'it takes about two minutes to politicise a hooker'.[14]

St James was a fierce defender of the heavily policed 'sexual deviants' in her San Francisco community. 'It's well past time for whores to organize', she said in an interview. 'The homosexuals organised and now the cops are afraid to harass them anymore.'[15] In the 1970s, an era when sex workers had barely any public platform, she organised for gay liberation alongside Harvey Milk, and identified herself openly as a 'whore' when she spoke frankly to *Rolling Stone* about her vision of liberating female sexuality from the 'pussy patrol' of the state. She formed Call Off Your Old Tired Ethics (COYOTE), got the practice of quarantine and forced medication for arrested sex workers overturned in California, and hosted 12,000 attendees at her 'Hookers Ball' events, including celebrities and politicians.[16] Connecting prostitution with pro-pleasure, pro-queer politics – in the midst of 1970s counter-culture – proved to be an effective way of getting sex workers' rights on the radar.

In 1974, sex workers in Ethiopia joined the newly formed Confederation of Ethiopian Labour Unions and engaged in strike action that helped to bring down the government.[17] In Europe the modern movement is generally considered to have begun in 1975, when sex workers in France occupied churches to protest criminalisation, poverty, and police violence. This sparked similar sex worker organising in London, where the English Collective of Prostitutes occupied churches in King's Cross, London, in 1980.[18] More recently, sex workers were deeply involved in anti-gentrification protests around Gezi Park in Istanbul, Turkey.[19]

In the UK, the 1970s and 1980s sex workers' rights movement was deeply entwined with the 'wages for housework' campaign. Marxist feminists named the value of women's unpaid reproductive and domestic labour and demanded a radical reorganisation of society to value women's work. Around that time, the feminist group Wages Due Lesbians linked domestic work, sex work, and the work of heterosexuality in a solidarity statement against a 1977 vice crackdown: 'Wherever women succeed in winning some of the wages due us, it is a strength to all of us and proof that women's services cannot be taken for granted'.[20]

Throughout the 1980s, the sex workers' rights movement became increasingly international. The First and Second Whores' Congresses took place in Amsterdam and Brussels, and new sex worker led groups began emerging from Australia, Thailand, Brazil, South Africa, and Uruguay, among other places.

In 1997, 4,000 sex workers made history with the first National Conference of Sex Workers in India, organised by the Durbar Mahila Samanwaya Committee (DMSC). At a follow-up event in 2001, their number rose to 25,000 who came to Kolkata to make their demands known, with signs proclaiming: 'We want bread. We also want roses.'*

In Bolivia in the mid-2000s, 35,000 sex workers from across the country participated in a huge series of collective actions against police violence and the closure of workplaces. 'We are fighting for the right to work and for our families' survival', said Lily Cortez, leader of the El Alto Association of Nighttime Workers, surrounded by prostitutes who had sewn their mouths shut in protest. 'Tomorrow we will bury ourselves alive if we are not immediately heard'.[21]

Some went on strike by refusing to go for mandatory sexually transmitted disease (STD) testing 'until we can work free from

---

* The slogan 'bread and roses' originated in a 1912 strike by women textile workers in Massachusetts; they demanded not only better wages but also respect and decent working conditions. See R.J.S. Ross, 'Bread and Roses: Women Workers and the Struggle for Dignity and Respect', *Working USA* 16 (2013): 59–68.

harassment'.[22] Others blockaded traffic or went on hunger strike.[23] 'We are Bolivia's unloved,' said Yuly Perez from the sex workers' union National Organisation for the Emancipation of Women in a State of Prostitution. 'We are hated by a society that uses us regularly and ignored by institutions obligated to protect us ... [We] will fight tooth and nail for the rights we deserve.'[24]

'All Hell Broke Loose – Between the Prostitute and the Movement'

Despite their precocious feminism, prostitutes' relationship with the wider feminist movement has always been fraught. In the mid-nineteenth century, as middle-class women emerged into the public sphere of the professions, a new kind of role was invented which married the ideal values and attributes of middle-class femininity to paid employment. In part, this can be thought of as a feminist project, as the alleged moral superiority of these women justified their taking a more public role in society, including working outside the home, the legal right to own property, the vote, and so on. But the creation of professionalised caring roles, such as philanthropic and social work, was about employment that *reproduced* rather than upset gender roles. These women were reasserting their position in a class hier-archy over working class people, particularly working class women and children, who were targeted as recipients for maternalistic and coercive forms of 'care'.[25]

This led to the development of what anthropologist Laura Agustín terms the 'rescue industry', meaning the various systems of social rewards associated with 'reforming' prostitutes as well as protecting children and rescuing animals.[26] (This new kind of philanthropic role implicitly bracketed children, animals, and prostitutes together, which gives a sense of how women who sold sex were viewed at the time.) The rescue industry enabled middle-class women to claim a space as citizens and political agents in the public sphere – at the expense of their working class sisters, whose lives were increasingly policed.[27] In 1877, the National Society for the Prevention of Cruelty to Children (NSPCC) became embroiled in controversy when it prosecuted an upper-class family for child cruelty for the first time; it had 'already prosecuted thirty-eight cases of cruelty amongst poor and uneducated people'.[28] Even when their interests temporarily aligned, as in their shared struggles against the Contagious Diseases Acts of the 1860s, suffragists and other feminists failed to see sex workers as their equals. (Likening sex workers to animals persists in some feminist anti-prostitution activism, with prostitutes sometimes compared to service dogs, pets, and Pokémon.)[29]

Feminists' discomfort with proximity to sex workers reached a fever pitch during the so-called 'sex wars' of the 1980s and 1990s. In this era, radical feminists locked horns with 'pro-sex' feminists over the issues of pornography and prostitution.[30] The radical-feminist perspective on sex work holds that it reproduces (and is itself a product of) patriarchal violence against women. This analysis could extend to all heterosexual sexual behaviours, as well as public sex and kink (commonly known as BDSM, for 'bondage, domination, submission/sadism, masochism').

The focus in this era was on censoring porn and 'raising awareness' rather than addressing prostitution through criminal law directly, but a nonetheless vehement anti-prostitution stance became commonplace in the feminist movement. Writer Janice Raymond stated that 'prostitution is rape that's paid for', while Kathleen Barry said buying and selling sex was 'destructive of human life'.[31]

The defence of porn and prostitution that followed in response was based on ideas of sexual liberation through nonconformist sexual expression, such as BDSM and the 'queering' of lesbian and gay identities. Many 'pro-sex' or 'sex-radical' feminists posited that not only could watching porn be gratifying and educational, it could upend patriarchal control over women's sexual expression.[32] Moreover, that the sex industry was sticking two fingers up at the institution of marriage, highlighting the hypocrisy of conservative, monogamous heteronormativity. While some people who fought for sexual liberation were sex workers – such as LGBTQ and AIDS activist Amber Hollibaugh – many sex radicals advanced their arguments from a non–sex worker perspective. Defending porn often meant defending *watching* it, rather than performing in it.

Radical feminists famously described sex radicals as 'Uncle Toms'*
pandering to the primacy of male sexuality, while they in turn were
derided as 'prudes'[33] invested in preserving sexual puritanism. Rather
than focussing on the 'work' of sex work, both pro-sex feminists
and anti-prostitution feminists concerned themselves with *sex as
symbol*. Both groups questioned what the existence of the sex industry implied for their own positions as women; both groups prioritised
those questions over what material improvements could be made in
the lives of the sex workers in their communities. Stuck in the domain
of sex and whether it is 'good' or 'bad' for women (and adamant that
it could only be one or the other) it was all too easy for feminists to
think of The Prostitute only in terms of what she represented to them.
They claimed ownership of sex worker experiences in order to make
sense of their own.

Anti-prostitution activist Dorchen Leidholdt spoke to this feminist
impulse; 'this de-individualized, de-humanized being has the function of representing generic woman ... She stands in for all of us,
and she takes the abuse that we are beginning to resist.'[34] It was in
this context that former prostitute Andrea Dworkin's work became
highly influential in the movement, and set a new tone for criticism
of sex work. The Prostitute, she said

> lives the literal reality of being the dirty woman. There is no meta-
> phor. She is the woman covered in dirt, which is to say that every
> man who has ever been on top of her has left a piece of himself
> behind ... She is perceived as, treated as – and I want you to remem-
> ber this, this is real – vaginal slime.[35]

Her confrontational writing style – and her experiences in the sex
trade – helped to legitimise and normalise similar usage of graphic

---

* The term 'Uncle Tom' is derived from Harriet Beecher Stowe's 1852
novel *Uncle Tom's Cabin*. It is used to describe someone who is meek, submissive, emotionally attached to or 'selling out' to a dominant oppressive order.
Although some considered Beecher Stowe's novel progressive at the time, the
term 'Uncle Tom' evokes an anti-Black caricature and is now considered anti-
Black. See Alison Phipps, 'Sex Wars Revisited: A Rhetorical Economy of Sex
Industry Opposition', *Journal of International Women's Studies* 18:4 (2017),
306–20.

and misogynist language in 'feminist' discussions of sex workers and their bodies. Barry, a contemporary of Dworkin, likened prostitutes to blow-up dolls, 'complete with orifices for penetration and ejaculation', while Leidholdt wrote that 'stranger after stranger use[s] her body as a seminal spittoon ... What other job is so deeply gendered that one's breasts, vagina and rectum constitute the working equipment?'[36] Academics Cecilie Høigård and Liv Finstad wrote of women who sell sex that 'at the core they experience themselves as only cheap whores'.[37]

Sex working feminists have long found themselves harshly excluded, and not only by de-humanising language in academia, but by explicit lack of invitation into spaces. Kate Millett recalls a feminist conference on prostitution, held in 1971. Disgruntled working women arrived to demand a seat at the table:

> An inadvertent masterpiece of tactless precipitance, the title of the day's program was inscribed on leaflets for our benefit: 'Towards the Elimination of Prostitution'. The panel of experts included everyone but prostitutes ... all hell broke loose – between the prostitute and the movement. Because, against all likelihood, prostitutes did in fact attend the conference ... They had a great deal to say about the presumption of straight women who fancied they could debate, decide or even discuss what was their situation and not ours.[38]

Unlike the hostile environment of radical feminism, sex radicals were welcoming and supportive to sex workers. This influence helped shape the movement's growth. In 1974, COYOTE hosted the first National Hookers' Convention. The bright orange flyer nodded to the way prostitutes had been shunned from the women's movement: emblazoned with a hand touching a vulva, it proclaimed, 'Our Convention Is Different: We Want Everyone to Come'.[39]

In the following decades, advocates from Amber Hollibaugh and Annie Sprinkle, to Kathleen Hanna and Amber Rose have linked sexuality to sex worker issues. Many sex workers have worked in the HIV/AIDS and LGBTQ movements, and been involved with riot grrrl, SlutWalk, consent awareness, sex education, and non-monogamy.

However, as we explore in depth in chapter 2, sex positivity can be a counterproductive point from which to start a conversation about the actual conditions of the sex industry. Working class sex workers and sex workers of colour have long criticised the race and class privilege of these politics; labour rights and safety are not the same as pleasure, and those who do experience sexual gratification at work are likely to be those who already have the most control over their working conditions.[40] As conversations about prostitution have rapidly widened and grown more complex in the age of the internet, sex workers have noted the way that a focus on sex positivity has become a defensive response to stigmatising media representations of prostitutes.[41]

Recent years have seen a significant shift in the sex worker movement away from protective 'Happy Hooker' myths, towards a Marxist-feminist, labour-centred analysis.[42] Sex workers who are survivors have become more vocal in the movement, citing their experiences of violence and criminalisation as a driver for their activism.

Anti-prostitution activists, too, are often drawn to feminism through their own histories of surviving violence. They often identify heavily with pro-criminalisation survivors of prostitution, also called 'exited women.' Through their harrowing testimonies of violence – and firm stance on the punishment of men who buy sex – Exited Women come to be regarded as the ultimate symbol of female woundedness, with the criminalisation of clients as feminist justice.

This sense of 'ownership' that many feminists have over prostitution sparks debates about who is entitled to speak as a sex worker, or on our behalf. It is common for anti-prostitution feminist commentators to claim that sex worker activists are paid shills – illegitimate fronts for exploitative bosses, pejoratively nicknamed the 'pimp lobby'.[43] When sex workers held a protest in the French Senate in 2009, one politician deemed them 'pimps dressed as prostitutes'.[44] In 2016, the Irish anti-prostitution organisation Ruhama accidentally forwarded internal emails to a student journalist. In them, Ruhama's chief executive muses that, should the young journalist produce a critical article, Ruhama can dismiss it as 'pimp-thinking'. Ruhama, caught out in writing, had to apologise.[45]

When Amnesty International announced their intention to support sex workers in their policy, anti-prostitution feminist campaigners flooded social media with the hashtag #NoAmnesty4Pimps.[46] They Photoshopped the iconic Amnesty logo, replacing the candle with an ejaculating penis above the slogans 'Protect the Male Orgasm' and 'Protect Male Entitlement to a Prostituted Class'.[47]

The way that sex workers' rights is merged with the interests of men in the feminist imagination makes it easy for non-prostitute women to turn away from us. As anti-prostitution campaigner Finn Mackay wrote, 'It is time to choose which side we're on, because the multibillion dollar "sex-industry" is doing fine and well, it does not need our support, it certainly does not need our protection.'[48]

Today, the anti-prostitution agenda focusses on eradicating sex work through harsher penalties for clients. Despite the fact that their movement is almost exclusively comprised of those who previously sold sex and those who have never sold sex, modern day anti-prostitution campaigning works to eliminate the means for other people to *currently* sell sex. Few in their number will themselves be materially affected by prostitution policy.

The relationship between survivor-led, sex positive, radical, liberal, libertarian, Marxist, and carceral responses to prostitution is as fractious as ever. Both anti-prostitution feminists and sex workers at times double down on their views as a kind of shield against traumatising encounters with their opponents, each believing that the other is the enemy. Hostile debates hinge on 'force' and 'choice', the spectre of sex trafficking, and the intersections of poverty and patriarchy. The few sex workers who speak out face pressures to conform to limiting narratives of their experiences. And regardless of how we share our stories, our movement continues to be attacked by those who reach for the 'happy hooker' strawman as a way to undermine our politics and derail more complex conversations. After all – as any woman knows – it is a struggle to be heard if your detractors can easily dismiss you as 'sluts'.

Cops, Borders, and Carceral Feminists

There is a huge emphasis on policing – including border policing – as the 'solution' to prostitution. This is the case even among those on the left. However, it is remarkable how little you will find *about* the police and borders in such discussions. These omissions have led to the illusion that one can discuss the laws that govern sex work without any discussion about *how* such laws are implemented and *by whom*. But laws are not just 'messaging'; they are what the police are permitted to do in the world.

The institutions of policing and borders may seem natural or inevitable, but they are recent inventions. Their modern forms date back only to the nineteenth century, and a look at their history illuminates their present.

In the southern United States, the first centralised and specialised policing organisations were slave patrols, whose major function was to capture and punish runaway slaves. Historians of the region argue that they 'should be considered a forerunner of modern American law enforcement.'[49]

In the early-nineteenth-century northern United States and in the United Kingdom, professionalised police forces were set up in response to a restive urban working class organising against bad working and living conditions. As historian David Whitehouse explains, the state needed a way to control burgeoning crowds, protests, and strikes without 'sending in the army', which risked creating working class martyrs and further radicalising the populace.[50] Thus the police were designed to inflict generally *non-lethal* violence to protect the interests of capitalism and the state. The situation is not so different today, with police citing 'authorisation from the president of McDonald's' to justify arresting restaurant workers protesting for better wages.[51]

Today's immigration controls are also largely a product of the nineteenth century. They rely on ideas of racial inferiority propagated by white Europeans to justify slavery and colonialism. Jewish refugees arriving in Britain in the 1880s and 1890s were met by a surge in anti-Semitism; anti-Semitic tracts claimed at the time that 'the white slave traffic [is carried out] everywhere ... by Jews'.[52] This racist panic led to the enactment of the Aliens Act of 1905, which contained the first recognisably modern anti-immigration measures in Britain.[53] In the US, the first federal immigration restrictions included the Page Act of 1875, the Chinese Exclusion Act of 1882, and the Scott Act of

1888. These targeted Chinese migrants, particularly sex workers, and devoted substantial resources to attempting to discern wives from prostitutes.[54]

Along with racism, anxieties about commercial sex are embedded in the histories of immigration controls. These are legislative spaces where race and gender *co-produce* racist categories of exclusion: men of colour as traffickers; women of colour as helpless, seductive, infectious; both as threats to the body politic of the nation.[55] These histories help us see that police and border violence are not anomalous or the work of 'bad apples'; they are intrinsic to these institutions.

The feminist movement should thus be sceptical of approaches to gender justice that rely on or further empower the police or immigration controls. Black feminists such as Angela Davis have long criticised feminist reliance on the police, and note that the police appear as the most benevolent protectors in the minds of those who encounter them the *least*. For sex workers and other marginalised and criminalised groups, the police are not a symbol of protection but a *real* manifestation of punishment and control.

Feminism that welcomes police power is called *carceral feminism*. The sociologist Elizabeth Bernstein, one of the first to use this phrase, uses it to describe a feminist approach that prioritises a 'law-and-order agenda'; a shift 'from the welfare state to the carceral state as *the* enforcement apparatus for feminist goals'.[56] Carceral feminism focuses on policing and criminalisation as the key ways to deliver justice to women.

Carceral feminism has gained popularity even though the police – and the wider criminal justice system – are key *perpetrators* of violence against women. In the United States, police officers are disproportionately likely to be violent or abusive to their partners or children.[57] At work, they commit vast numbers of assaults, rapes, or harassment.[58] Sexual assault is the second-most commonly reported form of police violence in the United States (after excessive use of force), and on-duty police commit sexual assaults at *more than double* the rate of the general US population.[59] Those are just the assaults that make it into the statistics: many will never dare to make a report to an abuser's colleague. Meanwhile, the very nature of police work involves perpetrating violence: in arrests or when they collaborate in incarceration, surveillance, or deportation. In 2017, there was outrage in the United Kingdom when it emerged that the Metropolitan Police had arrested a woman on immigration charges after she came to them as a victim of rape.[60] However, it is routine for police to threaten to arrest or deport migrant sex workers, even when the worker in question has come to them as a victim of violence.[61]

Carceral feminism looms large in sex-trade debates. Feminist commentators pronounce that 'we must strengthen police apparatus';[62] that criminalisation is 'the only way' to end the sex trade;[63] and that some criminalisation can be relatively 'benign'.[64] Anti-prostitution feminist Catherine MacKinnon even writes with ambivalent approval of 'brief jail time' for prostitutes on the basis that jail can be 'a respite from the pimps and the street'. She quotes like-minded feminists who argue that 'jail is the closest thing many women in prostitution have to a battered women's shelter' and that, 'considering the absence of any other refuge or shelter, jail provides a temporary safe haven'.[65]

Sex workers do not share this rosy view of arrest and incarceration. One sex worker in Norway told researchers, 'If a customer is bad you need to manage it yourself to the end. You only call the police if you think you're going to die. If you call the police, you risk losing everything'.[66] Sex workers in Kyrgyzstan, Ukraine, Siberia, Lithuania, Macedonia, and Bulgaria all view the police as more of a threat to their safety than any other group, according to research by the Sex Workers' Rights Advocacy Network (SWAN).[67] In 2017 in New York, a woman called Yang Song was caught up in an undercover sting at the massage parlour at which she worked. She had been arrested for prostitution two months earlier and had recently been sexually assaulted by a man claiming to be a police officer. (It remains unclear as to whether he was.)[68] When the police returned, looking to arrest her again for prostitution, she fell, jumped, or was pushed from a fourth-floor window. Yang Song died.[69]

On Speaking and Being Heard

Who are prostitutes? Ideas seem to lurch between contradictory stereotypes, perhaps unsurprisingly for a group more often spoken about than to. Much as immigrants are seen as lazy scroungers while somehow also stealing the jobs of 'decent people', sex workers are simultaneously victim and accomplice, sexually voracious yet helpless maidens.

When our society attempts to reconcile these wildly contradictory expectations, sex workers are asked to produce a spokesperson who 'represents the community'. This is impossible – just as there can be no one 'representative' token woman who can stand in every time 'women's issues' are on the table. One sex worker may be nothing like another in their identity, circumstance, health and habits. From the single mum with a weekday job in a Scottish massage parlour, to the young Cambodian bar hostess keen to travel to Europe, to the group of black trans sex workers forming political collectives in Cape Town, to the undocumented Nigerian migrant hustling on the streets of Stockholm, across the global north and south, across an age spectrum that spans many decades, sex workers are unimaginably diverse in race, religion, ethnicity, class, gender, sexuality and disability. To achieve anything like real representation, this book would need thousands of authors.

Many sex worker activists find their testimonies are dismissed in feminist spaces on the grounds that, by virtue of being activists, they are not representative; that they speak from an exceptional, privileged and anomalous perspective.[*] Questions over whether a sex worker is 'representative' become recursive: in their claimed eagerness to hear from 'the voiceless', anti-prostitution campaigners position anyone they *can* hear from as by definition someone who no longer needs

---

[*] In other words, the 'unrepresentative' or 'exceptional' categories can be bent and moulded to accommodate anybody: the only criterion is wishing to be heard on one's own terms. As Alison Phipps writes, 'for current sex workers, the condition for dismissal is being able to speak at all'. See Alison Phipps, '"You're not representative": Identity politics in sex industry debates', genders, bodies, politics, 31 August 2015, genderate.wordpress.com.

to be listened to. This is, of course, not a logic that anti-prostitution campaigners apply to their own voices.

The authors of this book could certainly not be described as representative of all people selling sex. Both of us are cisgender and white, born and raised in the global north, working in a country where the sex work we do is less criminalised, with middle-class educations and the access to power and capital that brings. It is not by accident that opportunities to speak on television, publish articles, and be appointed to salaried activist positions come to us or people like us. Just as in any radical movement, a select few activists often receive unfair credit for doing the same work that more marginalised sex workers, who cannot risk being public in their activism, are doing alongside them.

The existence of this book – which is written in English and which focuses on the UK, where we live and work – itself illustrates a way in which some modes of discussion are legitimised by society, while others go unrecognised. The service provision and community building created by marginalised, grass-roots communities is sometimes relatively unknown. These ephemeral forms of resistance can be incredibly joyful or life-saving, and the memories of them invaluable to a movement. On the other hand, books, blogs and policy documents are forms of advocacy that make easy passage into history. A book gives us a substantial amount of space to critically explore the sometimes painful aspects of sex work politics – space and nuance not afforded to people taking two-minute turns on a megaphone at a rally. This book is forged from our perspective, and our perspective is shaped by our privileges. However, we strive to include a range of sex worker voices in our writing – from triumphant, to reflexive, to critical, to mournful. All these forms of political speech are valid.

Sex workers sometimes pay a high price for political speech. In 2004, Argentinian trade union activist Sandra Cabrera was shot dead in her home in retribution for her work challenging police corruption and police violence directed at sex workers.[70] Her murder remains officially unsolved. Kabita Roy, an activist with a sex worker trade union in India, was murdered in the union's office in Kolkata in 2016.[71] In January 2018, three prominent sex worker activists were murdered in Brazil.[72] In 2011, criminal gangs murdered the president of a migrant sex worker trade union in Peru. Sex worker Angela Villón Bustamante, a colleague of the murdered trade unionist, said, 'It's not in the Mafia's economic interests that sex workers organise.'[73]

Nor is the high cost of political speech evenly distributed among sex workers. Precarious immigration status, fear of eviction and police violence, and potential loss of child custody mean that migrant and indigenous workers, the insecurely housed, and parents (particularly mothers) all face higher stakes when organising or speaking up than sex workers who have secure long-term tenancies, hold a passport or citizenship, or have no children. Cisgender sex workers are safer from these risks than transgender sex workers; white sex workers are safer than sex workers of colour.

Nonetheless, even as sex workers with relative power, demonstrating that we can speak for ourselves is often a gruelling task. The 'prostitution debate' is in many ways shaped far more by invisible actors – such as the media staffers who write article headlines and choose the photo that will accompany an article, or local government workers who process planning applications – than by anyone who actually sells sex. Even the most privileged sex workers take a considerable risk by becoming publicly known, so online anonymity is a vital tool of diverse speech. Yet this anonymity is often used to discredit us as nefarious 'sex industry lobbyists.' Websites where sex workers have anonymously connected with the public, with each other and with clients are rapidly being dismantled. As this book went to press, US president Donald Trump signed into law a bill that seeks to stop sex workers from communicating online, with disastrous implications not only for privacy and political advocacy, but for sex workers' safety and survival, too.*

---

* The Fight Online Sex Trafficking Act (FOSTA) and the Stop Enabling Sex Traffickers Act (SESTA) are, respectively, the House of Representatives and Senate bills, enacted 11 April 2018, that criminalise sites that host content linked to sex trafficking, or 'knowingly assist, support, or facilitate sex trafficking'. The text of the law is broad enough to refer not only to sex industry

We write this book with thoughtfulness about where we stand, but also with a sense of satisfaction that you will hold in your hand a book about prostitution *written by prostitutes*. This is, unfortunately, all too rare. Sex workers – not journalists, politicians, or the police – are the experts on sex work. We bring our experiences of criminalisation, rape, assault, intimate partner abuse, abortion, mental illness, drug use, and epistemic violence with us in our organising and our writing.* We bring the knowledge we have developed through our deep immersion in sex worker organising spaces – spaces of mutual aid, spaces that are working towards collective liberation. As two friends writing this book together, we strive to make the demands of our movement visible.

The man responsible for the killing spree in Thika, Kenya, was apprehended in 2010. He confessed and claimed that he would have continued killing until he'd reached a hundred prostitutes: 'I managed 17 and there were 83 to go.'[74] Aisha, a sex worker in Thika, who with her friends protested in the streets during the frightening time before he was caught, says, 'We wanted people to know that we call ourselves sex workers because it is the wheat our families depend on.' Even in the face of such overwhelming vulnerability, they openly identified themselves as sex workers in public for the first time, with bright red T-shirts and loud chanting.[75] As one sex worker at the protest remarked, 'The community should know we exist. And there's no going back.'[76]

---

advertising, but also to community organising or support spaces. At the time of writing, Backpage.com and several other major advertising platforms that enabled sex workers to identify both viable and dangerous clients had been taken down. More information is available at survivorsagainstsesta.org/documentation.

* Spivak, following Foucault, uses the term 'epistemic violence' to describe how oppressed peoples' ways of understanding and describing the world are suppressed, forcing them to use oppressors' concepts and language. She was talking specifically about colonised subjects, but the same point applies to sex workers and to women generally. See G.C. Spivak, 'Can the Subaltern Speak?' in Nelson, C. and Grossberg, L. (eds), *Marxism and the Interpretation of Culture*, Chicago: University of Illinois Press, 1988, 271–313. See also M. Fricker, 'Epistemic Justice as a Condition of Political Freedom?' *Synthese* 190:7 (2013), 1317–32.

1

Sex

We are anxious about sex. For us as women, sex can be as much a site of trauma – or uneasy compromise – as a site of joy or intimacy. Feminist conversations about sex work are often seen as arguments between those who are 'sex positive' and those who are 'sex negative.' The reasons for this will be explored in this chapter. We have no interest in positioning ourselves within that terrain. Instead, we assert the right for all women to be 'sex-ambivalent'. That said, the hatred of sex workers is rooted in very old and misogynist ideas about sex. Understanding those visceral responses of disgust is a key starting point for understanding all kinds of things about prostitution – including criminal law.

Is Sex Bad?

People are preoccupied with the *sexual* dimension of sex work. These anxieties manifest in ideas of bodily degradation and the threat that sex workers pose as the vectors of such degradation. The prostitute is seen as a disease-spreader, associated with putrefaction and death. We are envisioned both as removing corruption from society (a nineteenth-century French physician spoke of the 'seminal drain')[1] and as a source of contamination, disease, and death in our own right.[2] *Puta*, the Spanish word for prostitute, has links with the English *putrid*.* Another preoccupation holds that to have sex (or to have sex

---

* Most Romance languages use a variant of *puta* (Spanish), such as *putain* (French) or *puttana* (Italian) to mean 'prostitute', evoking the Latin *putida* ('stinking or rotting', giving us words like *putrid*), connecting to a long European tradition of associating sex workers with sewers or drains. D. Hopkins, 'Latin and Late Latin 'Puta "Concubine, Sexual Sleeping Partner" and Old French Pute', *Romance Notes* 45:1 (2004), 3–10.

in the wrong ways – too much, with the wrong person, or for the wrong reason) brings about some kind of *loss*. Often, contradictory ideas about sex and these visceral threats or losses are intertwined in cultural depictions of the sex worker – forming a figure that Melissa Gira Grant names the 'prostitute imaginary'.[3]

Sometimes the connection between these ideas is obvious. For the Victorians, the 'loss of virginity' risks ruin and a grim death from syphilis. The ruined woman is reconfigured as an agent of destruction, spreading disease in her wake. Sometimes the loss is a spiritual decline she precipitates in others; in 1870, for example, journalist William Acton wrote that prostitutes are 'ministers of evil passions, [who] not only gratify desire, but also arouse it [and] suggest evil thoughts and desires which might otherwise remain undeveloped'.[4] In *The Whore's Last Shift*, a 1779 painting by James Gillway, the tragic figure of a heavily made-up nude woman with hair piled high stands by a broken chamber pot in a dirty room, washing her filthy – and clumsily symbolic – white dress by hand.

Attitudes towards the prostitute imaginary can be read in context with the more familiar paradox around a specific body part. Ugly, stretched, odorous, unclean, potentially infected, desirable, mysterious, tantalising – the patriarchy's ambivalence towards vaginas is well established and has a lot in common with attitudes around sex work. On the one hand, the lure of the vagina is a threat; it's seen as a place where a penis might risk encountering the traces of another man or a full set of gnashing teeth. At the same time, it's viewed as an inherently submissive body part that must be 'broken in' to bring about sexual maturity. The idea of the vagina as fundamentally compromised or pitiful is helped along in part by a longstanding feminist perception of the penetrative sexual act as indicative of subjugation.[5]

The nineteenth century Contagious Diseases Act gave police the power to subject any suspected prostitute to a forced pelvic exam with a speculum – a device, still in use today, invented by a doctor who found gynaecological contact repellent, and who purchased enslaved Black women to experiment on.[6] In London in 1893, Cesare Lombroso studied the bodies of women from the 'dangerous classes', mostly prostitutes and other working class women, and women of colour, all of whom he described as 'primitive'. He asserted that prostitutes experienced increased pubic-hair growth, hypertrophy of the clitoris, and permanent distention of the labia and vagina, clearly believing that their unnatural deeds and their unnatural bodies were two sides of the same coin.[7] To him, the social and moral degradation they represented became legible in their physical bodies.

An 1880s novel describes a sex worker as 'a shovel full of putrid flesh', continuing: 'It was as if the poison she had picked up in the gases from the carcasses left by the roadside that ferment – with which she had poisoned a whole people – had risen to her face and rotted it.'[8] The body of the prostitute is out to hurt innocents: she is 'carrying contamination and foulness to every quarter', where '[she] creeps ... no precautions used ... and poisons half the young'.[9]

During World War II, the disease-ridden prostitute was imagined as the enemy's secret biological weapon. Posters depicted her as an archetypal femme fatale – with a cigarette between her red lips, a tight dress, and a wicked smile – above slogans warning that she and other 'pickups' were dangerous: traps, loaded guns, 'juke joint snipers', Axis agents, enemies of the Allied forces, and friends of Hitler.[10]

These questions about the duplicity of the sexualised body also come up around queer and gender non-conforming people. Trans women are often questioned about their 'biological' status: a demand that invariably reveals an obsessive focus on their genitals. A trans woman is constantly targeted for public harassment; at the same time, if she is 'read' as trans, she is seen to be as threatening as a man – accused of trespassing into bathrooms to commit sexual violence.[11] Conversely, if she can pass for cisgender, she is regarded as dangerous, liable to 'trap' someone into having sex with her unawares.[*]

---

[*] The animosity these themes bring up applies doubly to trans women who sell sex. Sex worker Jennifer Laude was murdered by a US Marine in the Philippines, where the 'trans panic defence' in this case reduced the sentence for murder by twenty-seven years. The jury heard that the perpetrator felt like he had been 'raped' upon discovering Laude's penis, and that he was a 'victim' of her fraud. M. Talusan, 'Jennifer Laude's death would've caused an outcry – if

Gay men have also been historically perceived through this mistrustful lens. Queer theorist Leo Bersani argues that gay men provoke the same sets of fears long embodied by the prostitute: a person who could either 'turn' decent men immoral or destroy them. The HIV crisis brought new virulence to these homophobic fears. An HIV researcher wrote at the time of the epidemic that, 'These people have sex twenty to thirty times a night ... A man comes along and goes from anus to anus and in a single night will act as a mosquito transferring infected cells on his penis.'[12] These fears about gay men as malevolent and reckless persist today. A Christian hate group that advocates against 'sodomist and homosexualist propaganda' was invited to the UN in 2017, and a feminist writer recently described a male HIV-positive sex worker as 'spreading AIDS.'[13]

To be associated with prostitution signifies moral loss. In 1910, US district attorney Edwin Sim wrote that 'the characteristic which distinguishes the white slave from immorality ... is that the women who are victims of the traffic are forced unwillingly to live an immoral life'.[14] This belief – that to be a sex worker is to live an 'immoral life' – has persisted. Mark Lagon, who led the US State Department's anti-prostitution work during the George W. Bush era (and went on to run the biggest anti-trafficking organisation in the US), wrote in 2009 that women who sell sex lead 'nasty, immoral lives' for which they should only not be held 'culpable' because 'they may not have a choice'.[15]

In the 2000s, the blog *Diary of a London Call Girl*, written by escort and anonymous blogger 'Belle de Jour', was a smash hit, leading to books and a TV show. After its author was named in 2009 as the research scientist Brooke Magnanti, journalists, like Lombroso before them, attempted to read her supposed moral loss in her physical body: 'I scrutinize [Magnanti's] face without quite knowing what I'm looking for ... dead eyes, maybe ... or something a bit grim and hard around the mouth.'[16] Sex work, categorised as the wrong kind of sex, is seen as taking something from you – the life in your eyes. In her imagined loss, Magnanti is transformed in the journalist's eyes into a threat, a hardened woman.

---

she wasn't transgender', *Guardian*, 28 July 2015, theguardian.com.

This supposed sexual excess, and the loss that accompanies it, delineates the prostitute as 'other'. The 'good' woman, on the other hand, is defined by her whiteness, her class, and her 'appropriate' sexual modesty, whether maidenly or maternal. Campaigns for women's suffrage in the late nineteenth and early twentieth centuries drew on the connection between women's bodies and honour and the honour and body politic of the nation. These campaigns were intimately linked with efforts to tackle prostitution, with British suffragists engaging in anti-prostitution work 'on behalf' of women in colonised India to make the case that British women's enfranchisement would 'purify the imperial nation-state'.[17]

This sense that people (particularly women) are changed and degraded through sex crops up in contemporary feminist thought about prostitution, too. Dominique Roe-Sepowitz, who runs a diversion programme for arrested sex workers in Arizona, claims that 'once you've prostituted, you can never not have prostituted ... having that many body parts in your body parts, having that many body fluids near you, and doing things that are freaky and weird really messes up your ideas of what a relationship looks like, and intimacy'.[18] Sex workers who go through that programme have to abstain not only from *selling* sex but also from sex with a partner.[19]

Even more punitive responses were common in the eighteenth, nineteenth, and even twentieth centuries. Orders of nuns across the world ran workhouses and laundries for 'fallen women' – prostitutes, unmarried mothers, and other women whose sexualities made their communities uneasy.[20] Conditions in these 'Magdalene laundries' were primitive at best and often brutal; even in the twentieth century, women could be confined within them for their whole lives, imprisoned without trial for the 'moral crime' of sex outside of marriage. Many women and their children died through neglect or overwork and were buried in unmarked graves. In Tuam, Ireland, 796 dead children were secretly buried in a septic tank between 1925 and 1961.[21] The last Magdalene laundry in Ireland closed only in 1996.

The Irish nuns who ran the Magdalene laundries did not disappear.[22] Instead, they set up an anti-prostitution organisation, Ruhama, which has become a major force in campaigning to criminalise sex work in Ireland, and now couches its work in feminist language.[23] The Good Shepherd Sisters and the Sisters of Our Lady of Charity continue to make money from the real estate where the Magdalene laundries stood, while largely stonewalling survivors' efforts to document or account for the abuses that took place there – and refusing to contribute to the compensation scheme for survivors.[24] There is a direct line between these religious orders and the supposedly feminist prostitution policy implemented in Ireland in 2016 (see chapter 7).[25]

Tropes about the prostitute body as a carrier of sexually transmitted destruction recur in ostensibly progressive spaces, as when a 'feminist' anti-prostitution organisation reuses World War II–era public-health posters, or when a prominent anti-prostitution activist tells sex workers' rights advocates that they could 'rot in HIV-infected pits'.[26] Sex workers observe such conversations to be laden with misogynist contempt, a ritual of political humiliation where our bodies are laid bare for comment. When we defend ourselves, our resistance outrages non-prostitute feminists, who seize on our obstinacy as proof that we love the sex industry and we love selling sex to men, that we're out to corrupt, and that we hate other women.

Witness, for example, a commenter on Mumsnet, the UK's most popular parenting forum, addressing a fellow community member with:

> You whores pander to men, you undermine women, you steal our husbands, you spread disease, you are a constant threat to society and morals. How can women ever be judged on their intellect when sluts make money selling their bodies? ... What you do is disgusting, letting men cum on your face? Vile and evil.[27]

Norwegian academics Cecilie Høigård and Liv Finstad write that the sex worker's vagina is 'a garbage can for hordes of anonymous men's ejaculations'.[28] We once witnessed a sex worker in an online feminist discussion being asked:

> What is the condition of your rectum and the fibrous wall between your rectum and your vagina? Any issues of prolapse? Incontinence?

Lack of control? You may discover that things start falling down/out when you're a little older. Are you able to achieve orgasm? Do you have nightmares?[29]

Such interrogation and commentary feels far from sisterly. It doesn't comfort or uplift sex workers to know that our being likened to toilets, loaves of bread, meat, dogs or robots is all part of a project apparently more important than our dignity.[30] Feminist women describe us as 'things' for which one can purchase a 'single-use license to penetrate'.[31] They gleefully reference the 'jizz' we've presumably encountered and our 'orifices' and tell us to stick to 'sucking and fucking' and leave feminist policy discussions to 'those of us who read the facts'.[32] Sex workers are associated with sex, and to be associated with sex is to be dismissible.

As Jo Doezema writes, within anti-prostitution feminism

> the echo … of the pornographic is notable. The prostitute not only lacks … she *is* lack. What [these] feminists most want of sex workers is that they close their holes – shut their mouths, cross their legs – to prevent the taking in and spilling out of substances and words they find noxious.[33]

Sometimes feminists' jibes are subtler than calling us 'holes', and these responses have much in common with the ways Victorians disciplined prostitutes into 'appropriate' modes of femininity and sexual continence. Contemptuous articles link sex workers with 'trivial', feminine-coded practices such as fashion, shopping, and selfies, or mock sex workers' discussions of 'empowerment'.[34] In an article expressing her feminist objections to the sex trade, one journalist writes that young women who 'dress like slags' in 'tiny skirts' *deserve* not to be taken seriously.[35] Rejecting a woman because of her appearance is simple misogyny, based on the idea that women who embody a particular kind of femininity are stupid, shallow or somehow inferior. The focus on feminine frivolities draws on pre-twentieth-century depictions of the prostitute as deviant and degraded in her rampant femininity, obsessed with luxury goods and sex. Through this lens, it's easy for non-prostitute feminists to portray sex workers as having no political literacy at all.[36] (Indeed, it is likely that a reviewer of this book will report that we claimed the sex industry to be *empowering* – and a conduit, presumably, to shoe shopping.)

Sex, in these discussions, is positioned as something intrinsically too special to be sold – something intimate reserved for meaningful relationships. Implicit in this view is the sense that sex is a volatile substance for women and must be controlled or legitimised by an emotional connection. One young feminist, for example, writes disapprovingly that sex work is increasingly acceptable to other young feminists because of 'hookup culture', adding, 'It's old-fashioned these days – almost prudish, perhaps – to believe that sex is somehow … inherently linked to your emotions or necessarily intimate.'[37] Yet for many people, sex can indeed be recreational, casual, or in some way 'meaningless'. The meaning and purpose of sex varies wildly for different people in different contexts or at different times in their lives. The sense that sex is *intrinsically, always* special rebounds on women, who are disproportionately seen as losing something when they have sex that is 'too casual'.* It is no coincidence that men who sell sex are not the focus of the same kinds of anxieties – men are seen as able to have casual, meaningless, or transactional sex with much less risk to their 'essential selves'.†

---

* Jay Levy quotes members of the Stockholm Prostitution Unit suggesting that trauma is a *prerequisite* for becoming a sex worker: 'You are raped, and then something is destroyed inside you, and then you can start selling sex'. See Jay Levy, *Criminalising the Purchase of Sex: Lessons from Sweden*, Oxford, UK: Routledge, 2015, 70.

† Though misogynist sexual standards are not applied to male sex workers, homophobic violence – from clients and from state actors – affects them hugely. While men who sell sex to men are stigmatised and criminalised all over the world, the eyes of the global anti-prostitution movement are rarely open to their experiences. Kenyan sex worker activist John Mathenge speaks to this feeling of abandonment: 'Male sex workers were dying in silence, as if we were nothing. We were burying people every month. In one week we buried four male sex workers. We buried some people younger than me, in their late teens and early twenties, and I started to wonder, will I die, too? … Silence was killing us … let the community see the male sex workers.' C.A. Mgbako, *To Live Freely in This World: Sex Worker Activism in Africa*, New York: NYU

In the UK, women 'rescued from brothels' are still sent to live with nuns.[38] The ultimate fallen women are sent to 'restore their dignity' among the ultimate chaste women. Women 'diverted' from the sex trade in the twenty-first century are overwhelmingly taught traditionally 'feminine' forms of employment – especially garment manufacture, but also baking, candle-making, and jewellery-making.[39] Motifs of purity are common in the jewellery produced by such projects.[40]

Is Sex Good?

In this context, where sex represents loss, threat, and bodily degradation, it is no surprise that some sex workers – and those who advocate for us – have responded by emphasising the *value* of sex. Sex work, they agree, *is* sex – but sex is, in fact, good. In agreeing that sex work is sex, they place commercial sex in a category with other kinds of sex which have traditionally been considered 'wrong' or degrading – for instance, queer sex or women having sex outside of relationships. These advocates push back against narratives that associate bodily or moral degradation with 'the wrong kinds of sex', instead asserting that sexual pleasure is a personal and social good. They position sex work as an adventurous, fulfilling, and sexy experience for the worker.

These politics are familiar in other contexts. For example, Jeannie Ludlow, an abortion rights advocate, notes that within pro-choice advocacy, there is a 'hierarchy of abortion narratives' and a category of 'things we cannot say':[41]

> There is a politically and socially constructed gap between what we experience at our clinics and how we talk about those experiences in public. When I began to notice this gap in my own speaking about abortion, I realized that it had been constructed in part out of political necessity. I was reluctant to close this gap for fear that I might, as one academic colleague accusingly put it, 'provide fodder for the other side'.[42]

Press, 2016, 146.

This 'defensive stance' leads to an emphasis on abortion stories deemed 'hyper-deserving' – for example, when the pregnancy results from rape. And in response to anti-choice narratives of grief and regret, we get feminist writing that describes an abortion as 'the happiest day of my life'.[43] Likewise, it is easy to find sex workers asserting, 'I love sex. I fucking love it.'[44] Sex workers who stray too far from this line fear being told that their stories are 'what gives those opposed to sex work their ammunition'.[45]

'Sex positive' advocacy gained increased momentum in the early 2000s in part because blogging emerged during the George W. Bush administration. The US government he led was propagating cartoonishly bad policies around contraception, sex education, LGBTQ young people, and sexual health. In response, liberal and feminist bloggers became particularly invested in producing non-judgemental information about sex and sexual health, and defences of pleasure, masturbation, queer sex, and sex outside of marriage. The increased accessibility and attractiveness of blogging technology made it possible to talk more openly about sex and pleasure. As a result, many sex worker writers became embedded in a blogging culture that was (perhaps rather too uncomplicatedly) pro-sex and pro-pleasure.

This discourse of sex positivity helped produce the figure we term the 'Erotic Professional'. Easily identifiable as one of the more vocal, visible figures of the sex worker movement, the Erotic Professional positions herself as answering a vocational 'calling' that seems to have barely anything to do with being paid.

In downplaying economic coercion and instead emphasising her pleasure and desire, the Erotic Professional attempts to make commercial sex more closely resemble the sex life that society is more ready to endorse – that for which women receive no payment. One escort, for example, is quoted in an interview as saying:

A prostitute will do everything for money. Not me ... I try to forget about the money ... it's very affectionate ... I don't even think about [payment] until the very end. I don't demand payment up front, because the guys I go with are always good people ... I also adore sex. I wouldn't be in this profession if I didn't like it. So, I found a way to make money doing something that I like.[46]

Often the Erotic Professional is a dominatrix or 'companion' – types of sex work in which the act of penetration is downplayed until it's practically incidental.

Blurring the lines between paid sex and recreational sex is a narrative readily available to many sex workers, as it is already present in much of the marketing directed at clients. Little is more consistently tempting for clients than the fiction that they are the object of the workers' genuine, irrepressible sex drive. The bored, libidinous housewife, the authentic 'girlfriend experience', ('It's very affectionate … I also adore sex') and the powerful, formidable dominatrix are socially palatable fantasy characters designed to entice and impress customers.

These sex positive politics create the illusion that worker and client are united in their interests. Both, we are told, are there for an erotic experience, for intimacy, for hot sex. Raising the subject of the worker's needs (for safety, money, or negotiating power) would spoil the illusion that the worker and client are erotically in tune, and that she's just as sexually invested in their encounter as he is.

In this rhetoric, the focus can easily shift to the needs and enjoyment of the client. Carol Queen's influential 1997 essay on sex positivity and sex workers' rights describes sex work as a 'life of sexual generosity' and has a subsection titled 'Why Johns Need Sex-Positive Prostitutes' – a subtitle it is hard for us to read without wondering, *who cares*.[47]

This approach reaches its apex in the 2011 documentary *Scarlet Road*, which follows sex worker Rachel Wotton in her relationships with two disabled clients. Rachel's advocacy makes little distinction between sex workers and sex buyers, and indeed focuses on the sexual rights of her clients. In the trailer for the film, Rachel tells us, 'I like the fact that my job always entails pleasure' and ends with 'I think there's a right to sexual expression' – eliding that what is being talked about is the sexual expression of *the client*, not the worker.[48]

This elision is harmful. The worker's interests are not identical to those of the client. Ultimately, the worker is there because they are interested in getting paid, and this economic imperative is *materially different* from the client's interest in recreational sex.* Losing sight of that leads to a politics that is inadequate in its approach to *workers'* material needs in the workplace.

As sex workers, we sympathise with the wish to over-emphasise pleasure, freedom, or power. This narrative may feel much better than being stigmatised as damaged, an animal or a piece of meat.

However, there is an obvious conflict of interest between a fantasy persona who loves their job and an activist who demands policy intervention to remedy the abuse of their human rights in the workplace. Using just one persona to assure your clients that you love your working conditions and *also* to highlight how inadequate they are is a difficult line to walk.

When sex workers market themselves as 'upscale' or 'exclusive', journalists often read this at face value and dismiss their voices as unrepresentative or privileged.[49] Honorifics like 'Mistress' or 'Domina' signal to the public that the politics of the sex workers' rights movement dovetail with the sexual roles we perform at work.† It suggests that these politics can be consumed *as sex*. Sex worker Lori Adorable writes, 'If we continue to play the same role outside the dungeon as we do within it, we will remain alienated from our basic labor rights as well as our labor.'[50]

These politics produce a further category of 'things we cannot say' – the perspectives of sex workers who hate sex work. For the Erotic Professional, the figure of the unhappy sex worker becomes the unacceptable 'other' who must be disavowed at all costs in their own fight

---

* However, as we shall see later, criminalisation – whether of the worker, the client, or both – pushes their interests to overlap, as both will have a shared interest in avoiding police detection in order that the interaction can proceed.

† A prominent recent example is Terri-Jean Bedford, lead plaintiff in the *Bedford v Canada* case, who worked as a dominatrix and made court appearances in leather outfits, brandishing BDSM equipment and cracking jokes about being hired as 'government whip'. H. Loney, 'Who is Terri-Jean Bedford, the dominatrix fighting Canada's prostitution laws', *Global News*, 20 December 2013, globalnews.ca.

for social acceptance. The idea of sex as a site of trauma prompts a knee-jerk dismissal, where anti-prostitution politics are discredited as mere 'prudishness'.[*] One activist writes, in response to sex workers discussing trauma,

> I am not a victim. My clients do not victimize me. If you are an independent provider not being forced, perhaps you should consider another line of work. How can your sex work be healthy if you resent men so deeply? ... You shouldn't be doing sex work!! *Healthy* sex work requires that you be empowered.[51]

Another sex worker activist responds callously to a former sex worker's claims that high numbers of people are raped in sex work, writing: 'Guess again, honey – I haven't been ... If you love yourself and believe that you deserve to be loved by others, when you choose to become a sex worker, then you'll probably be just fine. But if you don't, then you'll probably run into trouble.'[52] Like any victim-blaming politics, this is both harmful, *and* a misdirected attempt to feel 'in control' – to fend off the possibility of sexual violence.

Carol Queen, in the same sex positivity essay quoted earlier, explicitly excludes those who are not having fun, writing: 'I do not intend to encompass the experience of those whores ... who are not sex positive, and who act out the negative expectations imposed on them by a sexist and sex negative culture.'[53] Queen seems to position the workers' dissatisfaction at work as their own fault for being 'unenlightened'. A sex worker who is living precariously or in poverty, who is at risk of criminalisation or police violence, or who is being exploited by a manager or lacks negotiating power is not likely to be particularly 'sex positive' at work. These factors are structural, not a function of the worker's state of enlightenment.

Some activists become so invested in defending sexually empowered prostitutes that they downplay or even deny that the sex industry can be a site of abuse. This can quickly devolve into personal attacks,

---

[*] Journalist Laurie Penny, for example, invokes 'knickers in a twist' in the 'icy corridors of bourgeois moral opprobrium'. L. Penny, 'The most harmful effects of prostitution are caused by its criminality', *New Statesman*, 13 December 2012, newstatesman.com.

as typified by one North American sex worker and blogger who has written of the 'tragedy porn' of 'so-called survivors' with testimonies 'conveniently years or decades in the past, long enough for the evidentiary trail to have been washed away by their bucketfuls of crocodile tears'.*

Rape denialism is unconscionable and completely contrary to feminism. Those who are being exploited or harmed within commercial sex should be the central concern of the sex workers' rights movement, yet such politics actively push them away. Exited survivor Rachel Moran has spoken about the hurt such attacks have caused her, writing, 'My truths do not suit them, so my truths must be silenced.'[54]

Sex positive sex work politics are useful for the Erotic Professionals who advocate them *and* for carceral feminists who push for criminalisation. These groups *share an interest* in glossing over the material conditions of sex workers' workplaces. For Erotic Professionals, to raise such topics either spoils the advertising illusion or is detrimental to the self protective identity they've created. For carceral feminists, arguing about the 'meaning' of sex usefully conceals practical, granular questions about sex workers' access to power and resources at work – questions which, if examined, inevitably reveal that criminalisation cannot improve sex workers' lives.

Both sometimes represent the debate as a simplified binary opposition: 'Happy Hookers' (who enjoys sex work and thus support decriminalisation) versus 'Exited Women' (who experienced harm in the sex industry and therefore support criminalisation). For instance,

---

* M. McNeill, 'The Head of a Pin', *The Honest Courtesan*, 6 March 2017, maggiemcneill.wordpress.com. See also: M. McNeill (@maggie_mcneill), Twitter, 6:12pm, 30 March 2016: 'Dear soi-disant "trafficking victim": Your story would be a lot more believable if 1) you hadn't waited decades to tell it, until all possible evidence is long gone; 2) you had some kind of police report, names of your supposed 'traffickers', addresses, ANYTHING really 3) there had ever been any actual investigation into the incredibly serious crimes you allege, which in real life are generally acted upon no matter HOW long after the fact; and 4) if your story wasn't EXACTLY like other "sex trafficking" narratives in every important detail, when IRL the details of similar crimes are often dramatically different from one another. https://maggiemcneill.files.wordpress.com/2012/04/mind-witness-testimony.pdf ... Love, Maggie.'

anti-prostitution feminist and theatre-maker Grace Dyas characterises the debate thusly:

> The exited perspective says, *you need to see the harm done to me
> and the harm done to women every day*. The other side is like, *you
> need to see I am enjoying it* ... So many women involved in sex work
> don't want to be there ... But the others are saying, '*We're also here;
> we're enjoying it*'.[55]

Dyas fails to acknowledge the prostitute experiencing harm or coercion who disagrees that criminalising commercial sex will necessarily
bring her justice. She neglects to consider any concrete reason for this
disagreement, attributing it instead to 'enjoyment'.

Similarly, anti-prostitution campaigner Julie Bindel described the
group 'Survivors for Decrim' as 'the pro-prostitution lobby, co-opting
the language of abolitionists to further your cause'. The group's representative explained in reply, 'We're people who currently or formerly
have sold/traded sex, who are survivors of violence or trauma, and
who have a different perspective from you on how to deliver safety
for people selling sex. That's not pro-prostitution or co-opting.'
Bindel then claims, 'Your wording implies you describe yourselves as
survivors of the sex trade, which clearly is not true ... You're intentionally misleading the public.'[56] The implication seems to be that to
'legitimately' be a survivor requires you to agree with certain politics
around the sex industry. Those who support the decriminalisation of
commercial sex are cast as 'illegitimate' survivors.

For anti-prostitution feminists, survivors who advocate decriminalisation constitute a category that cannot – or should not – exist.
Those who experience sex work as miserable, violent, or exploitative
but continue doing it are left politically bereft, pushed out by pro-sex
politics in the sex worker movement and invisible to (or strategi-
cally unacknowledged by) carceral feminists, who consider the only
legitimate victim to be one who has exited or will imminently exit
prostitution. As Canadian prostitute and writer Sarah Mann argues,
'Unhappy whores are stuck seeking political representation among
either a camp that disavows their experiences or a camp that disavows their rights.'[57]

While the idea of selling sex as joyful sexuality is entirely at odds with the experiences of most prostitutes, we are not arguing for the focus on the sexual act to be completely discarded. (By the end of the following chapter, the tension between understanding sex work as *sex* and understanding sex work as *work* will become clearer.) As sex worker Pluma Sumaq writes:

> Looking at the sexual nature of prostitution is essential to understanding prostitution. How could it not be? ... Intimacy, sex and sexuality not only activate some of our deepest fears, but also some of our deepest woundings ... Prostitution presents us with a reality that is sometimes too emotionally painful to unravel because as we attempt to do so, we begin to realize that it is our reality too. Sex and intimacy are personally also our own struggle.[58]

Being critical about sex positivity in the sex worker movement should not mean pretending sex is incidental. We can explore the sexual experiences of people in the sex trade in a way that respects the diversity of those experiences – whether they are bad or good – and doesn't overwhelm the conversation about labour rights.

Thinking about sex work only as sex also allows any survivor of any sexual violence to claim the (real or imagined) traumas of sex workers as their own. In an article about brothel work in Germany, journalist Sarah Ditum imputes that a sex worker named Josie is experiencing daily trauma – based on the disclosure that she brings numbing cream to work in case a client is heavy-handed with a vibrator. In response, Ditum writes, 'Prostitution [is] an institution that insists on the dehumanisation of women, the grinding away of our souls so we become easier to fuck, easier to use, easier to kill.'[59] The use of 'we' and 'are' suggests that the experiences of a sex worker – in this case, Josie – are a struggle shared with all women. (Of course, the same cannot be said in reverse; 'women's liberation' is not always shared with prostitutes.)[60] So eager is she to link her own feelings to the vibrator story that Ditum neglects to ask whether the worker would like to see her workplace criminalised or not.

Feminist writer Gloria Steinem, too, typifies this when she writes: 'Our spirits ... break a little each time we see ourselves in chains or full labial display for the conquering male viewer, bruised or on our knees.'[61] The language of the paragraph flickers between two perspectives: Steinem-as-viewer ('our spirits break a little each time we see') and Steinem-as-performer ('ourselves in chains or full labial display'). Rendering the sex worker a symbol enables anti-prostitution campaigners to treat themselves and their concerns as interchangeable with those of sex workers, re-inscribing these concerns as representational rather than asking more granular questions of labour rights. As Melissa Gira Grant writes,

> An image of a woman in porn can be seen to stand in for 'all women', whereas an actual woman performing in porn is understood as essentially other. So 'defending women from images of women in porn' is a project that's understood (by some feminists) as a broader political project, whereas the labor rights of women who perform in porn are considered marginal.[62]

A sex worker may describe a bad experience as a labour-rights violation, sexual abuse, or simply a shitty day at work. Regardless, their testimonials are not merely symbols to be interpreted by non-prostitute feminists, especially not as part of rallying for the criminalisation of their income. Current workers are the experts on what *current working conditions* in the sex industry are like. It is frustrating to sex workers when the exited or non-prostitute perspective are centred, and our voices are treated as optional extras.

The difference between prostitutes and non-prostitutes and between current and former sex workers is fundamental not because of *identities*, but because of the *material conditions* of those who sell and trade sex. Only some people are *actually having sex for money* in the here and now – and others are not. No matter what stake they feel they have in the debate, non-prostitute and exited survivors cannot justifiably talk over sex workers who are still selling sex.

The difficult truth is that harm will come to people selling sex tonight, tomorrow, and for the foreseeable future. Nonetheless, for many people, doing so remains the only viable way to survive. The politics of Happy Hookers and Exited Women have no space for the existence of the unhappy sex worker, whose inconvenient truths disrupt the comforting delusion that prostitution is a sexual orientation. Instead, she is forced – usually by economic necessity – to continue choosing survival over a noble exit, and she reminds us that capitalism cannot be magicked away with liberal or carceral solutions. For this person, sex work *may* be sex – but it is also *work*, in a world that allows no alternative. Understanding what work is, however, is easier said than done.

2

Work

I've heard some of my white friends say that they're in prostitution because of the power. Well, for Black women it's for the money.

– Gloria Lockett[1]

Prostitution is not productive. The only 'product' of the sex trade is an orgasm for a man. That's not productive, that's not 'work'.

– Sharon Hodgson, Labour MP[2]

Capital had to convince us that [housework] is a natural, unavoidable and even fulfilling activity to make us accept our unwaged work. In its turn, the unwaged condition of housework has been the most powerful weapon in reinforcing the common assumption that *housework is not work*, thus preventing women from struggling against it, except in the privatized kitchen-bedroom quarrel that all society agrees to ridicule, thereby further reducing the protagonist of a struggle. We are seen as nagging bitches, not workers in struggle.

– Silvia Federici, *Wages Against Housework*

Is Work Good?

As a society, we obsessively valorise work as a key locus of meaning, status, and identity in our lives. At the same time, we struggle with shit jobs, falling wages, and the correct suspicion that what many of us do for money all day contributes nothing of real value to our lives or communities. Instead, we mostly just make profits for people further up the chain. In this confused and confusing context, to *do what you love* is deeply aspirational, a lean-in fantasy that gives an individual the illusion of control, a daydream of power in the office – and, in reality, a significant class-marker. The women interviewed in magazines about their morning routines are invariably early risers not because they're cleaning the office in question, but because they're running it – and we are taught a moral lesson connecting their happiness to their productivity, to the accoutrements of their good life: the high-end gym, the smiling personal assistant, the architecture firm, the fresh flowers. They are here to show us: *work is good*.

The Erotic Professional and the anti-prostitution activist share the assumption that work is good. The Erotic Professional, as we saw in the last chapter, cultivates an image of professionalism and economic achievement, emphasising her specialised skills, equipment, and talent. Her narrative includes the status symbols associated with success: a large income, leisure time, a good education, homeownership, and so on. Positioning herself within a context of luxury goods and conspicuous consumption is also an advertising strategy; it signals to wealthy clients that she is on their level, and that spending substantial sums on specialist forms of sex (or 'connection') is legitimate.

Along with sex positivity, the idea of the disabled client is often crucial to the politics of work that the Erotic Professional espouses. The disabled client, more than other men, typifies the figure of the *deserving* client. His need – seen as primarily a need for intimacy and connection rather than carnal passion – both professionalises and sanctifies the sex worker, portraying her in the soft, flattering light of a physical therapist or disability-rights advocate, and granting her work legitimacy through this lens. Not only does the Erotic Professional derive authentic pleasure from her work, but she does so within a framework of social value: who could deny such a man – depicted as desexualised, unthreatening and deserving – the intimacy and connection he craves? This is a patronising, ableist way to view disabled people. It is also an inadequate approach to sex workers' rights, which should hinge on workers' rights to safety, not on the purported social value of the work.

Through these fantasies and elisions, the Erotic Professional upholds mainstream notions of who deserves what. She agrees that *prestigious* work deserves respect and rewards – she merely wishes to expand our collective understanding of what prestigious work *is* to include herself, with her high income, her BDSM vocational calling, or her therapeutic approach to the deserving disabled client. The Erotic Professional's political expression regularly includes the claim that the sex industry is amazing to work in, much more so than any other job. This line of argument makes the purpose and demands of the sex workers' rights movement unclear: what problem are we trying to fix, if the situation is already perfect?

In a sense, anti-prostitution feminists implicitly agree with the Erotic Professional. They, too, think that the question of whether sex work is work should primarily be fought on the terrain of whether sex work is *good* work. They merely disagree that commercial sex could ever fall into the category of 'good work'. They therefore position work *in general* as something that the worker should find fulfilling, non-exploitative, and enjoyable. Deviation from this supposed norm is treated as evidence that something cannot be work. 'It's not work, it's exploitation' is a refrain you hear again and again.[3] One feminist policymaker in Sweden told a reporter, 'Don't say *sex work*, it's far too awful to be work.'[4] Awfulness and work are positioned as antithetical: if prostitution is awful, it cannot be work.

Anti-prostitution feminists and even policymakers often ask sex workers whether we would have sex with our clients if we weren't being paid. Work is thus constantly being re-inscribed as something so personally fulfilling you would pursue it for free.[5] Indeed, this understanding is in some ways embedded in anti-prostitution advocacy through the prevalence of unpaid internships in such organisations. Equality Now, a major, multimillion-dollar anti-prostitution organisation, instructs applicants that their eight-to-ten week internships will be unpaid (adding that 'no arrangements can be made for housing').[6] Such posts are common: Ruhama advertises numerous volunteer roles that could easily be paid jobs. In 2017, a UK anti-slavery charity came under fire in the national press for advertising unpaid internships.[7] In 2013, Turn Off the Red Light, an Irish anti-prostitution NGO consortium, advertised for an intern who would not be paid the minimum wage. The result of these unpaid and underpaid internships is that the women who are most able to build careers in the women's sector – campaigning and setting policy agendas around prostitution – are women who can afford to do unpaid full-time work in New York and London. In this context, it is hardly a surprise that the anti-prostitution movement as a whole has a somewhat abstracted view of the relationship between work and money.

Work may be mostly positive for those who can largely set the parameters of the conversation, like high-profile journalists. However, this does not describe reality for most women workers or workers in general (or even many journalists).* Most workers suffer some unfair conditions in the workplace and would not, as a rule, do their jobs for free. Work is often pretty awful, especially when it's low-paid and unprestigious. This is not to say that this state of affairs is good, or that we should accept it because it is normal, but nor is it useful to pretend that work is generally wonderful and exclude from our analysis the demands of workers whose experience does not meet this standard.

As with other jobs that women do, sexist devaluation of 'women's work' erases the emotional labour and hustle that constitutes the bulk of sex workers' actual efforts, reducing our job to simply being available for penetration at all times. Indeed, one of the key ideas used to treat prostitution as 'not-work' is the idea that we are simply holes: that we are offering up *purchased consent*. 'A man paying a woman for sex does so on the premise that he can do what he likes with her body in the time he has purchased it', writes one UK feminist.[8] Although perhaps easy to distractedly nod along to, commentary such as this reveals itself, upon closer inspection, to be perpetuating what it claims to condemn. A massage therapist who – like a sex worker – sells time and services rather than a physical product is not doing so 'on the premise that [a client] can do what he likes with her

---

* Sexual harassment and racism remain rife in the media, and journalists higher up on the chain are notorious for stealing ideas and credit from younger and more marginalised journalists, particularly women, people of colour, and working class and disabled people. The prestige of journalism jobs can be used against early-career journalists, who face being told – explicitly or implicitly – that if they won't do this job or stay quiet about that problem, there are a hundred others who will.

body in the time he has purchased', and to make such a statement about a massage therapist would be obviously horrifying. That it can be claimed about sex workers shows how deep the belief goes that women who sell sex give up all bodily boundaries: it is a belief shared – and mutually reinforced – by those who assault us and those who imagine themselves our defenders.

Not only are such claims misogynist, they are also absurd. Consider common sex-industry acronyms such as OWO ('oral without', i.e., a blowjob without a condom) in adverts posted by workers and reviews posted by clients. The existence of such terminology speaks to a *shared expectation* that sex workers have boundaries to which they expect clients to adhere. After all, if boundaries become meaningless after money changes hands, why do these adverts and reviews bother to convey – in sex-industry jargon created specifically to communicate these details – that Mia sells oral sex with a condom while Jade offers 'oral without'? Mia or Jade's specifications around condom use would become irrelevant if their consent had actually been 'purchased'.

Just as forcing a massage therapist to give you oral sex would constitute sexual assault, because she is *not* giving you the 'right' to her body when she sells massage services, forcing a sex worker to (for instance) have sex without a condom constitutes rape *precisely because* the sex worker has *not* sold the right for a client to use her body 'as he likes in the time he has purchased it'. In this way, a sex worker is no different from an actor who knows the difference between performing a love scene and having her breasts groped after the cameras have stopped rolling, or the movie's producer pressuring her to give him a 'massage' in his trailer. If we are serious about safety for sex workers in a post-Weinstein era, we will extend to them the same faith we give to film stars in their ability to differntiate between sexual touch at work and sexual touch that – even *in the workplace* – is assault.

Our ability to understand such assaults as rape depends on *not* understanding sex work as purchased consent, wherein sex workers hand over control of our boundaries and bodily rights with the exchange of cash. As sex worker Nikita told the 2017 Annual General

Meeting of Amnesty International UK, 'Part of believing me when I say I have been raped is believing me when I say *I haven't been.*'⁹

We live in a culture where it is assumed that to penetrate someone sexually is intrinsically an act of dominance and to be sexually penetrated is to be made subservient. This means that the mistreatment of sex workers begins to seem natural. If we who sell sex are already degraded through penetration, then the further degradation of being written about as garbage cans, flesh holes, sperm receptacles, orifices, or blow-up dolls is seen as fact rather than as actively reproducing and perpetuating misogynist discourse – and all in the name of feminism.

In being candid about bad workplace conditions, sex workers fear handing a weapon to political opponents; their complaints about work paradoxically become 'justification' to dismiss them as not 'real workers'.¹⁰ As one prominent UK feminist joked, 'Ever thought about having multiple penises shoved up you as a career? ... The longer you do it the more your earning potential decreases, but they say there's a fetish for everything!'¹¹ The joke is that sex workers 'mistakenly' think that what they do is work, even when that work can be sexist and ageist. Of course, if being subject to sexist and ageist discrimination at work excluded someone from the category of worker, *most* older women workers would be excluded: the gender pay gap increases with age.¹² If the only 'real' worker is one who suffers no workplace oppression or exploitation, then *all* organising for workers' rights becomes superfluous.

Some workers are lucky enough to have good pay, meaningful work, and autonomy, but most of us feel the sharp edge of exploitation in some way. Perhaps your boss took a cut of your tips, or forced you to work on your partner's birthday or during your grandfather's funeral. Perhaps you've started to resent the way your time-sheets always seem to entail an extra fifteen minutes of unpaid work at the end of the day, or how long you spend on your commute – time that's not only uncompensated but actively *expensive*. You're paying to get to work, and the company you work for is absorbing the benefit. In an important sense, waged work *is* exploitation. In a capitalist economy, bosses generate profits by paying you less for your labour than the money they make when the product of your labour is sold. It is not reasonable to assume that any kind of work – including sex work – is generally good.

Is Work Bad?

In the Parliament building, the small group of sex workers who had traipsed through the rain to meet with a Scottish government minister were asked to speak briefly about why we had entered prostitution. We went around the table. One single mother with several children explained that she got into sex work to support her family; another explained that, as an undocumented migrant, sex work was one of the few jobs available to her; a third explained that when she came out as trans and started her transition, she lost her mainstream job. A man talked about the homophobia he had experienced in other workplaces.

The minister was not impressed. She observed that we all seemed to have started selling sex in order to *get money*, in a tone suggesting not only that she was slightly incredulous, but that selling sex in order to earn an income seemed terribly mercenary to her. She contrasted our stories with those of sex workers who use drugs – *they* weren't in prostitution for economic reasons, were they?

Of course, sex workers who use drugs certainly *are* in sex work for economic reasons – either to get money with which to buy what they need (like housing or drugs) or as part of a direct trade for these same things. In the cacophony that followed the minister's question, as everybody tried to speak at once, this central point was lost.

People sell sex to get money. This simple fact is often missed, forgotten, or overlooked. This can be because sex workers are stigmatised to the extent that their motives are pathologised; it becomes inconceivable that people could do something considered so strange and terrible for the same mundane, relatable reasons that govern everybody else's everyday lives.* (Doubly so if they are sex workers who use

---

* The nineteenth-century French physician Louis Fiaux said prostitutes in his studies displayed 'the psychology of a child, the inattention of the young savage, the ... emptiness of a prehistoric brain still bathed in animality'. C.

drugs.) Sometimes the centrality of money is more deliberately hidden because to do so serves a political purpose. If a right-wing politician downplays the extent to which sex work is about generating a decent income and instead emphasises the extent to which it is driven by a 'criminal underworld', he can sidestep awkward questions about the connections between prostitution, poverty, and government policy – and align anti-prostitution measures with populist 'tough-on-crime' approaches. For example, Texas has some of the most extensive laws in the United States when it comes to criminalising pimps, traffickers and criminal gangs – but the state legislature has repeatedly failed to fund services for sex trafficking victims, let alone fund programmes that would meaningfully address poverty and failures in the child-welfare system.[13]

Pathologising sex workers as unable to make 'good' decisions, rather than seeing them as people largely motivated by familiar, mundane needs, can lead to disastrous consequences. In 2013, a Swedish family court ruled that a young mother named Jasmine did not know what was best for herself; the court saw her sex work not as a flexible job that gave her a livable income while caring full-time for her children, but as a form of 'self-harm'.[14] The judge ruled that as she was engaged in self-harm, that she was unable to care for her children, and disregarded her warnings that her ex-partner was violent. Her ex was awarded child custody. When she visited him in order to see the children, he stabbed her to death.

Dismissing Jasmine's prosaic, material reasons for doing sex work was key to the state's fatally inadequate response to her needs. The belief that sex workers aren't making – and can't make – good decisions leads us not to a feminist utopia, but to coercive, punitive modes of 'reform'.

Downplaying the practical and economic dimensions of prostitution also does some ideological heavy lifting for anti-prostitution feminists. For example, Catherine MacKinnon writes, 'If there were no buyers, *there would be no sellers*, namely traffickers.'[15] MacKinnon's

Bernheimer, *Figures of Ill Repute: Representing Prostitution in Nineteenth-century France*, Cambridge, MA: Harvard University Press, 1989, 211–12.

misidentification of 'people who sell sex' as 'traffickers' erases the fact that people who sell sex might be driven by economic need – a need which will not be solved by attempting to eradicate prostitution through criminal law. After all, if we forget for a second that people go to the streets because they need money, we needn't grapple with what will replace the income they lose – or what the implications will be for their safety when they desperately try to recoup that income.[16]

Remove money from the conversation and sex workers seem bizarre or broken. As one academic writes, 'The notion that prostitutes have distinctive personal biographies has a long and unhappy history: male myths about "the psychopathology of the prostitute" persist' – and, in the twenty-first century, these myths have a feminist veneer.[17] The sex worker, it is stated or implied, is not capable of understanding her own best interests and is instead acting out her childhood trauma. Anti-prostitution campaigner Kat Banyard, for example, argues that assuming a history of childhood sexual violence among sex workers 'makes sense' because 'common consequences of childhood sexual abuse include difficulty asserting boundaries'.[18] Sex working survivors have pushed back on this attempt to pathologise their lives. As Lori Adorable writes, 'It's not because of some kind of permanent "damage" or trauma-reenactment compulsion. It's because [childhood sexual abuse] survivors often lack family support.'[19] In other words, people who have fled an abusive family home have a compelling need to avoid returning to it and may sell sex as a strategy to avoid such a return. This is a material need, not a pathology.

'Economic necessity is the main imperative for women becoming involved in prostitution', according to UK Home Office researchers.[20] Academic Julia Laite writes, 'Several late-nineteenth-century studies found that up to half of the women selling sex in Britain had been domestic servants, and that many had hated it so much they had willingly left service.'[21] Laite quotes a 1920s sex worker asking an arresting police officer, 'What will you give me if I do give this up? A job in a laundry at two pounds a week – when I can make twenty easily?'[22] Writing in the 1980s, sex worker Nickie Roberts echoes these perspectives:

Working in crummy factories for disgusting pay was the most degrading and exploitative work I ever did in my life ... I think there should be another word for the kind of work working class people do; something to differentiate it from the work middle class people do; the ones who have careers. All I can think of is *drudgery*. It's rotten and hopeless; not even half a life. It's *immoral*. Yet as I say, it's *expected* of working class women that they deny themselves everything ... Why should I have to put up with a middle class feminist asking me why I didn't 'do anything – scrub toilets, even?' than become a stripper? What's so liberating about cleaning up other people's shit?[23]

Through the lens of economic need, people's reasons for engaging in sex work reappear not as aberrant or abject, but as a rational survival strategy in an often shitty world. As another set of researchers note, women 'are more likely than men to be unemployed, to be under-employed and to be low paid'; in the face of these obstacles, 'prostitution can be the more attractive option'.[24]

Dudu Dlamini, a sex worker in South Africa, says,

I had already been in Cape Town cleaning people's fucking bloody houses. I'd done lots of washing for people in different houses. I'd wake early in the morning and open the windows, clean, cook, make porridge for their children, take their children to school, and do their ironing just for a place to sleep, for a plate of food, not even a cigarette on top of it. So I was *done* with that.[25]

A migrant woman in the UK who sells sex in a flat says, 'This job is better; the money is good and quick. The cleaner job was really hard work and no good money. I still say I'm a cleaner, I have to lie, but I don't want to be one.'[26]

Race and disability are key factors in sex work demographics. Pluma Sumaq writes that, for many people of colour, 'Prostitution is not what you do when you hit rock bottom. Prostitution is what you do to stay afloat, to swim rather than sink, to defy rather than disappear.'[27] An anonymous Māori mother writes,

My body isn't capable of working a 40-hour week, nor allowing me to become qualified at something that pays well. I'm disabled from working, and I'm part of a society that doesn't take care of people like me, people like my daughter [who is also disabled] ... Being a sex worker means I can work when I am able and have days off when I'm not ... I can spend lots of time caring for my daughter.[28]

Like other marginalised groups, LGBTQ people are over-represented in sex work.* Discrimination, rejection, and abuse – both at home and in wider communities – increase their precarity and vulnerability in a homophobic and transphobic society, leaving prostitution as one of the remaining viable routes out of destitution. Trans women in particular often find that formal employment is out of reach. Increased school drop-out rates, lack of family support, and lack of access to adequate healthcare (including the means to finance gender-affirming treatment) leave them exposed to poverty, illness, and homelessness. One-quarter of homeless youth in London are LGBTQ, and of that group nearly seventy per cent were forced out by their families.[29]

It is very difficult to prevent anyone from selling sex through criminal law. Criminalisation can make it more dangerous, but there is little the state can do to physically curtail a person's capacity to sell or trade sex. Thus, prostitution is an abiding strategy for survival for those who have nothing – no training, qualifications, or equipment. There are almost no prerequisites for heading out to the streets and waiting for a client.† Survival sex work may be dangerous, cold, and

---

* 'A larger proportion of the transgender community is involved in sex work compared to the proportion of the population of cisgender women who are sex workers. This is indicative of the often marginalized status of transgender people in society. Deeply-embedded prejudiced attitudes inhibit LGBTI people from accessing education, thus impacting their access to livelihood options and housing. These individuals also tend to have less access to justice and to social support services due to stigma and institutionalized discrimination.' Amnesty International, 'Amnesty International policy on state obligations to respect, protect and fulfil the human rights of sex workers', POL 30/4062/2016, 26 May 2016, amnesty.org, 5–6.

† Many sex workers cite other positives to opting to work on the street – for instance, the sense of community or camaraderie, and complete flexibility. Street-based sex work has the lowest barriers to entry of any form of sex work. For instance, if your drug use, mental health, or caring responsibilities make sticking to a routine or turning up to pre-arranged shifts difficult, you can

frightening – but for people whose other options are worse (hunger, homelessness, drug withdrawal) it's there as a last resort: the 'safety net' onto which almost any destitute person can fall. This explains the indomitable resilience of sex work.

For some anti-prostitution campaigners, concerns about the sex industry stand in place of a wider critique of capitalism. 'Why is the Left in favour of the free market only when it is women's bodies being bought and sold?' asks Julie Bindel.[30] This question either misunderstands or misrepresents the argument. What the Left actually favours is *labour rights*, to redress the balance of power between employers and workers. In a capitalist society, when you criminalise something, *capitalism still happens in that market*. When we are asked, in a capitalist society, to choose between criminalising commercial sex and *de*criminalising it, we are not offered an option for the 'free market' to *not* govern the proceedings. Look at the United States, where the use, sale, and distribution of drugs is, for the most part, criminalised. If, in Julie Bindel's analysis, it can't be a capitalist market because it is criminalised, are those activities therefore happening on a communist or socialist basis? Maybe the US drugs market operates as a gift economy?

In fact, as the US drugs market devastatingly illustrates, capitalism is in many ways at its most intense in criminalised markets. This is because in criminalised markets there can be no regulations, no workers' rights. With commercial sex criminalised, *there can be no workers' rights*, whereas with commercial sex decriminalised, people who sell sex can access labour law. The left supports the *de*criminalisation of sex work because the left supports workers having rights.

The high prevalence of marginalised people in prostitution is seen as evidence for its predatory strangeness, but in reality, it reflects the normalised, systemic failures of mainstream society. This reflection is so sharp it makes people uncomfortable – but rather than

---

work around that through street-based sex work. You don't need to pay for a space to work in or specialist equipment (for example, BDSM-related kit or club-specific outfits). As such, people often opt for street-based sex work when they have very few resources to spare, as a way of surviving catastrophes such as homelessness.

seeing that the source of their discomfort is the economic inequalities that produce this situation, they 'other' the problem by locating its source in prostitution. A similar dynamic can be seen in punitive responses to homelessness, such as fining people for begging or rough sleeping and installing 'anti-homeless spikes' to prevent them from using doorways for temporary shelter. An Oxford city councillor gave too-explicit an account of the underlying reasoning when he said, 'I would like to go to some of these rough sleepers and say, "You are a disgrace." I don't think it would do any good, but they ought to have more respect.'[31] It's not hard to detect a commonality here with responses to street-based sex work, not least in how so many policy advocates emphasise decreasing the *visibility* of street-based sex work (rather than, say, increasing sex worker safety or decreasing poverty) as a key metric of success. The visibility of homelessness and street-based sex work makes people angry with those who are sleeping rough or selling sex outdoors.

To say that prostitution is work is not to say it is *good* work, or that we should be uncritical of it. To be better than poverty or a lower paid job is an abysmally low bar, especially for anyone who claims to be part of any movement towards liberation. People who sell or trade sex are among the world's least powerful people, the people often forced to do the worst jobs. But that is precisely why anti-prostitution campaigners should take seriously the fact that sex work *is a way people get the resources they need*. Instead, this is airily dismissed – losing a bad job, we're told, is no big deal.[32] Losing jobs is how we achieve social change, we're told. Anti-prostitution feminist Meghan Murphy writes, 'I suppose we shouldn't try to stop the oil industry because people will lose jobs? It isn't super progressive ... to defend harmful practices lest people lose jobs.'[33] Those who make these arguments imagine 'changing society' through taking something away. (Of course, many of these jobs are not directly analogous to sex work: oil workers, bankers, and nuclear scientists are not already at the bottom of the social pile.) But people with relatively little are right to be fearful when their means of survival is taken away. British miners in the 1980s didn't strike on the basis that mining was the most wonderful job – they were simply correct in their belief that, once mining was taken from them, Thatcher's government would abandon their communities to desperate poverty. Likewise, few sex workers would object if you sought to abolish the sex industry by ensuring that they got the resources they need *without having to sell sex*.

Instead, however, one Labour politician cites what she considered to be sex workers' 'low' income to argue that reducing it even further could not be a real concern.* It is *when* people's incomes *are* low that reducing them is a terrifying prospect; it is when jobs *are* bad that workers most need workers' rights.

Outsiders often think that selling sex must be a pretty horrible job, and many sex workers would agree. However, these sex workers may locate the problem not in *sex* but in *work*. Striking workers rely on their ability to refuse wages: the temptation to break the strike increases as your money runs out. In any negotiation, the most power is held by the side which is most able to walk away. We see this asymmetry of need within sex work – as anti-prostitution feminists often like to point out, no man *needs* to buy sex; it is ultimately a recreational activity. Sex workers, however, *do* have a need. As Dudu Dlamini says, 'What it's all about is money ... What am I gonna eat with my kids? My kids are hungry now. I need quick cash ... I felt,

---

* When Scottish Labour politician Rhoda Grant sought to criminalise the purchase of sex in Scotland in 2012, she faced criticism from sex workers regarding fears over loss of income and resulting poverty. She responded by citing research showing that the average sum earned by a sex worker in an encounter with a client was thirty-seven pounds, 'dispelling the myth' that sex work is a lucrative career. The obvious implication is that this is already such a 'low' amount that reducing sex workers' income could not be a serious concern, but thirty-seven pounds per client – which might be twenty minutes to an hour's work – is *not* an obviously low sum to women otherwise earning the minimum wage, at the time, of £6.19 an hour (the research focuses on highly marginalised women working in a deprived part of England, so the prospect of even that wage was probably not available to them). Ms Grant – who earns £67,000 a year – and her doubly oblivious approach to money, poverty, and work in many ways exemplify carceral feminist thinking about economics and the sex industry. See R. Grant, 'Proposed Criminalisation of the Purchase of Sex (Scotland) Bill (2): Summary of Consulation Responses', Scottish Parliament, 2013, www.parliament.scot.

"I will go. I will survive. And I will come back with money. I will take care of my kids."[34] In an important sense, clients are not the demand but the *supply*; for sex workers, clients represent the supply of resources into our lives.

We have witnessed clients using internet forums to organise a boycott against escorts in their area, forcing them to all drop their rates. The clients are, of course, easily able to forgo the luxury of commercial sex – and, as a result, their ringleader knows that the escorts are likely to yield, as he and his buddies can outlast the workers indefinitely. The person selling sex *needs* the transaction far more than the buyer does; this need makes the sex worker vulnerable. In the same way, a street-based worker suffering a lack of business after a police crackdown becomes desperate, and desperation makes them less able to refuse unfair demands. Compromise means capitulating to the client's fears about avoiding the police; if he wants to do business in an unlit park at midnight to stay hidden, then he can make that demand or simply leave without paying. People are attracted to the concept of a Nordic-style law that criminalises only the sex buyer, and not the prostitute – but any campaign or policy that aims to reduce business for sex workers will force them to absorb the deficit, whether in their wallets or in their working conditions. As a sex worker in the Industrial Workers of the World observes,

> I find that how easy, safe, and enjoyable I can make my work is directly related to whether I can survive on what I'm currently making ... I might be safer if I refused any clients who make their disrespect for me clear immediately, but I know exactly where I can afford to set the bar on what I need to tolerate. If I haven't been paid in weeks, I need to accept clients who sound more dangerous than I'd usually be willing to risk.[35]

When sex workers speak to this, we are often seemingly misheard as defending some kind of 'right' for men to pay for sex. In fact, as Wages For Housework articulated in the 1970s, naming something as *work* is a crucial first step in refusing to do it – on your own terms. Marxist-feminist theorist Silvia Federici wrote in 1975 that 'to demand wages for housework does not mean to say that if we are paid we will continue to do it. It means precisely the opposite. To say that we want money for housework is the first step towards refusing to do it, because the demand for a wage makes our work visible, which is the most indispensable condition to begin to struggle against it.'[36] Naming work *as work* has been a key feminist strategy beyond Wages For Housework. From sociologist Arlie Hochschild's term 'emotional labour', to journalist Susan Maushart's term 'wifework', to Sophie Lewis's theorising around surrogacy and 'gestational labour', naming otherwise invisible or 'natural' structures of gendered labour is central to beginning to think about how, collectively, to resist or reorder such work.

Just because a job is bad does not mean it's not a 'real job'. When sex workers assert that *sex work is work*, we are saying that we need rights. We are not saying that work is good or fun, or even harmless, nor that it has fundamental value. Likewise, situating what we do within a workers' rights framework does not constitute an unconditional endorsement of work itself. It is not an endorsement of capitalism or of a bigger, more profitable sex industry. 'People think the point of our organisation is [to] expand prostitution in Bolivia', says ONAEM activist Yuly Perez. 'In fact, we want the opposite. Our ideal world is one free of the economic desperation that forces women into this business.'[37]

It is not the task of sex workers to apologise for what prostitution is. Sex workers should not have to defend the sex industry to argue that we deserve the ability to earn a living without punishment. People should not have to demonstrate that their work has intrinsic value to society to deserve safety at work. Moving towards a better society – one in which more people's work *does* have wider value, one in which resources are shared on the basis of need – cannot come about through criminalisation. Nor can it come about through treating marginalised people's material needs and survival strategies as trivial. Sex workers ask to be credited with the capacity to struggle with work – even to hate it – and still be considered workers. You don't have to like your job to want to keep it.

3

Borders

It is common for sex workers' rights advocates to argue that sex work is different from trafficking. This serves as a kind of rhetorical dividing line: it says, 'We do not have to talk about this. It is a different category of thing'. This is not the argument we are going to make. The reality is both more complex and more important.

Trafficking is a topic that rightly concerns progressives. It speaks to global inequalities of power, money, and safety. It is legitimate to be sympathetic to sex workers' rights perspectives and also have big concerns about trafficking into the sex industry.

Sex trafficking is often presented as *the* iteration of human trafficking – to the extent that the two phrases often seem to mean the same thing. Given how strong this link is in the public mind, you might be impatient for this chapter to discuss commercial sex, not borders. However, a major problem with the way these ideas are lumped together is that trafficking into the sex industry is, in fact, only one symptom among many in the much larger process of undocumented migration.[*] Commercial sex within this context cannot be properly understood without talking about migration. Exploited people – working in the sex industry, in car washes, in hotels, or in freezing cabbage fields in Lincolnshire – are victims of problems that are *systemic* and largely originate from the state, rather than from individuals.

---

[*] *Undocumented migration* means people crossing borders without papers. We also use the phrase *irregular migration*, which speaks to how people may migrate through legal routes but, over time, become undocumented or insecurely documented – for example, by overstaying a visa or leaving an employer.

However, trafficking is often not clearly defined; people use the same word but mean different things by it. Focusing just on commercial sex, some people use *trafficking* to mean all prostitution, or all migration into the sex industry. Others mean all migration into the sex industry that involves help from a third party, even if that third party is not seeking financial gain (for instance, a friend or a relative). It might cover anyone who incurs debt in the process of crossing borders without papers, or who incurs such a debt and pays that debt off through sex work. It might mean anybody who works for a manager while selling sex – or it might mean all sex-industry workplaces where abuse occurs, regardless of the migration status of the workers. It might mean kidnap and rape.

Being specific about what kinds of situations are being discussed helps make sense of the conversation, even when the speakers disagree about the problems or the solutions. Trafficking is often presented as an 'apolitical' topic about which everyone can agree. As migration academics Bridget Anderson and Rutvica Andrijasevic write, approaching the topic of trafficking critically 'is akin to saying that one endorses slavery or is against motherhood and apple pie. Trafficking is a theme that is supposed to bring us all together.'[1] But once we drill down to specifics, genuine political fault-lines are revealed. Everyone does not agree.

Governments, NGOs, and corporations all fund policies and actions under the heading of 'anti-trafficking'. UK law defines *trafficking* as arranging or facilitating the arrival of another 'for the purposes of exploitation' using force, fraud, coercion, or in exchange for 'the giving or receiving of payments' (i.e., for money).[2] *Exploitation* is defined as 'slavery, servitude, forced or compulsory labour', the removal of organs, or general prostitution offences. This means, for example, that in countries where brothel-keeping is criminalised, arranging someone's travel so that they can work in a brothel becomes a trafficking offence. US law defines *sex trafficking* as 'the recruitment, harbouring, transportation, provision, or obtaining of a person for the purpose of a commercial sex act' – which, reading closely, we note does not necessarily entail the kinds of harms we might associate with the term 'sex trafficking'.[3] 'Harbouring', after all, can mean letting a sex worker friend crash at your place for a while. Some corporations are legally bound to do anti-trafficking work; for example, auditing for trafficking in their supply chains. Some do additional work – for example, retailers like Body Shop and AllSaints have launched awareness-raising campaigns, with a portion of their profit going to anti-trafficking work. Governments attempt to counter trafficking through legislation (for example, the UK's 2015 Modern Slavery Act), as well as trade deals and diplomacy.*

Broadly, most anti-trafficking NGOs come at the issue from either a human rights perspective, a carceral-feminist perspective, or a Christian perspective. Some mix two or more of these perspectives, but these three strands are the most useful for categorising these organisations' approaches. Generally, NGOs that approach the topic from a human rights–based perspective are doing work that is relatively unglamorous and not usually headline-grabbing; for example, they may be working on issues around cobalt mining in the Democratic Republic of Congo, fishing off the coast of Thailand, or migrant domestic workers in the United States.[4] Christian and carceral-feminist NGOs both tend to focus on trafficking into prostitution. Typically, their work tends to align around the goal of abolishing commercial sex through criminal law in order to 'end sex trafficking'.

Very few ordinary employees in these organisations are wealthy; most earn average incomes. Some grassroots anti-trafficking campaigners, like sex worker activists, struggle to earn a living. But, although individual activists may not feel it, a huge amount of money is poured into anti-prostitution work done through the prism of anti-trafficking. In 2012, in the United States *alone,* the collective budget

---

* For example, the US State Department issues an annual 'trafficking in persons' report, which ranks every country in the world in terms of how well the US perceives it to be tackling trafficking. A low ranking for several years can trigger trade sanctions. Countries with which the US wishes to express general displeasure – for example, Cuba or Iran – are often given low rankings despite a lack of data regarding how they are tackling the issue. See Alliance To End Slavery & Trafficking, 'Rankings Undermine Credibility of TIP Report: Malaysia, Burma and Qatar Upgrades Unjustified', press release, 28 June 2017, endslaveryandtrafficking.org.

of thirty-six large anti-prostitution anti-trafficking organisations (with many smaller organisations excluded from the calculation) totalled 1.2 *billion* dollars, while the US federal government budgets a further $1.2 to $1.5 billion annually for anti-trafficking efforts.[5] The vast majority of this money is spent on campaigning, as opposed to supporting survivors; in 2014, the United States had only about one thousand beds available for victims of trafficking.[6] (By contrast, in 2013, the collective budget for the sex workers' rights movement for the *entire world* was 10 million dollars.)[7]

Monstrosity and Innocence

Carceral feminists hold that if we could abolish prostitution through criminalising clients and managers, the trafficking of women would end, as there would be no sex trade to traffic them into. As the deputy prime minister of Sweden writes, 'It is very obvious to us that there is a very clear link between prostitution and trafficking ... Without prostitution there would be no trafficking of women.'[8] This perspective also views prostitution as intrinsically more horrifying than other kinds of work (including work that is 'low-status', exploitative, or low-paid), and as such, views attempting to abolish prostitution through criminal law as a worthwhile end in itself. For those who hold these views, defending sex workers' rights is akin to defending trafficking.

In these conversations, trafficking becomes a battle between good and evil, monstrosity and innocence, replete with heavy-handed imagery of chains, ropes, and cuffs to signify enslavement and descriptors such as *nefarious, wicked, villainous*, and *iniquitous*.[9] This 'evil' is driven by the aberrance of commercial sex and by anomalous (and distinctly racialised) 'bad actors': the individual villain, the pimp, the trafficker. A police officer summarises this approach as: 'we'll put all these pimps, all these traffickers in prison ... and that'll solve the problem'.[10] Numerous images associated with modern anti-trafficking campaigns feature a white girl held captive by a Black man: he is a dark hand over her mouth or a looming, shadowy figure behind her.[11]

Fancy-dress 'pimp costumes' offer a cartoonishly racist vision of 1970s Black masculinity, while American law-enforcement unashamedly use terms such as 'gorilla pimp' and link trafficking to rap music.[12] There is a horror-movie entertainment quality to this at times: tourists can go on 'sex-trafficking bus tours' to shudder over locations where they're told sexual violence has recently occurred ('perhaps you are wondering where these crimes take place')[13] or buy an 'awareness-raising' sandwich featuring a naked woman with her body marked up as if for a butcher.[14] Conventionally sexy nude women are depicted wrapped in tape or packed under plastic, with labels indicating 'meat'.[15]

Conversely, the victim is often presented with her 'girlishness' emphasised. Young women are styled to look pre-pubescent, in pigtails or hair ribbons, holding teddy bears. This imagery suggests another key preoccupation shared by modern and nineteenth-century anti-trafficking campaigners: innocence. A glance at the names chosen for police operations and NGOs highlights this: Lost Innocence, Saving Innocence, Freedom4Innocence, the Protected Innocence Challenge, Innocents at Risk, Restore Innocence, Rescue Innocence, Innocence for Sale.[16]

For feminists, this preoccupation with feminine 'innocence' should be a red flag, not least because it speaks to a prurient interest in young women. Conversely, LGBTQ people, Black people, and deliberate prostitutes are often left out of the category of innocence, and as a result harm against people in these groups becomes less legible as harm. For example, a young Black man may face arrest rather than support; indeed, resources for runaway and homeless youth (whose realities are rather more complex than chains and ropes) were not included in the US Congress's 2015 reauthorisation of the Justice for Victims of Trafficking Act.[17] Anti-trafficking statutes often exclude deliberate prostitutes from the category of people able to seek redress, as to be a 'legitimate' trafficking victim requires innocence, and a deliberate prostitute, however harmed, cannot fulfil that requirement.[18]

There is a huge emphasis on kidnapping and, correspondingly, heroic rescues. In the wildly popular action film *Taken* (2008), the daughter of the hero (played by Liam Neeson) is snatched by Albanian sex traffickers while on holiday in Paris. *Taken* typifies many real anti-trafficking campaigns, presenting trafficking as a context-free evil, a kidnap at random that could happen to anyone, anywhere. As if to emphasise the links between Hollywood and policy, the 'hero' is literally written into US law – the HERO Act (which stands for the Human Exploitation Rescue Operations Act) takes funding from Immigration and Customs Enforcement (ICE) to train US military veterans to fight trafficking.[19] (In *Taken,* Neeson has daughter-rescuing skills due to his time as a CIA agent.) Visitors to the website of the Freedom Challenge, an anti-trafficking NGO, are told:

> You crawl into bed and wrap yourself in your favorite blanket … You're alone, sleeping soundly and dreaming sweetly. Suddenly, a rustling in the next room jolts you awake. You … tiptoe across the cold floor and crack open the door. A bag is thrown over your head. You're carried away.[20]

A spokeswoman for another organisation told reporters that being 'stolen off the street' at random by human traffickers constituted 'a very big possibility' and warned people to stay in groups to avoid being kidnapped.[21] An anxious mother's claim that she thought her children were going to be abducted by traffickers in IKEA was shared more than 100,000 times on social media.[22] (All this resonates with nineteenth-century white-slavery fears; in 1899, a missionary with the Women's Christian Temperance Union reported 'there is a slave trade in this country, and it is not Black folks at this time, but little white girls – thirteen, fourteen, sixteen, and seventeen years of age – and they are snatched out of our arms, and from our Sabbath schools and from our Communion tables'.)[23] Slick, shareable videos depict young girls grabbed by strangers on the street, vanishing into vans.[24]

The plot of *Taken* repeatedly highlights the traffickers' nation-ality. After the film's success, Neeson had to issue a statement reassuring US parents that their children could go on school trips to Paris without being snatched by Albanian trafficking gangs.[25] 'The foreigner', writes historian Maria Luddy, has always been 'an inter-national figure symbolic of the white slaver.'[26]

The Role of the Border

People are not, en masse, being snatched off the street. A report from the UK's anti-slavery commission notes that cases of kidnap are very unusual, essentially because it would make little sense to 'give' someone the services of taking them across a border for free, when people are willing to pay up to thirty thousand pounds to be taken across that same border.[27] The vast, vast majority of people who end up in exploitative situations were *seeking to migrate* and have become entrapped in a horrifically exploitative system because when people migrate without papers they have few to no rights. Acknowledging that people who end up in exploitative situations *wanted to migrate* is not to blame them. It is to say that the solution to their exploitative situation is to enable them to migrate legally *and with rights*. Everything else is at best a distraction (sexy chains! evil villains!) and at worst, actively *worsens* the problem by pushing for laws which make it harder, not easier, to migrate legally and with rights.

You might be thinking that we seem to be talking about people smuggling rather than people trafficking, and that those two things are different. *People smuggling* is when someone pays a smuggler to get them over a border: in UK law, *human trafficking* is when someone is transported for the purposes of forced labour or exploitation using force, fraud, or coercion. It's tempting to think of these as separate things, but there is no bright line between them: they are two iterations of the same system.

Let's break it down. It is common for people to take on huge debts to smugglers to cross a border. So far, so good: clearly smuggling. But once the journey begins, the person seeking to migrate finds that the debt has grown, or that the work they are expected to undertake upon arrival in order to pay off the debt is different from what was agreed. Suddenly, the situation has spiralled out of control and they find themselves trying to work off the debt, with little hope of ever earning enough to leave. Smuggling becomes trafficking. The discourse of *trafficking* largely fails to help people in this situation, because it paints them as kidnapped and enchained rather than as *trying to migrate*. It therefore seeks to 'rescue' them by blocking irregular migration routes and sending undocumented people home— often the very *last* thing trafficked people want. Although they might hate their exploitative workplace, their ideal option would be to stay in their destination country in a different job or with better workplace conditions; an acceptable option would be to stay in the country under the current, shit working conditions, but the very worst option would be to be sent home with their debt still unpaid.

By viewing trafficking as conceptually akin to kidnap, anti-trafficking activists, NGOs, and governments can sidestep broader questions of safe migration. If the trafficked person is brought across borders *unwillingly*, there is no need to think about the people who will attempt this migration regardless of its illegality or conclude that the way to make people safer is to offer them legal migration routes. *People smuggling* tends to happen to less vulnerable migrants: those who have the cash to pay a smuggler upfront or have a family or community already settled in the destination country. *People trafficking* tends to happen to more vulnerable migrants: those who must take on a debt to the smuggler to travel and who have no community connections in their destination country. Both *want to travel*, however, and this is what anti-trafficking conversations largely obscure with their talk about kidnap and chains.

Our position is that no human being is 'illegal'. People should have the right to travel and to cross borders, and to live and work where they wish. As we wrote in the introduction, border controls are a relatively new invention – they emerged towards the end of the nineteenth century as part of colonial logics of racial domination and exclusion. (ICE, the brutal American immigration enforcement police, was only created in its modern form in 2003; the previous iteration of it is as recent as the 1930s, an agency called Immigration and Naturalization Services.) The mass migrations of the twenty-first century are driven by human-made catastrophes – climate change, poverty, war – and reproduce the glaring inequalities from which they emerge. Countries in the global north bear hugely disproportionate responsibility for climate change, yet disproportionately close their doors to people fleeing the effects of climate choas, leaving desperate families to sleep under canvas amid snow at the edges of

Fortress Europe. As migrant-rights organiser Harsha Walia writes, 'While history is marked by the hybridity of human societies and the desire for movement, the reality of most of migration today reveals the unequal relations between rich and poor, between North and South, between whiteness and its others.'[28]

A system where everybody could migrate, live, and work legally and in safety would not be a huge, radical departure; it would simply take seriously the reality that people are *already* migrating and working, and that as a society we should prioritise their safety and rights. Some journalists and policymakers argue that migration brings down wages. However, the current system, wherein undocumented people cannot assert their labour rights and as a result are hugely vulnerable to workplace exploitation, brings down wages by *ensuring* that there is a group of workers who bosses can underpay or otherwise exploit with impunity. Low wages and workplace exploitation are tackled through worker organising and labour law – not through attempting to limit migration, which *produces* undocumented workers who have no labour rights.

However, instead of starting from the premise of valuing human life, the countries of the global north enact harsh immigration laws that make it hard for people from global south countries to migrate. You don't stop people wanting or needing to migrate by making it illegal for them to do so, you just make it more dangerous and difficult, and leave them more vulnerable to exploitation. Punitive laws may dissuade some from making the journey, but they guarantee that everyone who *does* travel is doing so in the worst possible conditions. Spending billions of dollars on policing borders actively makes this worse, without addressing the reasons people might want to migrate – notably, gross inequality between nations, which in large part is a legacy of colonial – and contemporary – plunder and imperialist violence.

Thinking about how this plays out in practice may help illustrate the absurd cruelty of this set of systems. Again, let's keep commercial sex to one side for now, because it takes attention away from what is crucial here: *borders make people vulnerable*, and that vulnerability is what abusive people prey upon.

A citizen of France can purchase a French passport for under a hundred euros. If they then find themselves in Turkey, having a French passport means that they can purchase a ferry ticket to Greece – in other words, into the European Union – for less than twenty euros. Because this person can travel legally, they can travel cheaply, safely, and without the help of a people smuggler. In contrast, someone in Turkey with Somali travel documents, attempting to reach friends within the European Union, does not have the correct documents to take the tourist ferry. This person is likely to have to pay a smuggler. Because the smuggler is taking on a relatively high degree of risk – people smuggling is a serious criminal offence! – and because the person seeking to migrate is desperate to travel, the price point is high. The person without papers might be charged several thousand euros to make a similar journey to that of the tourist ferry, but in an unsafe, overcrowded boat.[29]

You can see this dynamic in action at the US–Mexico border. In 1994, the North American Free Trade Agreement (NAFTA) was signed. Two million Mexican farmers were forced off their land and into destitution while food prices within Mexico rose. As a result, a quarter of the population is regularly unable to afford sufficient food to avoid hunger.[30] During the same period, the border was increasingly hardened and militarised, making it more and more difficult for undocumented people to cross. (In 1992, the US Border Patrol had 3,555 agents on the southern border; by 2009, it had more than 20,000.)[31] Nonetheless, people continue to try, for the obvious reason that they are seeking to escape hunger and poverty and to send remittances home to mitigate the poverty of their families.

The clash between people's need to migrate and intensifying border fortifications has predictable outcomes. Migration scholars Nassim Majidi and Saagarika Dadu-Brown write that intensifying border restrictions *creates* 'new migrant-smuggler relationships', adding that 'smugglers will take advantage of a border closure or restriction to increase prices'.[32] Since the early 1990s, the Border Patrol has recovered the bodies of 6,000 people on the US side of the border, with as many as double that number thought to be lying undiscovered in the desert.[33] Isabel Garcia, co-chair of a local US migrants' rights organisation, says 'we never thought that we'd be in the business of helping to identify remains like in a war zone, and here we are'.[34] The US Department of Homeland Security reports that, as the border hardened, the costs to migrants who hire smugglers significantly increased – yet the proportion of migrants using the services of smugglers *also* increased, from 45 per cent to around 95 per cent.[35] Even as the inability to cross borders legally directly pushes would-be migrants into the arms of people smugglers, it increases the fees these smugglers can charge. As ethnologist Samuel Martinez writes, 'We have known for more than a decade that higher and longer walls, increased Border Patrol surveillance, and heightened bureaucratic impediments to immigration have deflected immigrants into the grip of smugglers.'[36] This pattern repeats at borders around the world. In Nepal, the International Labour Organisation found that banning women under the age of thirty from emigrating (which aimed to tackle their exploitation) had instead 'strengthened unlicensed migration agents', increasing the ability of these agents to entrap women in exploitative situations.[37]

This interplay is familiar to us in other contexts. When abortion is criminalised, women seeking abortions turn to back-street abortionists – some of whom will be altruistic, many of whom will be unscrupulous.[38] Although the pro-choice movement obviously decries people who charge exploitative fees to perform criminalised abortions in unsafe or neglectful ways, we also recognise that these bad actors are not aberrant villains who have come out of nowhere.* Instead, the criminalisation of abortion has *directly created* the market for unscrupulous abortion providers. Rather than simply 'cracking down', the policy solution that has put them out

---

* For example, Irin Carmon has argued convincingly that Dr Kermit Gosnell's notorious abortion practice in Pennsylvania, which led to the death of at least one woman, *was directly produced by anti-abortion laws closing many reputable clinics* in the state. This meant that many women – especially low-income women – had no local, accessible, affordable clinic to turn to before they passed the gestational limit for legal abortion, which pushed them into the arms of Gosnell, who would perform dangerous, no-questions-asked, illegally late abortions for cash. See I. Carmon, 'There is no Gosnell coverup', *Salon*, 12 April 2013, salon.com.

of business where it has been implemented is, of course, access to safe, legal, free abortion services. People living in places like England and Canada who can access free abortion services do not tend to pay people to perform dangerous back-alley procedures. Why would they? In the same way, people who can cross borders legally do not pay someone to smuggle them across. Like the people who perform illegal abortions, smugglers are not inexplicable villains; instead, *the criminalisation of undocumented migration has directly created the market for people smuggling.*

Many people engaging in undocumented migration agree to repay the debt that they take on to pay a smuggler through work in their destination country. This is common sense: people who are driven to migrate to escape poverty or war cannot normally produce large sums of money up front. Again, criminalisation directly creates conditions where harm can flourish. As a smuggler is *by definition* acting outside the law, and the migrant is already breaking laws in crossing the border, there is no legal recourse when the smuggler breaks the agreement or changes the terms. Often this happens midway through the journey or upon arrival in the destination country – points in the process where the person has little way of backing out, and has to accept these new conditions, however unfair.

Even in the best-case scenario, when an undocumented person finds work that is completely independent from the smuggling networks they used to cross the border, their lack of legal immigration status means they are intensely vulnerable to exploitation or other forms of abuse at the hands of their employer. They have little to no recourse to employment law; making themselves visible to state authorities as part of attempting to access justice or redress for workplace abuse will simply lead to their deportation. The Platform for International Cooperation on Undocumented Migrants (PICUM), an NGO network which defends undocumented people in Europe, writes,

> As undocumented migrants are limited to the informal sector, they often work without an employment contract meaning they have significant difficulties to prove labour-relations in a court of law. Even when a contract has been signed, it is usually considered invalid,

due to the irregular status of the worker, and thus unenforceable
... Further, if an undocumented worker reports violence or criminal
labour exploitation to the police, they face arrest and deportation,
rather than protection and justice.[39]

Focus on Labour Exploitation (FLEX), an NGO that tackles the
exploitation of migrant workers in Europe, notes that 'fear of immigration authorities is a major barrier to reporting for undocumented
workers ... The threat of reporting to police or immigration authorities is routinely used by unscrupulous employers to hold workers in
abusive situations.'[40] FLEX cites an example of two undocumented
men who were forced to work without pay in a laundromat. Their
employer claimed that their pay was going towards their residence
permits; however, 'the employer never arranged the promised residence permit, and instead threatened the men with reporting them
to the police if they complained ... The two men were too afraid to
disclose their situation to the labour inspectors.'[41] Carolina Gottardo
of the Latin American Women's Rights Service points out that 'when
women are undocumented and employers know about it, they are
very easy prey for very serious manners of labour exploitation'.[42] To
talk about this is not to digress from sex trafficking; it is to understand the broader, state-led systems which *produce* exploitation for
undocumented people.

Let's look at another example of this dynamic: a situation where
an employer controls a migrant worker's visa. Abdul Azad took on
debt to come to the UK on the promise of a well-paid job in a restaurant. Upon arrival, he discovered he would be working for no pay,
in conditions of absolute squalor in an isolated hotel in the remote
countryside. He had not entered the country illegally, but his visa
was dependent upon his employer, and Azad feared he and the other
men trapped at the hotel would be deported, with their debts unpaid,
if they contacted the police. His employer, he says, would 'show us
copies of our visa on his computer and say, "Here is your name. I will
cancel your sponsorship any time. This is my power."'[43] Abdul was
not wrong to fear this: when his case came to the attention of the
police, his employer was jailed – but Abdul was deported.[44]

Both the US and UK typically tie domestic workers' visas to a specific employer. As a result, a staggering 80 per cent of migrant domestic workers entering the US find that they have been deceived about their contract, and 78 per cent have had employers threaten them with deportation if they complain.[45] In the UK, these 'tied visas' were only introduced – by Prime Minister Theresa May, who was home secretary at the time – in 2012, so it is possible to see their effect very clearly. Migrant domestic workers who entered the UK after 2012 on a tied visa are *twice as likely* to be physically abused by their employers as those who arrived on a visa that gave them the right to change employers.[46] Compared to migrant domestic workers on the previous, more flexible form of visa, those on tied visas are substantially more likely to be underpaid, assaulted, and overworked, to be expected to sleep on the floor, and to have their passports confiscated by their employers.[47] Punitive immigration law produces harm.

However, much mainstream trafficking discourse characterises the abuse of migrants and people selling sex as the work of individual bad actors, *external* to and *independent* of state actions and political choices. Sometimes this discourse works not only to obscure the role of the state but to absolve it. One feminist commentator, for example, writes of the sex trade that 'criminalisation doesn't rape and beat women. Men do'.[48] From this, we might conclude that changing the law is pointless because, what makes women vulnerable is simply *men*. This may feel true for women who do not have to contend with immigration law, police, or the constant fear of deportation, but we can see from the results of tied visas that the legal context – including migration law – is heavily implicated in producing vulnerability and harm.

For undocumented migrant workers looking to challenge bad workplace conditions, penalties do not stop at deportation; instead, these workers face criminalisation if they are discovered. In the UK, someone convicted of 'illegal working' can face up to fifty-one weeks in prison, an unlimited fine, and the prospect of their earnings being confiscated as the 'proceeds of crime'.[49] This increases undocumented people's justified fear of state authorities and makes them even less able to report labour abuses. Such laws therefore heighten their vulnerability and *directly push* them into exploitative working environments, thereby creating a supply of highly vulnerable, ripe-for-abuse workers. Increasingly, border enforcement is infiltrating new areas of civic life. Landlords are now expected to check tenants' immigration status before renting to them; proposals have been floated to freeze or close the bank accounts of undocumented people, and a documentation check was introduced in England when accessing both healthcare and education, as part of an explicit 'hostile environment' policy (although both have been challenged by migrants' rights organisers, including in court). The UK devotes far more resources to policing migration than it does to preventing the exploitation of workers. Researcher Bridget Anderson notes that 'the [National Minimum Wage] had 93 compliance officers in 2009 and the Gangmasters Licensing Authority [which works to protect vulnerable and exploited workers] had 25 inspectors … The proposed number of UK Border Agency Staff for Local Immigration teams … is 7,500.'[50]

This is the context in which commercial sex frequently occurs. Undocumented or insecurely documented people are enmeshed within a punitive, state-enforced infrastructure of deportability, disposability, and precarity. *Any* work they do – whether it is at a restaurant, construction site, cannabis farm, nail bar, or brothel – carries a risk of being detained, jailed, or deported. In any work they do, they will be unable to assert labour rights. Even renting a home or accessing healthcare can be difficult. All this makes undocumented people more dependent on those who can help them – such as the people they paid to helped them cross the border, or an unscrupulous employer. It should therefore be no surprise that some undocumented migrants are pushed into sex work by those they rely on, or that some enter into it even if the working conditions are exploitative or abusive.

The experiences of a Thai woman working in the UK illustrate some of these complexities. She speaks of her high debt to get into the country and the bad working conditions and low pay she encountered in restaurant work, but also the higher pay she gets from sex work now that she has no debt to repay:

I came to work in England because there is no money in Thailand ... To come here so I made a contract with people, I had to give them back £22,000 ... I used to work and live in the same flat [a brothel], twenty-four hours a day, with three other Thai girls. We used to give her [the smuggler] all the money, except £200 to send to our families, but she did not take care of us ... we only had one egg per day to eat and she put washing-up liquid in the shampoo bottle. I paid up in eight months and was free. I work here [in a brothel] and in a restaurant now. The restaurant is better because it's got good reputation. Whereas here it's good money but bad reputation. Now I am okay, but I am only scared that immigration could come here and make me go back to Thailand.[51]

A Brazilian woman explains to the same researchers that if she had legal immigration status, she would do a different job than sex work: 'I decided to come to the UK because a girl I was working with in Spain took me here ... She was Brazilian as well. She had told me that the UK was better for work and I needed money ... If I was legal I would look for another job.'[52] Another migrant woman, who had also previously worked in Spain, notes that even decriminalising sex work does not make undocumented workers safe from the state: 'I felt more secure in Spain. I guess the only way would be to make it legal ... to work in brothels, but then that would not be enough because I could not be working there as I have no papers.'[53]

The constraints of immigration law come up again and again. One woman tells researchers, 'It is so difficult for Thai people to get a visa for the UK, why? If you want to come here to work you need to use these systems and people and it is very dangerous.'[54] Another adds: 'It is very bad, the girls want to go abroad and have a better life, but these people make money out of them, and on the other hand it's the only way to come! ... The Home Office should give more visas. It's difficult here if you are illegal!'[55] Nick Mai, who conducted the research, writes,

There is a direct correlation between the degree of difficulty in obtaining and maintaining documentation and the vulnerability of interviewees to exploitation, whether they work in the sex or in other

industries ... *Immigration status is the most important single factor*
engendering migrant workers' vulnerability to exploitation in the UK
sex industry. [emphasis ours][56]

However, the way trafficking is discussed allows exploitation to be
presented as unrelated to this system. For example, in 2018, news
agencies reported that German police had 'smashed' an organisation
that was trafficking Thai women into German brothels.[57] In response,
one anti-prostitution feminist in the UK noted, 'this is the problem
with legalising prostitution. Demand outstrips willing supply, and so
you get trafficking.'[58] The Thai media reported that the women in
question had been intending to migrate and had been aware that
they were going to be selling sex upon arrival. They had paid to be
smuggled into Germany, and had been deceived as to their remunera-
tion and the conditions in which they would be working.[59] In the
aftermath of the raid, the German authorities were weighing up the
possibility of prosecuting these exploited undocumented people *for
working without the correct visa*.[60]

To locate the problem in the existence of prostitution, as the UK
feminist commentator seems to, renders invisible the material things
that made them vulnerable to harm. Europe's border regime meant
they had to pay exploitative people huge sums of money in order
to be smuggled in, and that once in, they had zero access to labour
rights as their discovery by the state risked them being prosecuted.
These two factors combined to produce a situation wherein they
could be horribly exploited by their employers. None of this is to
downplay what happened to them – instead, it is to highlight the
inadequacy of a carceral 'anti-trafficking' response to their situation. Such an approach actively obscures the role of the border in
producing the harms they suffered, and compounds these harms by
rendering it prosaic that they face deportation and potential prosecution. Indeed, it is striking that although the spectre of commercial sex
attracted attention to this case among the UK commentariat, the idea
that this was an anti-trafficking raid – and therefore simply a 'good
thing' – foreclosed any interest in what happened to these people
after their discovery by the state. Their potential prosecution – and

inevitable deportation – become unremarkable and unremarked upon. As Nandita Sharma writes,

> Anti-trafficking policies do a great disservice to migrating people, especially the most vulnerable. By diverting our attention away from the practices of nation-states ... they channel our energies to support a law-and-order agenda of 'getting tough' with 'traffickers'. In this way, anti-trafficking measures are *ideological*: they render the plethora of immigration and border controls as unproblematic and place them outside of the bounds of politics. [emphasis ours][61]

Instead of locating exploitation within the state systems that push migrants into debt and force them to work in the grey economy with no workplace protections, anti-trafficking ideology locates exploitation in the figure of the villain. In Houston, Texas, one anti-trafficking organisation set up a 'museum of modern-day slavery'. In it they displayed a shackle dating from chattel slavery in North America, next to a high-heeled shoe. The shoe was titled 'A Modern-Day Shackle', and the caption reads:

> This shoe was found after [a] ... cantina known as Las Palmas was raided by law enforcement. Women are forced to wear clothing like this shoe to attract business. This type of clothing marks them as business property and is considered a modern-day shackle.[62]

The shoe is an ordinary high-heeled shoe of the sort that you can buy on any high street. For anybody to claim that it is 'considered a modern-day shackle' is an absurdly overheated fantasy. Comparing it to an actual shackle trivialises the real history of chattel slavery, a history which, as racial justice organiser Robyn Maynard writes, remains 'a living, breathing horror for anybody ... with Black skin in the Americas'.[63] This fantasy also obscures something real, which is that *a woman kicked these shoes off in order to run from the cops*.

As the caption notes, these shoes were found after a cantina was 'raided by law enforcement'. In choosing to see an ordinary shoe as a 'shackle' rather than identifying the key problem as criminalisation and the police, anti-trafficking activists misdirect attention away from the structures of the state and onto a fictional, shackle-wielding monster.

White Guilt and the 'New Slave Trade'

Trafficking anxieties have always been deeply tied to white national-ism. White women's bodies – threatened by prostitution – come to stand in for the body politic of the nation, threatened by immigra-tion. This is clearly legible in late-nineteenth-century concerns over 'white slavery', a panic that overtook Britain and the US in which campaigners thought that young white women were being lured into forced prostitution by Black and Jewish men. This panic was driven by the rapid growth of cities, women's increasing migration to cities as workers outside the home, and fears around women's economic independence, which combined with white-supremacist fears over 'race mixing' to create the conditions for a racist panic.

Academic Jo Doezema writes that the image of the white slave 'in her ruined innocence' represented 'the real and imagined loss of American rural innocence'.[64] Writing in 1909, the social worker and activist Jane Addams declared that 'never before in civilisation have such numbers of girls been suddenly released from the protection of the home and permitted to walk unattended upon the city streets and to work under alien roofs'.[65] Historians note that journalists' breath-less reportage of white slavery 'provided virtually pornographic entertainment to the reading audience'.[66] It was amid this obviously racist freak-out over swarthy men luring white innocents to their ruin that one of the first recognisably modern US anti-trafficking laws, the 1905 Mann Act, passed. The bill, which was ostensibly against forced prostitution, criminalised Black men in romantic relationships with white women.[67] In the UK, white-slavery legislation passed between 1885 and 1912 'created provisions to monitor and restrict the migra-tion of women'.[68]

Little surprise, then, given these origins, that anti-trafficking poli-cies are primarily either anti-migration policies, or anti-prostitution policies. Neither helps undocumented people, and both harm migrant sex workers, who are doubly in the crosshairs and disproportion-ately criminalised and deported. Abhijit Dasgupta of ActionAid Asia remarks that:

> anti-trafficking measures were being used internationally to prevent the migration of people, especially women who are driven by poverty and globalisation to move country. Governments claim that millions of women are being trafficked by a billion-dollar sex industry, but the UNHCR [United Nations High Commission on Refugees] and others have pointed out that because of tightening immigration controls, paying an agent is often the only way to migrate.[69]

Although racist panic about migration is never far from the surface of politics in countries that perpetrated and continue to benefit from colonialism, the last twenty-five years have seen an uptick in these anxieties. Campaigners often deliberately heighten this racism; for example, depictions of 'hordes at the border' featured prominently in the 2016 'Brexit' referendum on Britain leaving the European Union.[70] In 2017, a Conservative election strategist tweeted: 'I was in [the] 2005 Tory campaign – we worked assiduously to ramp up anti-immigrant feeling. And from [then–Labour Party leader Gordon] Brown on nobody challenged lies that immigrants took jobs, were here on benefits.'[71] That same year, Sarah Champion, the Labour Party's then shadow Secretary of State for Women and Equalities, wrote, 'Britain has a problem with British Pakistani men raping and exploiting white girls. There, I said it. Does that make me a racist or am I just prepared to call out this horrifying problem for what it is?'[72] Indeed, it is possible to trace these growing xenophobic and racist anxieties not just in phrases, tabloid headlines, and election strategies but in concrete and barbed wire. As geographer Reece Jones writes, 'as late as 1990, only fifteen countries had walls or fences on their borders. At the beginning of 2016, almost seventy did.'[73]

The history of the transatlantic slave trade and chattel slavery looms large in contemporary trafficking conversations – often in the form of claims, subtle or not, that modern trafficking is *worse* than chattel slavery. Politicians and police officers meet to tell each other that 'there are more slaves now than at any previous point in human history'; a UK former government minister insists that 'we are facing a new slave trade, whose victims are tortured, terrified East European girls rather than Africans'.[74] Matteo Renzi, then prime minister of Italy, wrote in 2015 that 'human traffickers are the slave traders of the twenty-first century'.[75] The Vatican claimed that 'modern slavery', specifically prostitution, is 'worse than the slavery of those ... who were taken from Africa'.[76] A senior British police officer remarked that 'the cotton plantations and sugar plantations of the eighteenth and nineteenth century ... wouldn't be as bad as what some victims [today] go through'.[77]

A 2012 anti-trafficking 'documentary' that was screened for politicians and policymakers around the world, including in Washington, London, Edinburgh, and at the UN buildings in New York, proclaims: 'In 1809 the cost of a slave was thirty thousand dollars. In 2009, the cost of a slave is ninety dollars.'[78] White people co-opting the history of chattel slavery as rhetoric is grim, not least because the term *slavery* names a specific legal institution created, enforced and protected by the state, which is nowhere near synonymous with contemporary ideas of trafficking. Indeed, the direct modern descendant of chattel slavery in the US is not prostitution but the prison system. Slavery was not abolished but explicitly retained in the US Constitution as punishment for crime in the Thirteenth Amendment of the Bill of Rights, which states that 'neither slavery nor involuntary servitude, *except as a punishment for crime whereof the party shall have been duly convicted*, shall exist within the United States, or any place subject to their jurisdiction' (emphasis ours).[79]

The Thirteenth Amendment isn't just a vestigial hangover. In 2016, the Incarcerated Workers Organizing Committee released a statement condemning inmates' treatment in the prison work system:

> Overseers watch over our every move, and if we do not perform our appointed tasks to their liking, we are punished. They may have replaced the whip with pepper spray, but many of the other torments remain: isolation, restraint positions, stripping off our clothes and investigating our bodies as though we are animals.[80]

There are more Black men in the US prison system now than were enslaved in 1850.[81] Seeking to 'end slavery' through increased policing and incarceration is a bitterly ironic proposition.

White people in Britain and North America have been very successful at ducking any real reckoning with the legacies of the slave trade. Historian Nick Draper writes, 'We privilege abolition ... If you say to somebody 'tell me about Britain and slavery', the instinctive response of most people is Wilberforce and abolition. Those 200 years of slavery beforehand have been elided – we just haven't wanted to think about it.'[82] By rhetorically intertwining modern trafficking with chattel slavery, governments and campaigners have been able to hide punitive policies targeting irregular migration behind seemingly uncomplicated righteous outrage.

Men of colour become 'modern enslavers' who deserve prosecution or worse. Their 'human cargo', figured as being transported against their will, are owed nothing more than 'humanitarian return', and the racist trope of border invasion is given a progressive sheen through collective shared horror at the villainy of the perpetrators. Meanwhile, in crackdowns and deportations, European governments position themselves as re-enacting and re-writing the history of anti-slavery movements to make themselves both victims and heroes. Of course, these actions by European governments do harm. For example, their policy of confiscating or destroying smuggling boats has not 'rescued' anyone, only induced smugglers to send migrants in less valuable – and less seaworthy – boats, leading to many more deaths.[83] This policy continued for years, despite clear evidence that it was causing deaths.[84] But, faced with twenty-first century 'enslavers', there is little need for white reflection. Instead, Renzi later wrote that European nations 'need to free ourselves from a sense of guilt' and reject any notion of a 'moral duty' to welcome arrivals.[85] At the time of writing, the Italian government's 'solution' to the migrant crisis is to pay for migrants to be incarcerated, stranded in dangerous, disease-ridden detention centres in Libya.[86] As Robyn Maynard writes,

By hijacking the terminology of slavery, even widely referring to themselves as 'abolitionists', anti–sex work campaigners ... in pushing for
criminalization ... are often undermining those most harmed by the
legacy of slavery. As Black persons across the Americas are literally
fighting for our lives, it is urgent to examine the actions and goals of
any mostly white and conservative movement who [claim] to be the
rightful inheritors of an 'anti-slavery' mission which aims to abolish
prostitution but both ignores and indirectly facilitates brutalities
waged against Black communities.[87]

What does the fight to save people from 'modern slavery' look like on
the ground? In 2017, police in North Yorkshire told journalists that
they were fighting to rescue 'sex slaves' and asked members of the
public to call in with tips, adding that the 'sex slaves' themselves 'are
prepared to do it [sell sex], they believe there is nothing wrong in it ...
We have just got to ... educate them that they are victims of human
trafficking.'[88] It seems fairly obvious that women who are 'prepared
to do it' and 'believe there is nothing wrong with it' will not particularly benefit from being 'educated' about the fact that they are victims
of trafficking – which in England and Wales means a forty-five-day
'respite period' (frequently disregarded) followed by a 'humanitarian'
deportation.*

In 2012, Alaska passed a law which essentially redefined prostitution as 'sex trafficking'. The *only* two people charged in the law's first
two years of the law were sex workers 'caught in ordinary prostitution stings'. One 'was charged with *sex trafficking herself* when the
state alleged that she "instituted or aided" in her own prostitution'.
In the other case, 'a woman was charged with multiple counts of

---

* 'The length of time confirmed victims have access to "move-on" support,
such as ongoing accommodation, counselling, expert advice and advocacy, will
be extended from 14 days to 45 days.' UK Home Office and Sarah Newton
MP, 'Modern slavery victims to receive longer period of support', 26 October
2017, www.gov.uk. Mark Shepherd, a lawyer at the UK-based Migrant Legal
Project, comments, 'In the young offender institutes I see many children ...
deported to Vietnam, without anyone doing anything about the fact they have
been trafficked.' M. McClenaghan, 'UK condemned for deporting survivors of
trafficking back to Vietnam', *Guardian*, 20 December 2016, theguardian.com.

felony sex trafficking ... for sharing space with other sex workers when she booked a duo [threesome] for herself and another worker with a police officer' who was posing as a client. After five years, the Alaskan state had not charged or convicted anyone with coercion, deception, or force relating to trafficking; the law had only been used against sex workers, their family members, and their landlords.[89]

In 2016, Irish police arrested four Romanian sex workers. Police claimed that the women had been trafficked but prosecuted them for brothel-keeping regardless – a 'crime' which simply entails sharing a flat, as sex workers often do for safety. The women stated in court that they were selling sex in order to send money home to their families in Romania. The police commented that '*they are four little girls* and they made full admissions that they were providing sexual services to a large number of men' (emphasis ours).[90] Their ages ranged from twenty-one to thirty. The police added, 'They were paying €700 rent to a greedy landlord for an apartment that they should have been paying €350 for. So, they were being used and abused by a lot of people.' The police took €5,000 from the women, and the court fined them another €200 each.[91] It is hard to see how taking all this money tackles the harm of an overpriced flat, and easy to imagine that these women might have preferred working in their apparently overpriced flat to being raided, being prosecuted, and having their cash taken as an 'anti-trafficking' initiative.

Anti-trafficking policing looks like border policing. In Canada, a 2015 human-trafficking raid on massage parlours led to eleven women being deported.[92] One migrant sex worker named Mi spent two months in a Canadian detention centre. 'They took away my phone and didn't allow me to contact my friends and family. [They] did not allow me to leave, as they said they had to protect me. They thought my friends and clients were bad people and dangerous for me. They did not allow my friends to be a bondsperson to get me out of those chains.' After Mi was deported, Canadian Immigration officials refused to return the $10,000 they'd taken from her, which included savings she'd brought with her when she moved to Canada.

Fanny, another migrant who was detained for eight days, said, of her arrest, 'it was very clear that [the police] were only looking for us as non-white workers. There were other women working in the same hotel who were white, and the police didn't bother them or even talk to them at all.'[93]

In October 2016, London police raided a series of massage parlours in Soho and Chinatown and arrested seventeen women on immigration charges.[94] In the northern UK town of Bolton, a 'crackdown on human trafficking and modern slavery' found two Romanian women who described themselves as sex workers. A local journalist writes that 'immigration officers served both women with papers instructing them to get a legitimate job … within 30 days or else risk arrest and possible deportation'. Meanwhile, the police forced the women's landlord to evict them.[95] In Northern Ireland, two asylum seekers – both homeless, one seventeen years old – were prosecuted for human-trafficking offences for the crime of smuggling *themselves* into Northern Ireland on false documents.[96]

Michael Dottridge, the former head of Anti-Slavery International, writes that on several occasions he has heard UK government ministers suggest that the police should destroy the basic shelters that migrant people are living in at the French-British border of Calais, the site of a large refugee camp, as a way to 'stop trafficking'.[97] Police Scotland put out a press release noting that they had refused entry at the border to more than a hundred people as part of their anti-trafficking work – offering as an example a Romanian woman who 'had previously worked as a prostitute in Glasgow'. The BBC reports, 'She was refused admission at Glasgow in May 2017, then again in Liverpool in July 2017 and was encountered recently at Belfast docks attempting to get to Scotland. She was removed to Romania.'[98] The same report describes another Romanian woman refused entry at the border because she was known to the police to be a sex worker. The police knew she was a sex worker because of an incredibly traumatic event. When she had previously worked in Scotland, she and another worker were held hostage in a flat in Falkirk by a client with a knife; they both were raped and the other woman, Luciana, was killed. On this basis, immigration police detained her at the border and deported her while claiming a humanitarian anti-trafficking mantle.[99] There are more examples of cases like this than could fit into one book.

At borders all over the world, sex workers are treated as both villain and victims. Homeland Security officially ban anyone who has sold sex in the previous ten years from entry into the United States, along with spies, Nazis, and terrorists.[100] The border to the United States is a No Man's Land – and people detained at a Port of Entry have few rights. No warrant, or even reasonable suspicion, is legally required for agents to demand passwords and search through electronic devices like phones or laptops, or even to clone all the data they find.

Sex workers attempting entry into the US for any reason can be questioned and detained for hours or days before being sent back. The numbers of people affected by this have risen significantly since the start of Trump's presidency. Many in our community – including personal friends – have spoken to the trauma of been stopped at customs and put through twelve-to-forty-eight-hour ordeals in which they were denied food, rest or medication. They were often handcuffed or shackled to chairs, including in public areas of airports, where immigration enforcement agents subjected them to the humiliation of excessive frisking and invasive bodily searches, and deliberately withheld sanitary products. No filming or recording of border agents is allowed, and many of them use illegal tactics to force sex workers to sign an admission of guilt banning them from the United States for ten years.*

In the era of the War on Trafficking, the hypocrisy is galling. While their agents taunt sex workers with screenshots of escort sites and naked photos during interrogations, US Customs and Border Protection condemn the 'heinous' crime of sex trafficking on their website, and advertise job vacancies that smugly proclaim the 'vitality and magnitude' of their 'mission' to secure the nation from threats like human traffickers.[101] US lawmakers say equally poetic things about the tragedy of sex trafficking – and how appalling it is that

---

* Maggie's, a sex worker group in Toronto, have developed a document, 'Safer Border Crossing Tips for Sex Workers', which details recommended precautions for sex workers to take when travelling to the United States. It is available on the 'Resources for Workers' section of their website, maggiestoronto.ca.

the human rights of prostituted people are so violated – but do nothing to overturn the travel ban that meant current and former sex workers couldn't attend the 2012 International Aids Conference in Washington, D.C. to do valuable human rights work. Nor do they act to change these harrowing and traumatising experiences that sex workers are subjected to at the US border. Instead, they produce the 'Fight Online Sex Trafficking' Act and the 'Stop Enabling Sex Traffickers' Act (known together as FOSTA-SESTA), laws which claim to create safety – while in fact decimating the internet spaces that help sex workers protect themselves from rapists or earn what they need to keep a roof over their head.

This cruelty is not an accident. The UN Protocol to Prevent, Suppress and Punish Trafficking in Persons is not a human rights document – it is a descendant of the Convention Against Transnational Organised Crime.[102] As such, it is concerned with *criminalisation*, not healing (or even harm reduction) for marginalised people. As Dottridge notes, the only measures that are obligatory for all states to uphold are those linked to law enforcement. Protection measures, in contrast, are weak and optional.[103] The protocol merely suggests that states *consider* adopting 'measures that permit victims of trafficking in persons to remain in its territory, temporarily or permanently, in appropriate cases'.[104] It is much firmer on the 'repatriation' of victims, 'without undue or unreasonable delay', and firmer still on strengthening border control, instructing signatory countries that they 'shall strengthen ... such border controls as may be necessary to prevent and detect trafficking in persons'.[105]

None of this has gone unnoticed by the far right, with tabloid newspapers and white supremacists deploying the language of human trafficking as part of campaigns to 'turn back the boats'. One Canadian white nationalist travelled to Italy in 2017 to join a French far-right group's 'direct action' against arriving migrants, brandishing a banner reading 'NO WAY for human trafficking'.[106] British columnist Katie Hopkins praised an openly fascist youth organisation for 'shining a light on NGO people traffickers'.[107] Although unsubtly expressed, these far-right views have a huge amount in common with more mainstream and even feminist conceptions of human trafficking. The head of Frontex, the European border agency, has also claimed that NGO rescues in the Mediterranean were facilitating traffickers.[108] (Indeed, aid workers across Europe are increasingly facing prosecution under anti-trafficking laws for helping people migrate.)[109] Feminist anti-prostitution campaigners sometimes share hard-right reportage of sexual violence supposedly committed by refugees in Europe, with one such campaigner commenting that European countries should 'take in the women and children, but leave the nasty men home'.[110] Alice Schwarzer, a prominent German anti-prostitution feminist, draws extensively on the racialised figures of 'pimps and traffickers', linking migrant men of colour to sexual violence.[111] (Schwarzer uncritically recounts a police officer telling her that '70 to 80 per cent of all the rapes in Cologne [are committed by] Turks'.)[112] When sex workers organise against deportations, we are told – by those with ostensibly progressive politics – that they 'should be deported if [they have] no right to be in the country. Such women are being trafficked into [the] country. Do you support that?'[113]

Hard-right politicians are keen to enact anti-trafficking agendas. US President Donald Trump has described human trafficking as an 'epidemic',[114] while Theresa May is positioning the 2015 Modern Slavery Act (passed while she was home secretary) as central to her image and legacy.[115] Uncritical use of the term *trafficking* is doing the ideological work required for these contradictions to 'make sense'; it hides how anti-migrant policies *produce* the harm that we call trafficking, enabling anti-migrant politicians to posture as anti-trafficking heroes even as they enact their anti-migrant policies.

Where Next?

It should be no surprise that carceral feminists and sex working feminists have such difficulty even discussing this topic. We disagree not only on the solution but on the *problem*: for carceral feminists, the problem is commercial sex, which produces trafficking; for us, the problem is borders, which produces people who have few to no rights as they travel and work. The solutions we propose are equally divergent. Carceral feminists want to tackle commercial sex through criminal law, giving more power to the police. For sex workers, the solution includes dismantling immigration enforcement and the militarised border regimes that push undocumented people into the shadows and shut off their access to safety or justice – in other words, taking power *away* from the police and giving it to migrants and to workers.

However, we also want to gently criticise the sex workers' rights movement. A common refrain among people who advocate for sex workers' rights is that sex work and trafficking are completely different phenomena that should under no circumstances be conflated. It is easy to understand why: all across the world, the total criminalisation of prostitution is advocated for – or enacted – on the basis that it is 'tackling trafficking': arrests of sex workers' colleagues, partners, landlords, and managers are 'justified' on the basis that they are perpetrators; arrests of sex workers are 'justified' on the basis that they constitute rescue. Our movement is desperate to convince the public and the media that these arrests are not legitimate – and rather than problematising the framework of trafficking (which has taken us several thousand words!), they reach for the idea of the category error. They say that 'sex work is not trafficking', meaning, '*these* crackdowns are not legitimate'. When possible, we need to be pointing more clearly to the *border* as the problem. Otherwise the effect can be to disavow those working in exploitative or abusive conditions – to say, 'these issues are not our issues; these people are not the concern of our movement'. It places them outside the remit of 'sex workers' rights'. It implicitly accepts carceral 'raid-and-rescue' approaches, so long as the target is 'right'.

To say that 'sex work is not trafficking' mirrors the error of carceral anti-trafficking campaigners by positioning trafficking as an inexplicable evil, shorn of the crucial context of the conditions of migration and the impact of immigration enforcement on the labour rights and safety of migrants. To assert simply that sex work and trafficking are completely different is to defend *only* documented sex workers who are not experiencing exploitation but say nothing about those exploited at the intersection of migration and the sex industry. As a slogan, 'sex work is not trafficking' suggests that the current mode of anti-trafficking policy is broadly correct and merely – on occasion – misfires. In fact, of course, carceral anti-trafficking policy is *not* misfiring: like the global prison industrial complex, of which it forms a part, it is a system which is working in the way it is supposed to be. As the Migrant Sex Work Project writes, 'it is an intentional and effective system.'[116] Immigration and border control are crucial to maintaining the exploitation of workers and resources in the global south, and to maintaining an exploitable pool of undocumented and insecurely documented workers in the global north, while border policing and the incarceration of migrants funnel huge sums back and forth between corporations and governments.

Fundamentally, the claim that sex work and trafficking are different operates as a way of refusing to talk about 'trafficking', since such conversations are often used to attack us when we organise; people reach for any easy way to shut the topic down. But sex workers should start welcoming such discussions. They are an opportunity to talk about how border enforcement makes people more vulnerable to exploitation and violence as they seek to migrate – an analysis which should be central to sex workers' rights activism.

State borders and the architecture of coercion that surrounds them can now seem so natural it is difficult to imagine the world without them. People who migrate without papers are, after all, 'breaking the law', implying that punitive state action against them – such as incarceration and deportation – is legitimate. This is, in part, why we historicised border controls in the introduction: to recount the recent history of borders is to see that they are not natural or inevitable. It is beyond the scope of this book to fully detail a migration policy centred on human rights and safety of all people who seek to migrate. It should be clear, however, that attempts to limit migration are producing horrific harms, from exploitation and abuse in workplaces, to deaths at sea and in deserts. The wealth of a handful of the world's richest people would, if fairly re-distributed, be more than enough to ensure that everybody who needs to travel – and everybody who does not – could live in safety and dignity. In the meantime, everybody should be fighting immigration enforcement, which rips families and communities apart and imprisons people for years in detention centres.

To defend the migrant prostitute is to defend all migrants: she is the archetype of the stigmatised migrant. Borders were *invented* to guard against her. There is no migrant solidarity without prostitute solidarity and there is no prostitute solidarity without migrant solidarity. The two struggles are inextricably bound up with one another.

4

A Victorian Hangover: Great Britain

Partial Criminalisation: A legal model where some aspects of the sex industry – often the most visible, such as street-based sex work – are criminalised. Within England, Scotland and Wales, the acts of buying and selling sex are legal, but almost everything else is criminalised: for example, soliciting and kerb-crawling, working indoors with friends, or facilitating sex work.[1]

In the weeks leading up to Christmas 2006, sex workers in the small British town of Ipswich feared for their lives. The bodies of two sex working women had been found in the previous week, and the killer was still at large. Out in the quiet streets, a local-news film crew approached a young woman named Paula Clennell, one of the few who remained waiting for clients in the usual spot. When asked why she was risking her life out on the streets when a murderer was on the loose, she explained, 'I have to work. I need the money.'[2]

Paula, a mother of three in her twenties, had been selling sex for some time. After her children were taken away from her, she became depressed and by the winter of 2006, her dependency on heroin and cocaine had reached a stage where she needed an income of around one hundred pounds a day to support herself.* For Paula, as for so many people in similar situations, selling sex was the only viable way to obtain this kind of money.[3] A friend encouraged her to try indoor escorting in the hope it would be safer – as well as legal under British

---

* The day before she died she bought between five and seven deals of heroin and cocaine for £15 each, so costing somewhere between £75 and £105. Her ex-partner says that paying for drugs sometimes cost her thousands in a week. See Frith, M. (2006) 'Victim 4: Paula Clennell: 'It was the only way to fund her addiction' Independent, independent.co.uk. Parsons E, (2008) 'Ipswich murders: Miss F tells of cocaine habit' Daily Gazette, gazette-news.co.uk.

law – but in her situation, that level of organisation and financial overhead was unrealistic. Street work, though criminalised, meant she could sell sex whenever she wanted and return home with instant cash. She had no partner and no manager to split her money with.

A few days after her appearance on the news, Paula vanished. By Christmas, her body had been found, along with those of four other women. Steve Wright, a local man, was later found guilty of all five murders.[4]

Nine years later, Daria Pionko's smiling face jumped out of news reports. Daria was just twenty-one and had moved from Poland to Britain ten months before. Daria's mother, Lydia, described her as a kind-hearted and joyful girl who was always eager to help others.[5] A few days before Christmas 2015, a young man named Lewis Pierre kicked Daria to death in Holbeck, Leeds, in order to steal eighty pounds from her. Daria's body was discovered by her housemate and friend Karolina, who was also a street-based sex worker.

Daria had been working in the Holbeck 'managed area'. This is a place where street-based sex workers and clients can meet without fear of arrest, an arrangement the only one of its kind in Britain. (In most of Britain, sex workers who wait for clients in public places may be charged with 'soliciting' or 'loitering with intent to commit prostitution'. Their clients may also be charged with 'kerb crawling'.)

Daria had left the managed area with Pierre, as was compulsory: although sex workers can meet clients without fear of arrest in the Holbeck zone, *sex* there is not permitted – they are forced to leave the managed area and find a dark alley or patch of woodland where they can conduct business in secrecy. In doing so, sex workers risk arrest. They also, of course, are at risk of attack in these hidden spaces. When Lewis Pierre reappeared in the lens of the same CCTV camera that caught him walking away from the managed area with Daria, he had blood on his steel-capped shoes.[6]

In responding to such horrific stories, it is easy to make them purely about male brutality and the disposability of prostitutes.[7] These themes have resonance for us, too, as they surely do for any sex worker who has stepped into a car or a hotel room with a stranger. The emphasis on male violence as *the* conceptual framework through which to understand these murders allows non-prostitute women – who may themselves be survivors of male violence – to empathetically and discursively 'enter into' the experience of the prostitute. While this empathy is welcome, there is a danger that this sands away the specifics of Paula and Daria's lives and the lives and experiences of prostitutes as a whole, which then become draped around the figure of the 'everywoman'. As Beth Richie argues, the 'everywoman' victim/survivor concept was created in the 1970s as a strategic rhetorical move on the part of the nascent feminist movement to demand attention for the epidemic of male violence.[8] But this has transmuted over time into something closer to a focus on the 'default woman' – and the 'default woman' is certainly not a drug user or a sex worker. Nor is she a survivor of *state* violence. Daria and Paula's lives were shaped by specific realities, including the ever-present threat of criminalisation. These young women were acting rationally in a system designed to harm them at every turn.

Instead of asking questions about how the state makes women like Daria and Paula unsafe, media coverage tends to channel the worldview of their aggrieved neighbours.* The fact that selling sex is technically not a crime in Britain does little to render sex workers relatable – or grievable – in the eyes of police, residents or journalists. Sympathetic perceptions of sex workers are readily tossed aside for something more callous. Mike Veale, chief of the Wiltshire police, indicated that when a prostitute reports a crime, he takes her less seriously than other victims: 'If you have a six-year-old girl who has trauma in her vagina or anus you would expect me to believe her. If you have a drunken prostitute, making allegations regarding a bad debt, you have to make more of a judgement.'[9]

---

* A neighbour of one of the Ipswich victims remembers their own personal anguish prior to the killings, saying that a benign depiction of the women as victims in a BBC documentary 'did not really tie in with my memories. I seem to remember being regularly accosted on my way home by desperate, pushy and often abusive creatures who did not take no for an answer. I remember the distress of being offered "a really good oral for twenty quid" ... I remember seeing five girls "looking for business" in one stretch of about fifty yards.' M. Brain and G. Lawrence, '"Five Daughters" – messages for Neighbourhood Watch on street prostitution and drugs', *Propertibazar*, 2010, propertibazar.com.

Judgements of this type are not in short supply. A few years after the Ipswich killings, one journalist wrote, 'The girls killed in Ipswich were not working in the stupidly PC term "sex industry"; they were junkies ... Can we afford rehab for the girls in Ipswich – and everywhere else? Speaking as a taxpayer, I'd say: *erm, well, um. Good question.*'[10] Indeed, it seems the Ipswich killings, and the questions they raise, drew a particularly vicious strain of rhetorical cruelty into the public arena, suggesting that hatred of sex workers and collective guilt about social neglect are closely bound together. Another journalist called the five Ipswich women 'disgusting, drug-addled street whores' and bridled at what he considered excessive mourning, writing, 'We do not share in the responsibility for either their grubby little existences or their murders. Society isn't to blame ... death by strangulation is an occupational hazard.'[11]

Who, then – or what – is to blame? Why didn't Paula and her friends have access to a flat that they could have taken turns using with clients instead of being driven away, alone, in a car? Why was she paying five hundred pounds a day for opiates that the National Health Service could have provided in a safe version for a fraction of the cost? Why was she stuck trying to manage her trauma through street heroin instead of through more sustainable support services? Instead of being supported to be the loving parent she desperately wanted to be, Paula was left depressed and in profound poverty. For Daria, too, these questions bubble up painfully. An evaluation of the Holbeck managed area had already noted, months before Daria's murder, that the 'most notable time of risk for sex workers is *away* from the Managed Area'.[12] Women like Daria and Paula need so *little* – some basic safety and resources – that it is easy to imagine society meeting those needs. Yet, at the same time, they needed so *much* – in that to imagine a society that takes their safety seriously is to imagine a society profoundly transformed.

Low Class, High Class

As with much else in Britain – including immigration and drug use – class plays a huge role in the way sex work manifests and stratifies. Prostitution law is produced by archaic class structures and in turn produces a microcosm of that class system within the bounds of the sex industry, where values of decorum, propriety, decency, and discretion are reshaped to fit the world of commercial sex.[13] The law attempts to establish what is and is not respectable on the long spectrum of the sex trade – from bareback blowjobs against a parked car to sugar-babying in exchange for tuition fees – and appears to grant a degree of exemption to that which is discreet or invisible.

Technically, the only way to sell sex in Britain without getting into legal trouble is to work alone and indoors (and for migrants, with the relevant documentation). Labels like 'elite' or 'high class' often attach to those who more or less meet this requirement, and these terms signify the sex worker's position within the class strata of sex work, even though such phrases are primarily advertising keywords and frequently have only a tenuous link to a worker's actual socio-economic class.[*]

It is in more exposed spaces, like the streets or conspicuous red-light establishments, that sex workers are most often perceived as being 'low class', immoral, or simply a nuisance. This is also where they are seen to be the most victimised and exploited, which provides a convenient justification for ever harsher policing. Soliciting on the street, kerb-crawling, managing sex workers, and working in groups – even pairs – are all criminalised, along with 'procuring' or 'inciting' people into sex work. Sex workers seen to be breaking these laws are framed as an embarrassing stain on the fabric of British society – a terrible, hyper-visible burden on all who regard them. To take one revealing example, a neighbourhood group seeking the end of the managed area in Holbeck, Leeds, is named Save Our Eyes – and is far more concerned about the scourge of 'scantily clad' women in public spaces than the prospect of actual violence against those women.[14]

---

[*] 'It's this idea that [as Black sex workers] we don't have the same amount of worth. I think it links to ... this idea of Black people being "ghetto" and such. This is why my marketing, and that of others, has to focus on how highly educated I am, the languages I speak, and almost push away from my Blackness ... because it meant that I wasn't as "high-class" as my fellow colleagues.' Amber Ashton, quoted by A. Tierney, 'What Happens When Sex Workers Put Women of Color First', *Vice*, 12 January 2018, vice.com.

Where irate residents can't provoke police crackdowns on sex workers to 'clean up' the community, they sometimes resort to vigilante violence. When residents of Balsall Heath, Birmingham, mobilised against street-based sex work in the mid-1990s, sex workers were harassed and physically threatened, including with baseball bats and dogs; their windows were smashed; and a sex worker who objected was forcibly removed from a community meeting.[15] Vigilantes lit fireworks and pushed them through a sex worker's letterbox, and fired an airgun into her house.[16]

While street workers bear the brunt of public discontent, most sex work in Britain happens indoors – in the worker's flat or the client's flat, or in rented temporary apartments and hotels. But staying within the law is almost impossible when the law is broad enough to encompass basically everything prostitution entails beyond actual sex. To 'incite' someone does not entail force; it can mean simply supporting or advising them before they begin sex work.[17] When police attempted to close working flats in Soho, London, in 2013, they defined 'incitement' to mean calling a job applicant back to talk to them about potentially working in the flat.[18] Arranging a second sex worker's involvement in a threesome might also be 'causing or 'inciting'. A 'brothel' can be any property in which more than one prostitute works, even if they work at different times and never cross paths.[19] Persistent fears of such rules and their consequences (in particular, eviction and loss of child custody) have a pre-emptive disciplinary effect on all people selling sex across the breadth of the sex industry. They must take the risk and toe the line or, if they cannot comply with the law, are compelled to be absolutely undetectable in their activities.

With laws as complex and outmoded as these, confusion is common among sex workers. Opaque policing mechanisms lead many to simply assume – in the absence of concrete knowledge – that what they're doing must in some way be illegal. This suspicion that they will be treated as criminals significantly impacts their perception of their own human and labour rights. This makes it nearly impossible to *exercise* those rights in the workplace and diminishes their power to resist abuses from clients, employers, the police, and violent assailants. Activist Niki Adams, commenting on a series of violent gang burglaries of London brothels, spoke of 'incidents where women have been attacked and their attackers have told them brazenly that they know the women won't dare go to the police'.[20]

As well as risks to safety and security, this situation also produces a culture full of silences. Very few sex workers are prepared to step forward and speak in political spaces because the consequences of visibility can be so disastrous. The few that remain – including the authors of this book – are often dismissed as privileged, unrepresentative, or 'high-class' outliers, but rarely are these structures within sex work properly interrogated at the material level.[21] It's accurate to say broadly that the demographic within sex work politics most often given a substantial mainstream platform to speak publicly dovetails with the group that lives in metropolitan cities, commands higher rates, has access to more resources, and suffers the least criminalisation, but it is an egregious oversight to leave the analysis there. *Why* are these people the only voices you are hearing? What structures are silencing the others?[22] The mechanisms that produce the silence, precarity, and vulnerability of most sex workers are not natural or fundamental to society, just as the class system itself is not natural. Sex working feminists watch feminist discussions of the 'policing' of speech with wry amusement: for sex workers, policing is not merely a metaphor.

The War on Sex Workers Who Use Drugs

All five of the women Steve Wright killed in Ipswich in 2005 – Paula, Anneli, Gemma, Tania and Annette – were dependent drug users.[23] This detail, pulled out many times in the media over the following decade, is worth mentioning – though not because it allows us to allocate blame to 'junkies' or see their deaths as an inevitable and unfixable result of perceived fecklessness or self-destruction. Drugs, and the way the law shapes the lives of people who use them, are of direct relevance when examining why these women were working on the street and why they were vulnerable to Wright's attack. Ending the war on drugs is a sex workers' rights issue.

In Britain, a significant majority of criminalised sex workers (particularly those working outdoors) have experiences with drug dependency.* The most significant link between these two circumstances is money. Drugs can be expensive: for many people, selling sex is the only way to afford the drugs they need, and the level of their dependency dictates the amount they will need to work.[24]

Sex workers who use drugs are subject to the criminalisation of both drugs and prostitution, and these policies and consequences manifest similarly. Criminalising drugs not only creates even more risk of police attention and a criminal record, it also makes them illicit and therefore dangerous. As with soliciting laws, laws that mandate the arrest or dispersal of people engaged in drug use in public spaces lead to more clandestine behaviours, which can mean more dangerous drug usage, particularly rushed and risky methods of injecting.† Arresting local dealers (who often use drugs as well) pushes people to buy drugs from unfamiliar sources and prevents them from making better informed decisions about the transaction. Taking a risk on a dodgy-seeming client because you need the money is a gamble; so is using a prohibited substance which may be mislabelled, 'cut' with other things, or of unknown potency. In both situations, lack – whether of money or of safer drugs – pushes people into risk, and the risk you're willing to take grows the more you lack. The desire to avoid withdrawal – or poverty – changes people's behaviour in powerful ways.

People who use drugs also have their safety measures destroyed

---

* A survey of street sex workers in Bristol found that 96 per cent reported dependency on drugs or alcohol, and 60 per cent of those in turn reported injection-drug use. Heroin and crack cocaine were the most used illegal substances. See N. Jeal and C. Salisbury, 'A health needs assessment of street-based prostitutes: cross-sectional survey', *Journal of Public Health* 26:2 (2004), 147–51.

† 'Since people who use drugs are frequently criminalised, drug-using paraphernalia, such as syringes and needles, can be used as evidence of drug use by the police, and paraphernalia can be confiscated and/or destroyed by police. This impedes safer, hygienic use of drugs and serves as a disincentive for people who use drugs to carry sterile injection paraphernalia. This increases the likelihood of rushed injecting and needle sharing, increasing the risk of overdose and impeding efforts to prevent transmission of blood-borne infections like HIV and hepatitis.' International Network of People who Use Drugs, 'Consensus Statement on Drug Use Under Prohibition – Human Rights, Health, and the Law', 2015, 18.

by the police (much like sex workers).* Groups of people keeping watch over each other while they're high are vulnerable to arrest, as are those carrying their own clean, sterilised equipment. Both sex workers and drug users face discrimination in the media, in courtrooms, in healthcare, in dealing with social services, and in formal employment – doubly so for those who fall into both categories.[25] Sex workers who use drugs are intensely vulnerable to violence because they fear arrest on two counts – as the tragic case of Bonnie Barratt, who was murdered in London in 2007, shows. Bonnie's colleagues, like her, were both selling sex and using drugs. Before her death, they had noticed a particular client becoming rougher and more violent; despite this, they all felt unable to report him or ask for help. This was with good reason; Bonnie herself was arrested more than thirty times prior to her murder.[26]

Both groups are forgotten by politicians, even the more progressive of whom are rarely prepared to die on the hill of reforming drug and sex work laws in *favour* of those who use drugs or sell sex. When commentators engage with the topics of drugs and sex work, it's easier to summon the contemptible figures of the Pimp and the Dealer (or better yet, blame the evils of sex and heroin themselves!) than to examine the structural context of prostitution and drug use. Examining these contexts would mean answering for the way that governments – not individual villains – are failing two of the most vulnerable groups of people in society. As already noted, many people who use drugs sell sex to get money to pay for drugs. Sex workers who take drugs often do so to cope with the trauma of work that is often exacerbated by criminalisation. Examining this two-way connection between sex work and drug use renders people who use drugs and sell sex as ultimately rational, logical actors who are responding to their environment.

---

* Edinburgh police confiscated injection equipment when they did drug raids in the 1980s, reducing the number of needles in the drug-user community and forcing people to share needles when they otherwise might not. As a result, the AIDS crisis tore through the city's drug-user population with devastating ferocity, and Edinburgh became known as 'the AIDS capital of Europe'. Hundreds of people died. See L. Hunt, 'Aids taking heavy toll of city's drug users: Edinburgh feels impact of HIV', *Independent*, 5 August 1994, independent.co.uk.

This is a perspective that many people find challenging. (Even language pushes up against it. Rational people are often described with words that mean 'not using drugs': *sober, clear-headed*.) But thinking of sex workers who use drugs as people who are trying their best to survive in a bad situation is *necessary*. It pushes the public to think of them not as flawed or failing, but as dealing with the big and small ways that society is stacked against them. It also helps to identify the big and small changes that would make them safer, like safe injection facilities, clean needles, safe red-light areas, affordable housing, and an end to destitution.* Most starkly, prescription opiates would free people from long hours on the street to afford drugs, and instead connect them with healthcare and other services – giving them the knowledge and resources to manage their use safely.[27]

To some people, these forms of harm reduction – giving people heroin, needles and places to use these things – would seem shocking, but are they really more shocking than needless deaths? Sex workers and drug users in Britain are dying every week in the failed war on drugs. Twelve people died in the small Scottish city of Dundee in just one month in early 2018 because the drugs they were using were unsafe.[28] Current British drug policy amounts to a form of 'social cleansing'.

The drugs debate is steeped in the same injustice as the sex work debate. When *all* drug use is constructed as terrible, the differences between harms and more sustainable behaviours are flattened out, made invisible, or even reversed. British law is stricter on people smoking cannabis in a park than on people who sniff glue, despite the latter being far riskier. Both groups would be better served by being able to buy legal cannabis. Spice is a synthetic cannabinoid, more addictive than natural cannabis and much more dangerous; unlike cannabis, spice can cause serious bodily injuries and even deaths. It is the criminalisation of cannabis that caused spice to be developed and widely used: the creators of spice were taking advantage of a

---

* As far as we know, there has never been an overdose fatality at *any* supervised injecting facility anywhere in the world – a record spanning decades, more than ninety separate facilities and millions of individual opioid injections. P. Gregoire, 'Why Does Australia Still Have Only One Supervised Injecting Room?' *Vice*, 26 January 2016, vice.com.

temporary legal loophole, as the law cannot keep up with the rate that people can invent new compounds. The whack-a-mole game of criminalisation pushes people (both those who use and those who sell) to experiment with riskier and riskier substances in an attempt to keep just ahead of the law.

Precarious sex workers who use drugs are maligned and punished while the middle and upper classes enjoy cocaine, ecstasy, cannabis, ketamine, and LSD on a regular basis.[29] The lack of solidarity from middle-class drug users towards those who are more marginalised is particularly frustrating given that all drug users, regardless of social class, are affected – to a degree – by drug prohibition.[30] Maybe you were ripped off for a bag of 'weed' that was mostly herbs or felt a pang of fear in a nightclub watching a friend pop a mystery pill that you both hoped was ecstasy. Maybe your partner suffered the ill effects of a night on cocaine that had been cut with something cheaper. Across the board, criminalisation prevents people who use drugs from being certain what they are taking.

There's an argument that weed, pills and coke are 'not as bad' as heroin, crack cocaine, or crystal meth, but it is the *people using the drugs*, not the drugs themselves, who are branded 'good' and 'bad'. The history of drug prohibition has shown us that 'problematic people' favouring a specific substance is what renders that substance 'problematic', not the other way around[31]. It is easy to demonise a drug when demonised people are most strongly associated with it, and although Black British people use drugs at a far lower rate than white people, they are searched by police at a much higher rate as well as prosecuted more intensely if found in possession of drugs.[32]

The difference between the 'normative citizen' and the prostitute who uses drugs is a question first and foremost of circumstance and need: 'hard' drugs are a far more powerful way to cope with a difficult life than party drugs, and often easier to obtain than prescription drugs. Second, it is a difference of policing and social control. Who is targeted? Who can be criminalised? Who is deemed unworthy of a good life? Who is allowed to flourish and prosper?

Outdoors

The criminalisation of street-based sex work in Great Britain inten-
sified sharply in the early 2000s. First New Labour and then the
Conservatives created and retained new and punitive approaches, of
which the best-known was the Anti-Social Behaviour Order (ASBO)
and its successors.[33] (In 2014, the coalition government abolished the
ASBO but introduced a range of other similar orders aimed at tack-
ling 'anti-social behaviour', including the Crime Prevention Injunction
(CPI), the Criminal Behaviour Order (CBO), the Community
Protection Notice (CPN), dispersal orders and 'section thirty-fives'.
In order to not overwhelm the reader with acronyms, we have used
'ASBO' as an umbrella term, as it continues to be common parlance.)

The ASBO is *deliberately* broad and vague: it can target noise,
fly-tipping (illegal dumping), public drug use, graffiti, harassment –
and street-based sex work. Once an ASBO is issued, breaching it can
criminalise what would otherwise be non-criminal behaviour. For
example, someone can get an ASBO banning them from a specific
area. Breaching the ASBO by returning to that area can land them
in jail for up for five years, despite the fact that imprisonment for
soliciting was technically abolished in England and Wales in 1982.[34]
A women's charity conducted in-depth interviews with fifteen women
who work or had worked on the street, and found that eight had
received custodial sentences – ranging from a few weeks to six months
– for not paying fines or for breaching ASBOs.[35] As Cari Mitchell from
the English Collective of Prostitutes put it, 'In effect, ASBOs have rein-
troduced prison for an offence which is not imprisonable'.[36]

This has become even worse in recent years: the 2009 Policing and
Crime Act made it easier to prosecute street-based sex workers by
creating a new crime of 'persistently loitering for the purpose of prostitution'.[37] (What a gift from Britain's first female home secretary,
a self-declared feminist.)[38] And in 2013, the coalition government
introduced a mandatory rehabilitation period for those coming out
of prison on short sentences. As women's charity Nia write,

> The supervision [mandatory rehabilitation] period could have the
> potential of opening up access to services for women, although it is

questionable whether this will include specialist services for exiting. More worryingly though, such measures increase the risk that women on supervision who may breach certain conditions or face relapses could be further entrenched in the criminal justice system.[39]

In other words, a sex working woman could be sentenced to prison for breach of her ASBO conditions, and upon release, be *re-sentenced to prison* for breach of her 'post-release supervision' conditions. Welcome to the twenty-first century!

The introduction of the ASBO marked a new era of middle class disgust towards poor people. Not only did it bring in a new way to punish and persecute the working classes, but it turned jeering at 'junkies, hookers and chavs' into a national pastime.[40] The acronym has become a byword for public disgrace ('Sex-for-cash Asbo woman dodges prison')[41] and the injustice in the mechanism of the ASBO is often lost beneath the tabloid spectacle. Many British news outlets ran photos of one woman who was jailed after breaching her ASBO by simply visiting her client at his home. She was sentenced to three months and ordered to pay a fine towards 'victim services', despite the fact that there was no victim – he had given her keys and even showed up to defend her in court.[42]

In banning people from specific areas, the ASBO makes *explicit* what is largely *implicit* in other aspects of British prostitution law: dispersal and invisibility. It asks that street-based sex workers, who are overwhelmingly working class women navigating poverty and oppressive drug laws as best they can, remove themselves from the communities where they live, work, buy their groceries, meet their dealers, raise their children, and visit their GPs.* Breaching these dispersal orders

---

* People of all genders sell and trade sex. However, street work is largely done by women. This is especially the case for street-based work that is *visible to the police* as sex work – although cis and trans men sell sex on the street, they are more likely to be working opportunistically in or around bars or through dating apps, which is less detectable to the police, compared to loitering on a known stroll. There are two factors at play – first, that street work is already overwhelmingly done by women; second, that enforcement overwhelmingly targets women (and people the criminal justice system read as women). Thus, in this section we refer to women and street-based sex workers with a high degree of interchangeability.

is inevitable, because people cannot vanish from their communities as the ASBO asks them to. In this impossible demand, we glimpse how anti-prostitution law wishes the 'orderliness' of death upon those who most visibly sell sex. It is no coincidence that the police and the men who murder sex workers *share* a preoccupation with 'cleansing the streets'. (Peter Sutcliffe, the 'Yorkshire Ripper', infamously told his brother, 'I were just cleaning up streets, our kid. Just cleaning up streets.')[43] Police crackdowns on sex workers are routinely described as 'cleaning up' the streets;[44] a 2016 US anti-prostitution action was even named Operation Cleanup.[45] More practically, of course, it forces women to work in new, isolated, and unfamiliar places. The shared preoccupations of the police and the men who murder sex workers meet at their most lethal, devastating point here, in the figure of the woman working late and alone, far from home.

In Medway, Kent, sex workers' rights campaigner Ruth Jacobs obtained the arrest figures for a police-run project named Safe Exit. She found that far from safety or even exit, Safe Exit entailed a huge number of ASBOs and arrests: sixty-seven women were charged with prostitution offences over five years, with half of those prosecutions made just in 2010 and 2011.[46] In comparison, in other neighbouring Kent districts – Thanet, Gravesham, Shepway, Sevenoaks, Tonbridge and Malling, and Royal Tunbridge Wells – not one woman was slapped with an ASBO or charged with soliciting during those five years. Ruth told us that 'whistleblowers I spoke to ... said these women disappeared and some died because of this approach. The woman they held up as the poster success story [case study] for the scheme died – it's sickening.'[47]

These ever-tightening laws are also incredibly labyrinthine, with multiple, broad, overlapping modes of punitive state control: in addition to ASBOs, soliciting, and loitering, outdoor workers can also be prosecuted for public sex, issued with 'prostitute cautions' and with 'section twenty-ones' or 'section thirty-fives', arrested by immigration police, and de-prioritised for social housing.[48] Unlike an ordinary police caution, a prostitute caution can be handed out entirely at police discretion, and there is no right of appeal.* Like an

---

* Per the Crown Prosecution Service, an 'ordinary police caution' requires

ASBO, a prostitute caution appears on your record if you apply for jobs requiring enhanced disclosure.

Criminalisation is a multi-pronged trap. Convictions, ASBOs, and prostitute cautions hinder sex workers' ability to secure other jobs and lead to accumulating debts for fines, pushing them into continuing to sell sex. These fines are huge financial millstones, sometimes totalling hundreds of pounds. Prison sentences for breaches of ASBOs or pile-ups of fines mean that women lose custody of their children, that upon release they are made homeless, and that they lose any other job they may have had – again, all pushing them back into street-based sex work, where avoiding police makes them more likely to experience violence.

This means that for a woman on the street, punishment can trigger a vicious cycle of physical and legal risk. Yet even Holbeck with its managed area, about which countless headlines have blared titillated fury over *a legalised sex industry*, retains criminalisation for sex workers. Monika, held in Yarl's Wood Immigration Removal Centre after being arrested in Holbeck, told a reporter, 'It feels like I'm in prison ... The doors are locked. I never realised I wasn't allowed to be working ... Now I don't know what's going on. I feel like I'm going crazy.'[49]

In Redbridge, East England, after the local community pressured the police to 'take action' against street-based sex workers, they sharply increased arrests and cautions. Visible prostitution seemed to decrease, and the community – at least, community members who were not sex workers – responded with praise. Meanwhile, a young woman named Mariana Popa, who had arrived in the country just three weeks earlier and whose only other source of income was low-paid, cash-in-hand waitressing, needed money to support herself and her young family. She went out to work in Ilford, a few minutes' walk away. Late on the evening of 29 October 2013, a man approached

---

that there must be enough evidence of guilt that if the case was taken to court there would be 'a realistic prospect of conviction', and that the person receiving the conviction must admit guilt. A prostitute caution has neither requirement. See the Crown Prosecution Service legal guidances, 'Cautioning and Diversion' and 'Prostitution and Exploitation of Prostitution', available at cps.gov.uk.

Mariana and stabbed her in the chest. She staggered into a local chicken shop, desperate for help, but her injury was already too serious. Mariana died.

Monica Abdala, who runs an outreach service in the area, told a journalist, 'It does not help when the police do operations ... It makes the women spread out; it makes the women work harder. They have to go up alleys where there are no cameras.'[50] Women in the area were seen literally running from the police, ducking behind cars or taking off their shoes and leaving them on the pavement to get away more quickly.[51] Criminalisation pushed Mariana to work in ways that made her more vulnerable to the man who killed her. On the night of her murder, Mariana had been verbally admonished by the police *three times* and handed a caution.[52] She needed to work to pay off a soliciting fine she had received a few days earlier. (Another woman in the area at the same time had a fine totalling £1,350.)[53] Her reasons for working later than normal and in a more secluded way are clear – she desperately needed to avoid the police, to make the money that she needed and avoid another expensive fine.

Assistant Chief Constable Chris Armitt, then the police lead on prostitution in England and Wales, commented after Mariana's death, 'Where there have been robust and overt police enforcement operations, shortly afterwards we see that incidents of violence against sex workers increase.'[54] The Metropolitan Police in Redbridge, however, do not share his pragmatic view – or don't care. The borough where Mariana died continues to criminalise street-based sex workers aggressively; the local police hand out the highest number of prostitute cautions in London and boast on social media about their work.[55] The harms are obvious. 'We are not going to enforce our way out of this problem', comments Armitt. 'It simply won't work.'[56]

The hostility of the police towards sex workers, and the hostility of other residents towards sex workers is mutually reinforcing: a few weeks after Mariana was killed, a group of locals attacked another migrant sex worker in the area, beating her so badly she needed hospitalisation. No charges were brought.[57]

Indoors

Selling sex alone indoors is legal in Britain. Rivka Holden, a fifty-five-year-old sex worker in Colindale, preferred that her clients visit for an 'in-call' – a term for a pre-arranged appointment at a place of the sex worker's choosing. Lenuta Haidemac, an escort and mother of two from Skegness, could not work at home, where her children were. She did 'outcalls,' visiting clients at their own homes or hotel rooms. Both were murdered by men in cold blood, in horrifically brutal killings which resulted in long jail sentences. Lenuta's killer admired Jack the Ripper and scrawled 'Jack' onto her torso after stabbing and strangling her.[58] The man who murdered Rivka beat, stabbed, and strangled her. He later confessed in a phone call to a friend, 'I killed a person ... not a person, a whore.'[59]

For murderers like these, a sex worker is the go-to victim. The laws which encompass commercial sex make it all too easy to be reasonably certain your victim will be alone. The injustice is excruciating; not only did Rivka and Lenuta suffer unimaginably sadistic deaths, but it's likely things could have been different for them if they could have shared a workspace with a friend.

For many sex workers, working together in pairs or small groups is infinitely preferable to being alone with a stranger who has the power to maim or kill them. Indeed, although anti-prostitution campaigners sometimes portray sex workers' wish to work in pairs legally as illustrating the intrinsic danger and aberrance of prostitution, other occupations widely acknowledge that working alone can be dangerous.[60] After the presumed murder of estate agent Suzy Lamplugh in 1986, estate agents were advised to work in pairs where possible or have a 'buddy' keep track of their whereabouts.[61] The Royal College of Nursing produces similar advice for health care workers, as does the British Association of Social Workers.[62] Unison, one of Britain's largest trade unions, highlights that working alone renders many workers vulnerable to violence and suggests working in pairs.[63] For exactly the same reasons, small groups of people may opt to sell sex from the same flat.* Often such an arrangement will involve

---

* Occasionally people suggest that advocating for sex workers to share

taking turns in one bedroom, while the person who is not with the client sits in a nearby room out of sight. As sex worker Claire Finch said, 'My main thing was safety. It's not safe to work on your own. With two of us you had back-up, you had camaraderie.'[64]

However, as Finch found out, sharing work spaces is illegal in Britain where two or more sex workers constitute a 'brothel'. This penalty applies whether or not both people see a client at the same time – or even on the same *day* – and regardless of whether one person has greater power than the other. In other words, although it *can* criminalise managers, this law can also be used to criminalise two workers for sharing a flat. Finch and her friends, who were all women in their forties, emphatically stated that their arrangement was one of equal power and mutual safety. Despite this, *twenty police officers* broke down Finch's front door and searched her house, confiscating her cash, her laptop and her phone.

This is routine. In 2015, Jean Urquhart, a politician in Scotland, presented evidence to the Scottish Parliament that arrests and prosecutions that use the brothel-keeping law to criminalise sex workers sharing a space happen all the time. Urquhart wrote:

> Small groups of women working together for their safety and well-being continue to be arrested and charged with brothel keeping in Scotland. In Aberdeen, women were arrested, prosecuted or convicted [of] brothel-keeping in November 2013, December 2013, March 2014, April 2014, May 2014, October 2014, February 2015

---

premises is 'victim-blaming', because it implies that sex workers who *chose* to work alone and then were attacked in some way did not take necessary precautions. This would be more convincing if those who made this argument were trying to change the law to force *all* women workers to work alone – after all, in this analysis, surely a social worker who takes a colleague with her on a home visit is *also* implicitly victim-blaming any colleagues who, for whatever reason, do not do the same. It is perfectly possible to think, as we do, that no one should have to change their behaviour to avoid violence *and* to think that for the state to criminalise basic safety measures is incredibly harmful. Someone might find it terrible that women often opt to walk home late at night in pairs or groups, but unless they are advocating to *criminalise* walking home after dark with a friend, they are putting a bizarre burden on sex workers, who just want to use the same safety measure without risking arrest.

and then in May 2015. In May 2013, women were being prosecuted for working together in Paisley and in November 2013 'brothels' were raided in Glasgow and five women were arrested and taken to court. *There is no suggestion that these women were doing anything other than renting apartments together to work in safety given that they were all working as sex workers themselves and not as bosses or managers.* (emphasis ours) [65]

Local police forces can decide how 'proactive' they want to be about hunting down these shared flats. Urquhart's research highlighted the particularly aggressive enforcement in and around Aberdeen. For several years, online forums where sex workers share information had been buzzing with concern about Aberdeen – warning that if you're working in Aberdeen, *you need to be alone.* * Otherwise, you'll be arrested. It's crucial advice: a brothel-keeping prosecution can ruin your life, even more so if you're a migrant or a mother. It's advice that Jessica McGraa likely heeded: in February 2016, she was working alone in Aberdeen and was so wary of the aggressive enforcement in the city that, when a client's manner alarmed her, she called a friend, not the cops. (As a mother, a sex worker, and a Black woman, Jessica had multiple reasons to worry that she would not be treated well by the police.) The client raped and then murdered her. [66]

In 2013, Renata K. and Anna W. were selling sex in Leeds. They were working for an exploitative manager and wanted to escape. [67] So, along with a third friend, they left their manager and set up in a flat in Bradford where they could see clients and share bills. It was an equitable and friendly working space. This did not, however, stop the police from raiding the flat, seizing the 672 pounds they found there, and arresting the women. During Renata and Anna's trial (the third woman fled to Poland before the trial), the judge and *even the prosecutor* agreed that the flat was being run as an 'informal co-operative'. [68] Nonetheless, Renata and Anna were convicted of brothel-keeping.

In August 2017, three Romanian sex workers were arrested for sharing premises in the West Midlands, and in July 2017, police

---

* To protect sex workers' privacy, we are not linking to this online forum.

in Swindon raided a flat to find three Romanian women working there.[69] The police recounted what happened next proudly on social media, writing:

> All three women had been advertising sex work online via a website called adultworks [sic] ... The women were spoken to and no offences of trafficking or coercion were disclosed. They were very open about their sex work, and confirmed the profiles on adultworks [sic] were their own, which they had set up and paid for ... the women state that they do sex work of their own volition, because they can earn more money [through it] than back in Romania.[70]

The local paper reports that 'all three women were arrested for brothel offences' and deported.[71] The Swindon police describe these arrests as 'a very positive outcome' on the grounds that 'the women are now safe and away from their clients and no longer vulnerable to the risks of off-street sex work'.[72] It's hard to imagine many things less 'safe' than to be arrested, to have your money stolen, to be taken to an immigration detention centre, and to be deported, unable to say goodbye to your friends or partner.

In 2017, the Metropolitan Police left a note at a suspected brothel (which was only on their radar because it had been subject to an armed robbery), warning, 'Any female at this address now, who is found at this same address in the future, is very likely to be arrested.'[73] This threat clearly does not distinguish between workers and managers. Even police and prosecutors know – and openly acknowledge, in court and on social media – that these raids are *not* targeting or finding managers, let alone crime bosses: they are targeting and arresting sex workers.

The definition of brothel-keeping is so capacious as to easily facilitate the criminalisation of sex workers: a brothel can be any place where 'more than one woman offers sexual intercourse, whether for payment or not' or that is 'resorted to for the purposes of lewd homosexual practices'.[74] In other words, a flat-share where both housemates regularly have casual *non-commercial* sex could theoretically count as a brothel under British law. In reality, of course, the law is not used to criminalise casual sex, aside from the occasional sex-club raid.* Regrettably, it is much easier for us to imagine a mainstream feminist campaign in Britain working to remove casual-sex-havers from this law – on the basis that the symbolism of their inclusion is unfortunate – than to imagine such a campaign working to defend sex workers.

Ultimately the police target sex workers rather than people having one-night stands because, even indoors, sex workers are seen as disorderly in ways that other people engaging in indoor heterosexual copulation are not. Look at the reaction of a homeowner when they find that the photogenic little apartment that they've put on Airbnb has been used by a sex worker. Such scenarios are described as 'traumatic', despite the fact that Airbnb landlords have presumably had to come to terms, in general, with the thought of people having sex on their property. Commercial sex, then, is evidently different and alarming.

There is also a more prosaic reason for the police to focus on paid sex: the opportunity to confiscate cash and other assets. Under the Proceeds of Crime Act of 2002, British police have the power to confiscate assets they *suspect* are the result of criminal activity.† Even if no crime is ever proven, it falls on the suspect to prove in court that the assets were earned legally – a nearly impossible task with a cash-based business like sex work.[75] Between them, the police and the Crown Prosecution Service can each pocket 50 per cent of whatever is taken, giving the police a significant incentive to use these powers extensively.[76] And, as Alex Feis-Bryce, former chief executive of sex worker safety charity National Ugly Mugs, points out, it is also significantly more tempting for the police to target unarmed women selling sex (and working with cash) than to go after the professional criminal gangs for whom the law was originally intended.[77]

---

* Beginning in 2013, police in Edinburgh have raided and closed a number of 'saunas', a category including both commercial brothels and venues where men meet to have *non-commercial* casual sex. See A. Fogg, 'Why are Edinburgh's seamier saunas under attack?' Guardian, 24 October 2013, theguardian.com.

† American readers may notice the similarity to 'civil asset forfeiture' laws in the United States, which are also abused to confiscate huge sums of money from sex workers. See E. Nolan Brown, 'Sex Work and Civil Asset Forfeiture Increasingly Go Hand in Hand', *Reason*, 28 August 2015, reason.com.

As a result, the theft of sex workers' money in police raids on brothels is routine and goes beyond merely confiscating the occasional eighty pounds. In October 2016, when the police raided massage parlours in Soho and Chinatown, London, and took seventeen women to deportation centres, they also removed thirty-five thousand pounds.[78] They even took money from individual women's lockers.[79] Sex worker Janice had thirteen thousand pounds taken from her in a brothel raid and it was never returned to her, even after she was found not guilty: 'They even tried to take my home. I was left with nothing after a lifetime of hard work. I'm not young anymore and don't know how I'll manage. My life has been turned upside down.'[80] Anti-prostitution policing thus becomes legalised theft.

The brothel-keeping law harms not only those who are caught – i.e., arrested or prosecuted – but also every sex worker who *worries* about being caught. People change their behaviour out of *fear*. It also enables the police to use criminalisation as a threat. A sex worker we know who reported a violent crime was told, in her local police station, 'You do realise you're at risk of eviction if you carry on telling me what you are telling me?'[81] Another young woman we know approached the police about a man who was stalking her, only to have them investigate *her* for brothel-keeping – because one day a week she advertised 'duos' from her flat.

Criminalisation grants the police power over sex workers, and at the same time creates points of leverage which can be exploited by predators. We have both experienced phone calls from people *claiming* to be clients, asking, 'Do you work alone then, love?' and had to gamble, in that moment, with two competing problems. Is he seeking to rob or assault me, in which case I should put him off by telling him I work with a friend? Or is he a cop seeing if he can make a brothel-keeping arrest that day, in which case I should put him off by assuring him that I work alone?

As we see again and again among our friends, two people working together in a flat are powerless in the face of a landlord who can charge extortionate rent – or explicitly blackmail them – under the threat of reporting them to the cops. The same two workers have little defence when a client decides that this culpability is leverage he can use to assault them or to evade justice. A few years ago, two London sex workers (we will call them Lily and Jane) were working together in a flat as a safety measure after one of them was feeling shaken up after a recent incidence of violence. While Lily and Jane were working, a client of Lily's turned aggressive. Jane came into the room to back Lily up. The client, instead of becoming chastened, became even more confident, telling them, 'You can't call the police on *me* – there's two girls here! This is a *brothel!* I'm gonna call the police on *you!*' This is the kind of man given power by brothel-keeping laws.

In a *collective* workplace, *all* the sex workers risk criminalisation. But a sex worker who works with an agent or manager (in a brothel, massage parlour, walk-up, sauna, or escort agency) is not criminalised – that buck is passed to the boss who organises or facilitates their work. This, along with the safety that comes with having another person on-site, makes employment in brothels and parlours attractive to many sex workers. Thus, the law's failure to distinguish between these two kinds of set-ups *pushes sex workers into the arms of managers*. It also allows managers to extract more profit from sex workers' earnings – some of the manager's 'cut' comes out because they are shouldering the threat of criminalisation.

Being self-employed can be difficult. For sex workers who are carers, parents, or students, it can be a reasonable alternative to hand over some proportion of income to a boss who takes care of the logistical demands of commercial sex: answering the phone or email, running a website, setting up advertising, holding the money during the booking, organising the rental of the premises, providing equipment, and organising the cleaning of the venue. Rather than self-employment swallowing their free time and personal space, they can do one or two shifts a week and leave the job behind as soon as they step out of the door.

While the sex worker isn't breaking the law when they're working for a boss, the workplace is still an illegal one. When your workplace is criminalised, there are no employment tribunals, no HR departments, no legal contracts or health and safety inspectors - and therefore extremely limited recourse when your working conditions are bad. Your employer may threaten you with the sack if you decline to provide services to a client. They may fail to stock provisions like condoms, verbally abuse you, arbitrarily dock your wages, coerce you into longer shifts, or subject you to sexual harassment. They may simply be negligent in their obligations to provide basic safety, such as failing to pick up the phone in an emergency or to step into the room when you call for them. You have only two choices: do nothing or make a police report.

Assuming that you need the money, this presents a conundrum. If you call the police, the response will be a raid – resulting in the closure of your entire workplace, a lost job for you and every other worker there, and potentially deportations. A raid poses other risks, too, like the confiscation of money, belongings, or drugs. Many managers or agency owners firmly discourage reporting sexual violence to the police and emphasise to their employees that raising the alarm on a rapist will put everybody out of work. Almost all sex workers are in the job because they need the money. When made to pick between their income and making bad bosses or rapists accountable, the sex worker often has no choice but to tolerate bad conditions. Sex workers effectively protect their abusers in the same way some survivors of domestic violence have to protect partners upon whom they are financially dependent when police are called out. As grassroots feminist groups have noted, a heavy-handed police response is, in some cases, worse for survivors than nothing at all.

In these ways, 'pimping' laws limit victims' responses to abusive managers. Yet people who would be willing to decriminalise the selling (or even buying) of sex often still wish for penalties against third parties. The idea that a third party should be involved in the transaction strikes people as intuitively wrong – exploitative at a fundamental level.

Such an assumption can only survive by obscuring the mundane realities of sex workers' everyday lives. A spouse or partner who helps answer emails or schedule appointments, a receptionist who works the phones for tips in a brothel, or a sex worker who sublets her flat to a friend in times of illness or injury are all vulnerable to pimping laws. This means that should something happen – for example, if your workplace is robbed by armed men – you will probably hesitate to call the police for help, for fear of endangering others.

At a brothel in Bournemouth, Christy Norman – a seventy-year-old cleaner who worked just two days a week – helped a client who had collapsed by calling an ambulance and administering CPR. When the paramedics arrived with police, Norman was arrested and charged with running a brothel.[82] Despite her obvious goodwill, she was found guilty, thus ensuring that no sex worker or brothel employee in Dorset will ever feel confident calling the authorities in an emergency again.

Many sex workers (including, at times, the authors) proactively seek out managed sex work rather than independent work for the reasons highlighted above. These people would prefer enhanced power *within* their relationships with bosses rather than that relationship being criminalised. The reason is that workers generally want to *keep their jobs*, with improved conditions. That is a standard trade union demand. Likewise, the feminist movement would not celebrate a woman losing her job in the aftermath of reporting workplace sexual harassment – that would be easily recognised as harmful, not a victory. But the criminalisation of our workplaces means sex workers *lose our jobs* if we report abuse.

However emotionally satisfying it may be to punish people like managers, that doesn't mean it will have good consequences. The reality is that criminalisation is not a deterrent for the most abusive. Commenting on the failed war on drugs, former undercover police officer Neil Woods observes that his successful efforts to bust drug dealers simply resulted in ever more violence:

> Every year the police get better at catching drug gangs, and the gangsters' most effective way of fighting back is upping the use of fear and intimidation against potential informants. The most efficient way to stop people grassing them up is to be terrifying. In other words, organised crime groups were getting nastier and nastier as a direct result of what I was doing ... It's a classic arms race.[83]

The relatively easy-going 'mom-and-pop' operations are quickly shut down and replaced by organisations that are prepared to be more mercenary, by murdering not only police informants but anyone who accidentally leads the police to them.

The same process plays out in the sex industry. The advertising platform Escort-Ireland is well known for subjecting escorts to exploitative practices, and for allegedly committing cyberattacks against potential rivals. It rose to near-monopoly status in the wake of a police crackdown on the previous system of newspaper ads for escorts.[84] In attempting to eradicate prostitution – and instead vandalising the systems that sex workers need – prohibition cultivates ruthlessness.

Looking the Other Way

Despite all this, the solidarity shown to sex workers fighting the criminalisation of sex work in Britain – from ASBOs, fines, and jail to brothel raids – is at best uneasy. One feminist commentator, for instance, interjected into a debate about sex work policy to claim, 'Decriminalised [sex work] *is* the status quo in the UK. If that harms [sex workers], then how will extending it be better?'[85] (Sex workers are used to having to argue that criminalisation is bad; it is a new and regrettable ideological shift to have to explain that criminalisation *exists*.) When the National Police Chiefs' Council issued new guidance suggesting that brothel raids and enforcement against street-based sex workers be halted, anti-prostitution feminists were among those who objected.[86]

This type of feminist tends to have trouble with the terminology of the debate, regularly seeming to confuse very different legal models: calling the Swedish model 'decriminalisation', treating 'decriminalisation' and 'legalisation' as interchangeable, and, during a tense debate at a UK Amnesty Annual General Meeting, claiming the United States – which has full criminalisation – is an example of 'the Swedish model' (see chapter 6).[87] Whether they spring from intention or accident, these politics leave criminalised women out in the cold. The feminist movement cannot fight what its activists cannot name.

Indeed, many anti-prostitution feminists actively support some form of criminalisation. Much of the mainstream feminist movement gave support to a 2014 report from a group of MPs recommending the continued use of ASBOs against women who sell sex as well as a law proposed by Scottish Labour politician Rhoda Grant that sought to retain the criminalisation of soliciting.[88] Scottish politician Trish Godman, who proposed to criminalise both the purchase *and the sale* of sex is feted at feminist conferences.[89] Anti-prostitution feminists are so focussed on criminalising *clients* that when a legislative proposal contains this measure, they support it – seemingly without checking the 'detail' of what the proposal includes for sex workers.

The arrests of sex workers as a result of Britain's broad brothel-keeping laws may represent 'collateral damage' to some feminists that on some – silent – level they are genuinely sad to see, albeit while believing it 'necessary for the greater good'. For others who feel anger towards sex workers, despite their claims of sympathy, such arrests might scratch the itch to see punitive state action. (As one such woman memorably told a sex worker, 'Frankly I've got to the point if it takes a few lives like yours to save one eleven-year-old … I'll deal.')[90] One UK-based feminist anti-prostitution organisation gives out guidance on 'how to spot an illegal brothel';[91] they seem unconcerned about the arrest, prosecution, theft of money, and deportation that sex working women may be subject to as a result of their 'guidance'. In Glasgow, a feminist-aligned 'support service' claims that arrest can be *helpful* to women in prostitution. Its manager tells a journalist, 'We don't wait until [prostitutes] say they want to exit and we share all our info with police … We try everything to engage with them. That could be a [criminal] charge, which puts them in a system where they have support.'[92]

After a 2016 brothel raid in Leeds, an officer told reporters that the purpose of the crackdown was to 'protect the vulnerable … They don't necessarily see they're being taken advantage of and it's part of our job to make them aware.' When the sex workers told the raiding officers that they were, in fact, migrant workers in possession of their passports and house keys, with freedom to come and go as they pleased, they were evicted and issued with deportation orders.[93] Despite the obvious injustice of these raids, only sex workers protested; mainstream feminists and the anti-trafficking movement remained resoundingly silent. As an activist with UK collective Sex Worker Advocacy and Resistance Movement (SWARM) commented to us, 'These raids are violent and abusive. As usual, the support of anti-prostitution feminists is nowhere to be found when migrant sex workers are arrested, evicted or deported.'[94]

In the aftermath of the arrests in Swindon, sex workers organised to stop the deportations of the Romanian women.[95] Most anti-prostitution feminists made no comment, but one speculated that maybe the Romanian women were pimps after all.[96] The idea that a workplace might have three managers and no workers, and moreover that the 'managers' would all be migrant women in their twenties advertising their own sexual services online is patently absurd. Its absurdity speaks, as gender studies academic Alison Phipps has noted, to just 'how far people will go to avoid extending solidarity to those they disapprove of'.[97]

Almost everybody with any flavour of feminist politics proclaims not to want those who *sell* sex to be arrested. However, that sex workers patently *are* arrested as a result of brothel-keeping laws is, for most anti-prostitution feminists, unmentionable – because the legal model they are pushing for retains and even strengthens these exact same laws (see chapter 6). The fundamental awkwardness of this truth – one that ultimately reveals dedication to something other than sex working women's welfare – creates a frustrating culture of unseeing and unknowing among the feminist left. They stick their fingers into their ears while sex workers try, with increasing frustration, to make the impact of criminalisation clear to them.

The situation for sex workers in Scotland, England, and Wales is bad and getting worse. Harsh drug laws, intensifying poverty, and ever grimmer policies targeting migrants all act in concert with multi-layered and complex forms of criminalisation targeting commercial sex. Carceral feminism offers sex working women meagre solidarity. We turn next to the situation for sex workers elsewhere in the world, to explore in other contexts how criminal law (or its absence) shapes the experiences of people who sell sex.

5

Prison Nation: The United States, South Africa, and Kenya

Full Criminalisation: A legal model where the sex worker, the client, and third parties (such as managers, drivers, or landlords) are all criminalised. Also seen in Uganda, Russia, Iran, Pakistan, and China.

> I picked prostitutes as my victims ... because they were easy to pick up without being noticed. I knew they would not be reported missing right away and might never be reported missing. I picked prostitutes because I thought I could kill as many of them as I wanted without getting caught.
>
> – Gary Ridgway, the 'Green River Killer'*

Ideological Battleground

You'd think almost everybody would agree that full criminalisation, where the prostitute, client, and anybody else associated with the transaction can *all* be arrested, is a brutal, clumsy, unjust system. It should be obvious that the act of selling sex is a non-violent survival strategy – yet, if the sex worker is classed as criminal, their relationship with police becomes automatically adversarial; selling

---

* Ridgway is the most prolific known serial killer in US history, having murdered at least forty-eight women and girls (and very likely many more) around Seattle in the 1980s and 1990s. The women he attacked were mostly but not exclusively sex workers; disturbingly, he viewed his murders as a continuation of law enforcement against them. After his arrest in 2001, he remarked to police, 'I thought I was doing you guys a favor, killing prostitutes ... Here you guys can't control them, but I can.' See S.J.A. Talvi 'The Truth About the Green River Killer', *Alternet*, 11 November 2003, alternet.org.

sex becomes much more dangerous; lives are destroyed by even the shortest jail sentences; and those saddled with criminal records are, paradoxically, trapped in long-term prostitution when employers won't touch them. New Yorker Sarah Marchando was arrested for prostitution-related offences seven times in two years. 'It wasn't like I could just say, "Hey, let me go get a job," because I am not stable. I can't get stable if every time I turn around I am in jail again.'[1]

While the 'prostitution debate' might seem to play out among progressives, criminalising the prostitute is rooted in disgust and hatred – entangled with misogyny, racism, and fear of the visibly queer or diseased body. These coalesce into the belief that the prostitute is a threat who must be warded off through punishment. It is these reactionary politics doing most of the ideological work that sustains full criminalisation. Nonetheless, occasionally someone attempts to put a progressive gloss on such a system. One local paper reports that 'Sergeant Coleman of the Prince George's County Vice Squad says his goal is to help, not hurt, the women he arrests.'[2] An Arizona police officer speaks of a new era of sympathetic 'victim-centred' policing but adds that 'some arrests are still required to protect victims from abusive pimps, and an arrest sometimes motivates a victim to re-examine her life'.[3]

Many anti-prostitution writers barely touch on the topic of full criminalisation, clearly considering the case to be closed. Feminist campaigner Julie Bindel opens her recent book *The Pimping of Prostitution: Abolishing the Sex Work Myth* by detailing the 'two legal models' (the 'Nordic Model' as one, versus either legalisation or decriminalisation as the other).* There is no reference to the legal regime that arrests women like Sarah Marchando. This might suggest that the real battle is elsewhere, or perhaps that it *goes without saying*.

Full criminalisation, however, persists in dominating the globe. Russia, South Africa, the United States (aside from a few Nevada counties), China, and Kenya, among others, all fully criminalise prostitution. All the harms that flow from other, more 'subtle' forms of

---

* While for Bindel, these two models are 'Legalisation/Decriminalisation' and 'The Nordic Model',' we consider them to be three distinct models out of the five detailed in this book, including this chapter.

criminalisation start here; these are harms which do not go without saying. For Marchando – and for the tens of thousands of sex workers (and people profiled as sex workers) arrested, prosecuted, incarcerated, deported, or fined in the US every year – it's a conversation that urgently needs to be had. 'If nobody says nothing, it is not going to be dealt with' she says.[4]

Alisha Walker and GiGi Thomas are two sex working women who, in separate instances, have had to defend their own lives (and, in Walker's case, also the life of a friend) against a violent male aggressor.[*] Each has been brutally punished for desperate, panicked acts of self-defence, for the preservation of their own lives. In a nation where 'stand your ground' laws protect the rights of some to use lethal force against perceived threats to their safety, there is a bitterly unfair double standard for such women.[†] It is no coincidence that both are marginalised because of race and gender: Alisha is a Black cis woman and GiGi is a Black trans woman. The criminalisation of prostitution robbed them of their right to safety, and the treatment of Black and trans women in the US 'criminal justice' system – a system never built to deliver justice for women like GiGi and Alisha – robbed them of their right to self-defence and their right to freedom.[5]

Amidst the increasingly visible resurgence of fascism, it is easy for some liberals to position themselves as 'good people' simply by being to the left of the most ghoulish and uncouth iterations of hard-right politics. Structural problems become personalised and pathologised in figures like Donald Trump. But nothing short of a radical transformation of 'criminal justice' will bring safety to women like Alisha and GiGi. This cannot be left to liberals, who, in misdiagnosing the

---

* C.S. Becerril, 'Why Is This Sex Worker In Jail For Surviving?' *Fader*, 16 February 2017, thefader.com. Gigi Thomas, 'I am a survivor of violence', *BPPP*, 31 January 2017, bestpracticespolicy.org.

† In a recent case, Marissa Alexander, a Black woman living in Florida – the same state where George Zimmerman was acquitted for killing unarmed Black teenager Trayvon Martin under a 'stand your ground' law – was given a long jail term for firing a warning shot towards her violent partner, despite not injuring anyone. S.R. Brown, 'Black woman's failed "Stand Your Ground" claim raises allegations of racial double standard', *New York Daily News*, 15 July 2013, nydailynews.com.

problem, risk strengthening the carceral state. (The Obama administration, for example, responded to the outcry over Black deaths at the hands of the police by channelling millions of dollars into police departments.)[6] Punitive state control snaps shut like a trap around women like GiGi and Alisha. Only through naming these modes of control and unsafety can we begin to unpick them.

Prison Nation

Mainstream feminism too often puts 'police violence' and 'male violence against women' into different conceptual categories – if, indeed, it considers police violence to be a topic of feminist concern at all.[7] This is especially the case for the violence that is 'normalised' as part of policing: arrests, most obviously, but also violations such as intimate searches, and harassment such as stop-and-frisk.[8] The result is that police violence gets left out of mainstream feminist anti-violence work. However, when we think of police violence not only as state violence but also (often) as *male violence against women*, the criminalisation of prostitution comes into focus in a new way: as a key driver of male violence against women.

The infrastructure of criminalisation saturates our political consciousness. It is the bobby on the beat, the jail on the Monopoly board, the crime-drama TV show (with its inevitable murdered prostitute), the car-chase footage on the news. In this saturation, such images are rendered mundane, sidelining questions of the legitimacy or purpose of these modes of control. As Angela Davis writes, the prison 'is one of the most important features of our image environment', yet it

> functions ideologically as an abstract site into which undesirables are deposited, relieving us of the responsibility of thinking about the real issues afflicting those communities from which prisoners are drawn in such disproportionate numbers. This is the ideological work that the prison performs – it relieves us of the responsibility of seriously engaging with the problems of our society, especially those produced by racism and, increasingly, global capitalism.[9]

Theorist Beth Richie uses the term *prison nation* to mean a 'broad notion of using the arm of the law to control people, especially disadvantaged people and people from disadvantaged communities'.[10] Her term encompasses not only the physical infrastructure of prisons and jails, but also 'surveillance, policing, detention, probation, harsh restrictions on child guardianship ... and other strategies of isolation and disposal'.[11]

Perhaps the key trick of the prison nation is 'now you see it, now you don't'. Prison vanishes people; criminalisation renders those same people hyper-visible. The deeply racialised, anti-Black figure of the Pimp looms large as the perpetrator of 'slavery' – while the prison system itself, one of the key material legacies of chattel slavery in the Americas, is filled with ever more Black inmates.

Through the intensifying militarisation of police departments, there is a direct link between the foreign wars at the frontiers of the contemporary American empire and the hyper-carceral state at home.[12] As the *New Yorker* reports, since the 1990s, 'local governments have received approximately thirty-four billion dollars in grants from the Department of Homeland Security to buy their own military equipment ... That brings the total [spent by American police departments on military equipment] to thirty-nine billion dollars – more than the entire defense budget of Germany.'[13] The same trend is visible even in the histories of policing; early-twentieth-century American policing drew on the US Army's experience imposing brutal colonial rule in the Philippines, just as UK policing explicitly drew on tactics developed by the British Army in subduing colonised populations.[14]

Communities feel the police are an occupying army; the police *feel themselves to be* an occupying army, and the police respond to the people they encounter with the hostility that engenders.[15] Some of the most powerful photography emerging from the ongoing fight for Black lives in the US speaks to the visual dimension of this: an iconic photograph taken in Baton Rouge, Louisiana, shows Ieshia Evans, a young Black woman in a summer dress, calmly facing down two oncoming police officers in full body-armour. Meanwhile, the overlapping military and prison industrial complexes drain hundreds of billions of dollars from the American public purse, outfitting the police who rushed Ieshia in futuristic 'protective' armour – alongside cuts to Social Security, healthcare, and education, and catastrophic divestment from Black communities.

The Crime of Sex Work

Prostitution arrests are racist. They have always been racist. In 1866, San Francisco police arrested 137 women, 'virtually all Chinese'; the police boasted that they had 'expelled three hundred Chinese women'.[16] In the 1970s, the American Civil Liberties Union found that Black women were seven times more likely to be arrested for prostitution-related offences than white women.[17] This disparity is no relic of the past: between 2012 and 2015, 85 per cent of people charged with 'loitering for the purpose of prostitution' in New York City were Black or Latinx – groups that only make up 54 per cent of the city's population.* Increases in prostitution enforcement mean increases in the arrests of women of colour. Between 2012 and 2016, the New York Police Department stepped up enforcement targeting massage parlours. As journalist Melissa Gira Grant details, during this period the arrests of Asian people in New York charged either with 'unlicensed massage' or prostitution went up by 2,700 per cent.[18] Arrests on the street target Black and Latina women – who may not even be selling sex – simply for wearing 'tight jeans' or a crop top. The NYPD do not arrest white women in affluent areas of the city for wearing jeans.[19]

Racial disparities play out, too, in terms of who is charged with what. As Andrea Ritchie writes, Black women are also far more likely than their white counterparts 'to be charged with a more serious prostitution offence'.[20] A relatively high proportion of people incarcerated in the United States for human trafficking offences are Black women in their twenties who, at the time of their arrest, were selling sex.[21] Such women are prosecuted as sex traffickers simply for sharing a

---

* 'Loitering' in this context simply means standing or walking around in a public place; inferring a person's 'purpose' in doing so is normally left to the discretion of the police. A.J. Ritchie, *Invisible No More: Police Violence Against Black Women and Women of Color*, Boston, MA: Beacon Press, 2017, 150.

workspace with someone else who is selling sex – and who turns out to be seventeen rather than eighteen. As attorney Kate Mogulescu asks, 'is this the purpose of our federal human trafficking criminal law? To prosecute 20-to-24-year-old women of color involved in the commercial sex industry?'[22] Ritchie details the case of Gloria Lockett, a Black woman who went on to co-lead the sex workers' rights organisation COYOTE and who was on one occasion arrested for 'felony pimping' for holding another woman's money for her. Racism meant Lockett 'was charged with felony pimping, while police charged the white women with simple misdemeanour prostitution'.[*]

Through the prism of a fully criminalised legal model, the idea that a sex worker should be punished for selling sex is often under-scored by a philosophy of deterrence – a short, sharp shock to bring them in line with 'decent values'. (As one New York politician put it, 'Sometimes you have to compel people to help themselves ... [they] might need the incentive of, "Listen, you know, you've got to stop this."')[23] But at the level of material reality, criminalisation is not just a helping hand or a slap on the wrist. Often, charges like 'breach of parole' (continuing to sell sex after having been previously appre-hended for it) generate much harsher penalties than the crime of prostitution itself, such as time in jail rather than a fine. Jail means that, if they have children, they will likely lose custody, and that upon release they are likely to be made homeless,[†] will struggle to find 'legitimate' employment, and may be barred from some kinds of social safety net provisions, such as public housing.[24] The criminal status of 'prostitute' is thus a trap.

Criminalisation is often a 'revolving-door of arrest and prosecu-tion'.[25] State-inflicted vulnerability is transfigured into what looks like 'justified' permanent disgrace. Sex workers with drug dependencies,

---

* People who sell sex themselves are regularly criminalised by legislation ostensibly intended for pimps, but this very fact enables those who oppose sex workers' organising to paint the movement as full of shady bosses. In other words, the very injustice that sex workers are attempting to highlight becomes 'justification' for dismissing us. Ritchie, *Invisible No More*, 150.

† Often simply through missing rent payments while incarcerated. In some jurisdictions, carers of children are given priority access to supported housing, so losing custody of children can lead to homelessness in its own right.

trying to deal with the pain of homelessness and the loss of children, are seen as steering their own chaotic downward spiral, which makes it easier to vilify them as 'deserving' punitive sanctions. Prostitution policing also forcibly administers the mantle of chronic disgrace in more direct ways, such as posting mugshots and full names from prostitution arrests on social media. In one recent case, a Florida police department outed a sex worker who tried to trade sex with an undercover officer for a fast-food meal. Her legal name and photographs were reproduced widely in the press, as if this were an amusing rather than horrifying abuse of a vulnerable person.*

Prior to 2011, a centuries-old law that criminalised 'crimes against nature' by solicitation (CANS)[26] resulted in some sex workers in Louisiana being placed on a sex-offender registry for fifteen years to life.[27] The sex workers placed on the registry were disproportionately Black or trans workers. To be placed on such a registry is in many ways to experience a profound social death: you are excluded from housing, from Social Security, from most jobs, and from your community. You can be barred from domestic violence shelters. You often cannot live or socialise unsupervised with children, even your own children. Your driver's license – which you need to produce during a traffic stop, or to buy alcohol, or to deposit money in your local bank – reads 'sex offender' in huge orange letters. People on the registry are assumed to be perpetrators of extreme sexual violence and as such are often subject to vigilante violence from neighbours. In the aftermath of Hurricane Katrina, the nearby state of Florida barred registered sex offenders from public hurricane shelters, directing them to jails instead.[28] Those prosecuted under federal law as traffickers – even those who have only 'trafficked' themselves, like the young Black women selling sex mentioned earlier in this chapter – are *still* placed on sex-offender registries.[29]

Anti-prostitution policing also severely obstructs sex workers from carrying and using condoms, exposing them to health risks such as unwanted pregnancy and HIV.[30] One sex worker in New

---

* We were not able to find reporting on this story that doesn't include the woman's name, and so cannot ethically provide a citation.

York had police officers open her condoms and 'drop them into the sewer, all the time, ten times a month'. Another US sex worker says, 'If I took a lot of condoms, they would arrest me. If I took a few or only one, I would run out and not be able to protect myself. How many times have I had unprotected sex because I was afraid of carrying condoms? Many times.'[31]

Andrea Ritchie writes that, in New York in the early 2000s,

the practice was so pervasive that many believed there was a 'three condom rule' – anyone caught with three or more condoms would be charged with prostitution ... In reality, there is no magic number. I have seen criminal complaints listing a single condom as evidence of intent to engage in prostitution-related offences.[32]

In a direct echo of what happened to Gloria Lockett, one transgender Latina woman told lawmakers that when she and a friend were arrested on the street, 'her friend was charged with loitering for the purposes of prostitution [a misdemeanour] and she was charged with promoting her friend [a felony] because she was carrying condoms'.[33]

As technology and commercial sex collide, anti-prostitution policing, too, is increasingly present online. In America, the 2010s have seen a war of attrition against online platforms that host sex workers' ads – sites from Craigslist to BackPage to RentBoy and Eros have shuttered their ads sections in response to attempted prosecutions or have been brought down by actual arrests.[34] RentBoy, for example, was suddenly pulled offline in the summer of 2015, when law enforcement raided its offices and indicted its chief executives.[35]

Losing these advertising platforms pushes sex workers onto the street, where their increased visibility makes them more vulnerable to arrest, or more likely to depend on managers. When San Francisco ad site and messaging board MyRedBook was taken down in the summer of 2014, local sex workers lost not only the ability to post free ads and screen clients online but a huge community resource – including harm-reduction information such as 'bad date' lists, which warn workers of violent clients.[36]

While we were writing this book, new laws which increase website providers' vulnerability to prosecution over hosting sex work ads were passed in the US legislature. SESTA-FOSTA (see footnote on page 20) censored a huge number of advertising platforms at once in spring 2018, rendering sex workers in the US and beyond *more* precarious, broke, and desperate almost overnight as their source of income vanished. SESTA-FOSTA *increased the power* of clients and would-be managers, as sex workers scrambled to find work in any way they could. One client wrote, 'I definitely think this will end up being a win for hobbyists [habitual clients] … prices will drop because providers [sex workers] will not be able to pull in new customers and have to take whoever they can get. Specials [such as sex without a condom] will become more prevalent … They will have to act friendlier and not have the luxury of turning away clients any longer.'[37]

Sex workers across the US reported that in the immediate aftermath of SESTA-FOSTA, they started getting a flood of texts, calls and other come-ons from wannabe-managers, looking to lure newly-desperate workers into potentially exploitative arrangements. As one sex worker said, 'There's always something in the message alluding to these bills that have just passed. *"Now you need me."* It's really creepy, because that exact thing is what the people who passed the bill thought they were fighting, and they've brought it into my life.'[38]

Another sex worker wrote, 'Once Backpage was seized, I saw workers in my area who'd only recently clawed their way up from street-based work and homelessness into the lowest rung of indoor work … get flung back into what they'd just escaped. St. James Infirmary reported four times as many street-based workers as before in the Mission district. The sex worker community online started to hear about workers going back out on the street and missing their check-in calls—as of April 14, just based on anecdotal data passed between us, 13 workers have gone missing and two have been confirmed dead.'[39]

It could seem paradoxical that these laws, which ostensibly aim to fight exploitation, instead *make exploitation easier* and more prevalent. But ultimately it is not a paradox: reducing sex workers' ability to connect with clients always increases scarcity and makes workers more vulnerable. What is new about SESTA-FOSTA is the way in which, in an increasingly interconnected world, the effects of crimi-nalisation in the US hit sex workers all over the world. Sex workers in the UK also had to scramble to move adverts onto different sites and servers, losing work in the meantime. The law thereby making these workers more precarious. Our community had to pool money and energy to help those who struggled as a result.

Criminalisation forces workers to compromise on some or all of their safety strategies in the hope of avoiding the police. At the same time, it signals to violent people that sex workers are in some sense 'legitimate' targets at the periphery of society. One sex worker in South Africa says that it used to be

> very good doing sex work because police officers were not on our case. I don't know what triggered it, but they started being on our case. So we needed to move to darker and shadier places to avoid the police, who were abusing us, and that's when we started being prey to our clients.[40]

Simply being a police officer opens up opportunities to perpe-trate harassment, abuse, extortion and rape. One young woman in Chicago reports, 'I was solicited by a police officer who said that if I had sex with him he wouldn't arrest me. So I did. Then afterwards he cuffed me and pressed charges anyway.'[41] Another says, 'I was going to meet a new john, it turned out to be a sting set up by the cops. He got violent with me, handcuffed me and then raped me. He cleaned me up for the police station and I got sentenced to four months in jail for prostitution.'[42]

Beside those illegal abuses of power, police having sex with prosti-tutes is formally endorsed by the state. Across the US, police officers routinely have sex during 'prostitution stings', conveniently arresting the worker only after the officer has ejaculated.* In Alaska, a pro-posed legislative measure to ban undercover cops from sexual contact

---

* The officer in question commented, 'If you are asking if I had an orgasm, yes. It was a job, sir … I didn't have pleasure doing this. I was paid to do it.' In other words, he was looking to criminalise sex workers, yet argued that, for him, having sex *as work* is legitimate. See 'Cop: Sex With Hooker Wasn't Fun, It Was Work', *Fox News*, 22 August 2008, foxnews.com.

with sex workers has met with resistance from the Anchorage Police Department, who have argued that abstaining from sexual contact makes it harder to prove prostitution is happening.[43] Would any sex worker consent to sex if they knew it was a prelude to being arrested?

Can Anti-Prostitution Law Be Progressive?

In Henrico County, Virginia, the women's jail is overflowing. They have had to order 200 roll-out beds. Women sleep on the floor in corridors, in communal areas, and between bunks in packed cells. Driving this spike in incarceration is the county's recent 'aggressive approach to prostitution and human sex trafficking', which has led to 'more women with lengthy arrest records in jail'.[44]

As we have noted, much anti-prostitution policing now comes with a progressive gloss. Sometimes arrest is spoken of as 'needed' to fulfil other goals: one policymaker, for instance, told a journalist that arresting prostitutes is necessary because if the police did not have the 'leverage' of arrest and prosecution, they could not coerce people into testifying against those the police deem to be traffickers.[45] Lauren Hersh, the New York director of feminist organisation Equality Now, writes that although arresting sellers of sex can be 'fraught with ethical dilemmas and possible human rights violations', it is nonetheless useful in a number of ways. For example, she writes, 'prosecutors may have an easier time maintaining reliable contact with an arrested victim'.[46]

Anti-trafficking work done by the state invariably starts with an arrest. The US media generally reports such arrests as 'rescues', thus framing the arrest of people in the sex trade not just somewhat progressive but actively humanitarian.[47] Few could object to fighting trafficking.

For those caught up in them, however, these arrests are profoundly traumatic. Celia, who has been arrested seven times, told researchers:

> These raids are ugly and horrible. They ... break the door, they come in with the guns out! In the beginning, it's frightening and upsetting.

[Law enforcement] could do anything, you don't know what they are going to do ... It's really horrible, sometimes if they are very angry, they don't let you get dressed. They take you in your work clothes ... One never lets go of the fear. Being afraid never goes away. They provoke that.[48]

Lily, arrested five times, says, 'They were wearing guns and uniforms, and it made me very scared. They didn't tell us anything. They treated us like criminals during the arrest and it was scary.'[49]

Aya Gruber, Amy Cohen, and Kate Mogulescu write that the US criminal justice system has recently undergone a shift towards what they term *penal welfare*.[50] This, they write, is the 'growing practice of using criminal courts to provide social services and benefits', adding, 'in an era in which "mass incarceration" is a familiar term and tough-on-crime and broken windows ideologies are falling into disfavor, penal welfare enables entrenched institutions of criminal law to continue to function despite a growing crisis in public confidence'.[51] One example is Safe Harbour laws, which entail putting underage youth who sell sex through a system of mandatory services – by arresting them and funnelling them through the criminal justice system. Researchers have found that these frequent arrests 'create instability and perpetuate youths' need to engage in survival sex', magnifying the very harms the system is ostensibly attempting to remedy.[52]

New York's human-trafficking courts are another example of penal warfare. Their adherents argue that they are a progressive shift towards services, premised on the idea that people arrested for prostitution should be treated as trafficking victims. Yet they nonetheless involve arresting a woman. (Red Umbrella Project report that over ninety-eight per cent of the defendants are women, whether trans or cis.)[53] She is then prosecuted for prostitution but can be sentenced to services instead of a criminal conviction. Black women are charged with 94 per cent of the loitering offences and 70 per cent of the prostitution offences that go through the Brooklyn trafficking courts.[54] And while there is outrage when immigration officials appear at these human trafficking courts looking for people to deport, it is standard practice throughout the US that a prostitution conviction 'renders an immigrant immediately deportable' – making the court's 'humanitarian' rationale for ongoing prostitution arrests ever harder to sustain.[55]

If the defendant has previous drug charges on her record, she may spend several weeks in jail awaiting 'evaluation' before being sentenced to 'months in an inpatient drug-treatment program that differs little from prison'.[56] Those with 'complex cases' may be subject to pre-trial detention; many cannot afford to bail themselves out, meaning that they are confined to New York's notorious Rikers Island jail while they wait for their case to be heard. The ostensible 'victim' status of the defendant inevitably comes into conflict with the fact that what the court exists to do is impose judgement, control and punishment. One prosecutor, declining to offer services to a young woman, explained:

> To have been arrested so many times for prostitution in so many different states. Obviously, she's a victim ... But still, she just has so many arrests, so ... I said that I will give her a disorderly conduct and time served and she can go back to California ... and it better be the last [arrest] because I don't want people coming into Queens [thinking], 'Oh you get a good disposition in Queens.'[57]

Defendants can be evicted or jailed 'for their own good'. One prosecutor argued, upon 'successfully' sending a woman to jail, 'I do not want to see Ms. F going back to her ex-boyfriend, whatever she thinks he is. In my eyes, that's the person that's exploiting her and that's just not a good situation, Judge. I am going to ask that she be remanded [to jail].'[58]

Even for women who do get services, the services available through the court are not necessarily those the defendants need. Defendants are often assigned activities of uncertain immediate value, like yoga, art therapy, or counselling, with the threat of re-arrest if they fail to attend.[59] Jenna Torres, a mother arrested while under the age of eighteen for prostitution in New York, writes,

> The treatment program the courts provided was not a good fit for me. I didn't need to be treated for sex work. That isn't an illness ... I really needed that time for more important tasks. The sessions

hampered my ability to create a better environment for myself and my children so I wouldn't have to rely on sex work … They gave me options that didn't fit my situation, suggesting that I just stop sex work and my life would be magically improved. Stopping sex work for me means not being able to make money.[60]

The court-mandated therapy forced Torres to drop out of college, as there wasn't time in her schedule to attend both. As the sex worker led project RedUp NYC writes, 'This cycle of criminalisation, especially for those who do not complete the mandated services, can make exit from the sex trade more difficult for those who want to.'[61]

There is no progressive version of full criminalisation. Abuses such as racist policing, corruption, and sexual assault are fundamentally bound up with the vulnerability of the sex worker who, when defined as criminal, has little recourse to justice or protection. Across nations where sex workers are criminalised, stories emerge of police officers capitalising on the weakness of their victims in order to inflict beatings, rape, and extortion to an extent where sex workers fear police more than clients, managers, or the public. 'Police are our biggest problem, more than anyone', comments a sex worker in Lagos, Nigeria. 'When he puts on the uniform, he thinks he can do whatever he wants.'[62]

Criminalisation dehumanizes people in sex work to the extent that members of the public often don't notice or care about their mistreatment. Russian murderer – and police officer – Mikhail Popkov managed to get away with killing eighty-two women over eighteen years as part of a crusade to 'cleanse' the streets of prostitutes.[63] (He sometimes found victims by offering them a ride in his police car, and was twice called in his official capacity to investigate murders he himself had committed.)[64] Chi Adanna Mgbako writes of a police officer in Uganda who 'has long made grotesque sport of tormenting street-based sex workers … stripping them naked, and parading them through town'.[65] Despite such public and visible abuse, when his victims filed complaints, he was merely transferred to another unit where, sex workers report, he has continued to force his way into the homes of pregnant and nursing women, 'dragging them out by the hair to dump them in the police station'. Mgbako recounts the story of a group of sex workers attacked by police officers in full view of a crowd of spectators, who goaded the officers to arrest the women and remove them, shouting, 'Take them, take them – this is our rubbish.'[66]

In South Africa, the brutal institutional legacy of apartheid combines with full criminalisation to produce particularly horrific abuse.[*] In Johannesburg, for example, the police habitually pepper-spray the genitals of sex workers.[67] Male sex workers and trans women are particularly targeted for violence. In one case, police in Cape Town are reported to have arrested a young male sex worker and then encouraged the men in his cell to sexually abuse him.[68] A court in Cape Town ruled that the police were arresting sex workers arbitrarily without intent to charge them – simply to abuse or harass them in the police van or the cells.[69]

Individual perpetrators, even the most terrifying and sadistic ones, are not freakish anomalies. They are a recurring symptom of any legal system that frames prostitutes as worthless and disposable criminals. In 2015, police officer Daniel Holtzclaw was convicted by an Oklahoma jury of eighteen counts of rape.[70] His victims were low-income Black women who either had criminal records or were engaging in criminalised behaviours, particularly drug use and sex work. Holtzclaw was emboldened to target these women because he knew that the huge power disparity between him and them meant he was unlikely to be held accountable. In the end, he was only caught because he assaulted Jannie Ligons, a woman without a criminal record – a woman who was not afraid to report him and whose report was taken seriously. This bare minimum of respect in the justice system was all that set her apart from the other victims.

---

[*] In a recent survey of over a thousand sex workers in South Africa, a majority (54 per cent) report experiencing some sort of physical violence in the previous year, including beatings, rape and other forms of sexual violence. Of those, 55 per cent name the police as among the perpetrators of that violence. NACOSA & Sex Worker Education and Advocacy Taskforce (SWEAT), 'Beginning to build the picture: South Africa National survey of sex worker knowledge, experiences and behaviour', report, 15 January 2013, available at hivsharespace.net or sweat.org.za.

Holtzclaw himself very explicitly named this logic when, after his conviction, he complained to an interviewer that Ligons was 'not innocent the way people think she is. She had a bust in the '80s ... but we couldn't present that to the jury. This is not a woman that, you know, is a soccer mom, or someone that's credible in society.'[71]

Clearly Holtzclaw – like other abusers and killers of prostitutes – subscribed to an idea that is corroborated by the laws he enforced: that the criminal body is a vulnerable one. The criminalised woman is easy pickings.

Disorderly Bodies

Cyntoia Brown's case briefly became headline news in 2017, when celebrities such as Rihanna and Kim Kardashian West drew attention to the horrific way she had been treated by the criminal justice system.[72] At sixteen years old, Cyntoia had been in an abusive relationship with a man who forced her to sell sex. She picked up a client, but once she was at the client's house, he threatened and assaulted her. She shot him in self-defence – but rather than being recognised as a traumatised young woman defending her own life, she was portrayed as a murderer and sentenced to half a century in jail. By the time Rihanna and Kim Kardashian publicised her case, Cyntoia was already twenty-nine; she has so far spent nearly fifteen years of her life incarcerated.

Cyntoia's case is unusual in that her youth at the time of her 'offence' made it easier for the public to sympathise with her. Indeed, prison-abolitionist organiser Mariame Kaba and sex workers' rights organiser Brit Schulte picked up on this, noting that the explosion of interest in Cyntoia was accompanied by images of her as a sixteen-year-old. Kaba and Schulte write:

> Is an adult, 29-year-old Black woman an unsympathetic victim? If so, why? Acknowledging trauma and resilience are often ignored in favor of the driving desire by the media and public to support only a perfect victim. Perfect victims are submissive, not aggressive; they don't have histories of drug use or prior contact with the criminal legal system; and they are 'innocent' and respectable.[73]

As we see time and time again, the requirements for the 'perfect victim' that Kaba and Schulte outline not only routinely exclude Black women from safety but actively sweep them up into the definition of *criminal*. Cyntoia's case briefly gained international attention, although as of this writing her appeal has been denied.[74] The cases of Alisha and GiGi, whose stories opened this chapter, have been taken up by sex worker organisers and by the wider 'Survived and Punished' movement to free incarcerated survivors of violence (a movement Kaba has been instrumental in organising).[75] But these cases are, of course, only the tip of the iceberg. In the US, the criminalisation of people attempting to survive is routine; for some, police attention means arrest as often as it means any kind of safety. The Atlanta Solutions Not Punishment coalition found that 'encounters with [the police] leave trans people less safe than they were before ... This is true even when we have called the police ourselves for help because we were in danger or to report a crime.'[76] Thirty-eight per cent of trans women of colour in Atlanta reported that when they called the police for help, they ended up getting arrested instead.[77]

Hillary Clinton's ill-fated 2016 presidential run was dogged by anger from the left, in part over her role in promoting the Violent Crime Control and Law Enforcement Act (known as the Crime Act), signed into law by her husband.[78] She infamously justified the 1994 act with reference to 'super-predators ... no conscience, no empathy, we can talk about why they ended up that way, but first we have to bring them to heel.'[79] In the 2010s, organisations like Black Lives Matter ignited public concern over deaths at the hands of the police and drew attention to how over-policing and mass incarceration disproportionately hit Black communities and perpetuate the systemic devaluation of Black lives. The Crime Act sent a hundred thousand more police onto the streets, earmarked nearly $10 billion for prisons, retained the racist 'hundred-to-one' sentencing ratio for crack versus powder cocaine, and continued with three strikes and mandatory minimum sentencing requirements that put hundreds of thousands of mostly Black and poor Americans in jail for long stretches for drug offences.[80]

Part of the aim of the law was to use 'mandatory arrest' policies to force police to take domestic violence more seriously. However, where the police weren't sure who was the aggressor (or felt unsympathetic to both parties), they often responded by arresting both perpetrator and victim. As a result, arrests of women shot up: in Los Angeles, the number of women arrested as a result of domestic-violence calls doubled in 1995; in Maryland, the arrest rate for women tripled between 1992 and 1996; in Sacramento, it went up by 91 per cent.[81] A key reason is that mothers were criminalised for 'failing' to protect their children from the man who was abusing both mother and child.[82] As researcher Susan Miller puts it, 'An arrest policy intended to protect battered women as victims is being ... used against them. Battered women have become female offenders.'[83] Black and Latinx women were disproportionately arrested.

When one young Black trans woman in Los Angeles called the police about her partner's violence, the police returned to arrest her for an old prostitution offence.[84] Tiawanda Moore, a young Black woman in Chicago, was sexually assaulted by a police officer when she called for help regarding her partner's violence.[85] When she sought to complain about the assault, she was dismissed on the grounds she had been a stripper.[86] When she recorded the officers talking about her in order to gather further evidence of the appalling way she was being treated, they arrested her and charged her with 'eavesdropping' – an offence that could have seen her jailed for fifteen years. (Thankfully, she was ultimately acquitted.)[87] These policies can impact doubly on sex workers: Black women in the sex trade are routinely subject to 'dual arrest' (when both parties involved in a domestic violence incident are arrested) if they call the police to report domestic violence.[88]

When it passed, some feminists hailed the 1994 Crime Act as a triumph because it included major legislation that sought to tackle violence against women – the Violence Against Women Act (VAWA).[89] In a 2015 *Feminist Current* essay titled 'A Thank-You Note to "Carceral"/"Sex-Negative" Feminists', writer Penny White typifies this mainstream feminist praise for the VAWA and the police, writing that feminists of the seventies and eighties were 'heroes' who 'paved the way for the Violence Against Women Act ... which gave law enforcement

1.6 billion dollars to investigate and prosecute sexual and domestic violence ... [This] transformed our culture into a *bigger, safer, and freer* space for women than I had ever dreamed possible.'[90]

Rhetoric like this doesn't just forget about victims of police and state violence – it throws them under the bus. Liberal commentator Amanda Marcotte caused outrage when she wrote an article titled 'Prosecutors Arrest Alleged Rape Victim to Make Her Cooperate in Their Case. They Made the Right Call', arguing that it was 'understandable' that prosecutors 'might try to do everything within their power to convict [the perpetrator]', including jailing his victim, adding that 'we have to decide what's more important to us: putting abusive men in jail or letting their victims opt out of cooperating with the prosecution as they see fit'.[91] Carceral feminism prioritises punishing wrongdoers above all else, even protecting victims.

These competing perspectives on the 1994 Crime Act speak to larger conflicts within the feminist anti-violence movement and illuminate some of the problems with seeing the police as the solution to violence against women. Identifying the problems of this law-and-order approach pushes us to locate violence against women within the broader texture of state violence – including arrests, deportations, evictions, loss of child custody, anti-homelessness ordinances, the war on drugs, gentrification, and racism in policing and in the criminal justice system. The fight for decriminalisation is just one strand. Working to end the power of the police to assault, arrest, prosecute or deport people in the sex trades is part of a larger struggle for safety, a struggle which includes freeing incarcerated survivors, ending cash bail, and fighting for investment in the things that make people safer – *not* cops and prisons.

Organising

In such an intensely criminalised context, organising and speaking out come with huge risks. The experience of Monica Jones is a case in point. Monica, a social-work student, sex workers' rights advocate, and Black trans woman, was arrested in Arizona in 2013. The day before her arrest, she had spoken against the punitive approach of local police at a sex worker rally, and on the day of her arrest, she had publicly tipped off sex workers about an upcoming police sting. She was convicted of 'manifesting prostitution' – a broad and ambiguous law that encompasses a range of everyday activities, including simply walking in the street. Campaigners often refer to it as the criminalisation of 'walking while trans', and sex worker led research elsewhere in the US has found that such laws are used overwhelmingly against Black women.[92] Monica's activism, race, and gender operated in concert to make her hyper-visible to the police. She was targeted for arrest in part because, as she told a journalist, 'I was very outspoken about the [arrests of sex workers], being out there protesting ... The police knew about me.'[93]

Sex worker activism is frequently on the radar of the police. In New Jersey in 2016, a sex worker was arrested as she left an activist meeting. Law enforcement officers were using sex workers' self-organisation as an opportunity to surveil and criminalise them. A colleague of the worker wrote about this incident in the local press, and on the day the article appeared, its author was herself arrested.

When almost two dozen sex workers were brutally murdered in Uganda, forty-four sex worker activists gathered for a crisis meeting in a hotel.[94] The main agenda of the meeting was to share safety advice while the killer was at large and to raise funds for the funeral of one of the murdered women. All forty-four women were arrested and charged with public-nuisance offences, held for two weeks in jail, and given large fines.[95] Incidents like this go largely ignored. While bravely planning more public actions relating to the murders in the following months, an activist from Ugandan sex worker group Women's Organization Network for Human Rights Advocacy (WONETHA) remarked, 'no other women's organisation is paying attention'.[96]

Despite this context of state surveillance mixed with feminist obliviousness, the sex worker movement in heavily criminalised countries buzzes with energetic grassroots organising. An uplifting 2012 video shows dozens of sex workers disrupting a special session of the US Congress on the global AIDS epidemic to draw attention to the failings of the President's Emergency Plan for AIDS Relief (PEPFAR). PEPFAR is the largest source of government funding for HIV/AIDS in the world, but requires recipient organisations to be explicitly anti–sex work (the 'anti-prostitution pledge').[97] Opening red umbrellas, they stormed the stage, loudly chanting 'Repeal the pledge! Reform PEPFAR!' One activist named Sharmus Outlaw addressed the delegates from the stage; 'Before I'm transgender, before I'm a sex worker, before I am anything, I'm human.'[98]

Sharmus Outlaw, tragically, died in 2017 as a result of a litany of failures in the US healthcare system relating not only to her poverty, but also to her status as a Black trans woman. A biopsy that she desperately needed was delayed for months because her healthcare providers claimed to be 'confused' about her gender marker on her documents. Although she was taken far too soon, Outlaw achieved a huge amount in her campaigning work for LGBTQ people, people living with HIV, and sex workers. Penelope Saunders, a close friend of Outlaw, says, 'she would say to me every time we met, "The girls need jobs. They need jobs!" Never has Sharmus backed away from defending someone who society has shunned or stigmatized.' Outlaw inspired and supported numerous other activists and never lost an opportunity to advocate for human rights and harm reduction, whether she was addressing politicians, or travelling home to see her family in North Carolina – trips on which she would take condoms and information on HIV and LGBTQ rights, in case she met people during the journey who needed help or advice. She did all of this tirelessly, while battling her own numerous arrests, living in poverty, and never even having secure housing of her own.[99]

African sex worker activism also keeps going in the face of adversity. Chi Adanna Mgbako writes that 'African sex workers, refusing to swallow the bitterness of their suffering, have sparked a sex workers' rights movement that is spreading like a brushfire across the continent.'[100] There are eighty organisations representing sex workers of all genders across twenty-seven African nations, with more than thirty sex worker collectives in Kenya alone.[101] Health Options for Young Men on HIV, AIDS and STIs (HOYMAS), for example, is a male sex worker led organisation in Kenya. It fights for access to HIV/AIDS services and hosts regular discussion groups among gay and bisexual men and men in the sex trade. One of its leaders is a plaintiff in a suit to overturn Kenya's anti-homosexuality law.[102] In Cape Town, South Africa, sex worker collective SistaazHood creates safe community spaces for street-working trans women and tackles transphobic police violence. Their efforts have ensured that when trans women are arrested, they are searched by women officers and not put in cells with cis men.[103]

Sex worker organising is often characterised by tenacity, creativity – and a touch of irreverence. In Kenya, three hundred sex worker activists, carrying brooms and mops, marked World AIDS Day in 2012 by cleaning a hospital. The action was designed to illustrate that sex workers are not a 'problem' but part of a solution, and that they want to help healthcare staff do their jobs better. John Mathenge Mukaburu, a Kenyan activist who helped to organise the event, explains, 'We wanted to sensitize the community and the health workers who often stigmatize us; we wanted to show them we need them, but they need us as well.'[104] In Russia, sex worker group Silver Rose joined the May Day march without authorisation to protest against 'rotten morals, social prejudices, capitalism and inequality'.[105] Sex worker Irina Maslova explained the decision to start the group: 'No organisation could [give us] legal advice at that time. Eight of us teamed up and decided to ruin this state system.'[106]

For sex workers, effective organising *has* to mean solidarity that branches out further than a single issue. The most criminalised and marginalised sex workers have more problems than the criminalisation of sex work. In Kenya, sex workers are part of Bunge la Mwananchi (The People's Parliament), an anti-poverty social movement for low-paid workers, street vendors, homeless people, bus drivers, squatters and other street-based communities that face harassment from law enforcement.[107] In the US state of Massachusetts, sex worker Caty Simon, whose organising work has included resisting the criminalisation of panhandling and fighting for legal needle exchanges, spoke at a local meeting to protest the implementation of surveillance cameras in the downtown area:

> As a harm-reduction activist, I must address the effect it would have on Northampton's illicit substance-using poor, who often are used as scapegoats to justify targeting all our poor people ... preventing their reintegration into the community when the solutions are clear – expansion of voluntary treatment and harm-reduction resources.[108]

Many activists focus on ensuring that sex workers' basic needs are met. Bonnie has been providing tireless outreach to street-based sex workers in Maryland, Northern Virginia and Washington, DC since 2001. Bonnie and other DC-based organisers, particularly Sharmus Outlaw, were key in overturning DC's 'prostitution-free zone' ordinance. She described her role to community site *Tits and Sass*:

> Up until very recently I provided housing. I had to stop, and now I provide referrals and transportation to shelters or transitional living or an affordable place to live, whatever is asked of me. My current venues are methadone clinics, BDSM clubs, immigrant sex work apartments, drug testing clinics ... I never leave someone who wants to be inside outside. What if it was the last time I saw that person? What if they were arrested for being homeless? It took eight years for us to rid D.C. of the prostitution free zone, which was profiling for standing, walking, or walking up to a car. How many people were killed and caged in that time?[109]

New York's Lysistrata Mutual Care Collective and Fund sprung up in the aftermath of the closure of BackPage's sex work ads section. Without it, many sex workers – particularly those closest to the poverty line – were stranded without a way to find indoor work. Through Lysistrata, sex workers share funds to see each other through times of scarcity.[110] As disabled former sex worker Sarit Frishman comments, 'There is no safety net for most of us. There's no such thing as a union or pension fund.'[111]

Peer-led sex worker activism is even more impressive given its shoe-string budgets. Funding is hard to come by. But persecution can provoke inspiration; activist communities in fully criminalised countries are often notable for their passion and solidarity. Sex worker Daisy describes the enthusiasm among Ugandan activists: 'Someone will be arrested today, stay in a police cell for a week, but the day they come out, before they even get home, they're talking [on behalf of sex workers' rights]. I think that's something to be proud of'. Maslova of Silver Rose says, 'I won't give up until sex work is decriminalised in Russia, even though I will be burned at the stake as a witch.'[112] This spirit of bold defiance is typical of the global sex workers' rights movement; there is a sense that change is coming.

Grassroots organizer Deon Haywood works with Women With a Vision (WWAV). From 2008 to 2013, they spearheaded the NO Justice campaign to get the CANS and sex offender registry penalties changed in Louisiana. After the passage of a new bill that meant no sex workers would be newly added to the register, they went on to lead a class action lawsuit that resulted in the names of 800 people being expunged from the list. One WWAV client, who had been on the registry since 1980, said at the time, 'I can taste my FREEDOM!'[113] It was a feeling of triumph shared by Haywood. 'I challenge those people who say that change can't happen in the South', she says. 'Because it did. And don't say the little man can't win, because we did.'[114]

We are all marinating in a culture which hates people who sell sex – as the persistence and prevalence of full criminalisation makes painfully clear. In the US, the mainstream feminist movement often pushes for *more* criminalisation without removing existing criminal laws.[115] It should be clear, however, that criminalisation does not *prevent* commercial sex – it does not deal with the root causes of *why* people sell sex, which is to get the resources they need.

6

The People's Home: Sweden, Norway, Ireland, and Canada

The Swedish Model: A legal regime that criminalises the purchase of sex and punishes third parties (such as managers, drivers, and landlords) while ostensibly decriminalising those who sell sex. Also called the Nordic model, sex buyer law, sex purchase ban, asymmetrical criminalisation, 'End Demand', *sexköpslagen*. **Also seen in:** Northern Ireland, France, Iceland.

When the Swedish parliament passed the *sexköpslagen* – or sex purchase ban – in 1999, feminist activists were ecstatic. Finally, they thought, they had achieved a feminist prostitution law – a law which aims to reduce prostitution but lifts the threat of criminalisation from the seller, instead placing it where the power really lies in the transaction: the punter and the pimp. Sweden would be a model for the world. They argued that criminalising the demand of the client and the profiteering of the manager would go some way towards shrinking the sex industry and redressing the huge power imbalances that make sex workers so vulnerable. Feminist professor Catherine MacKinnon describes this idea when she writes, 'Against his demand to buy her for sex, this [Swedish] law says she is not for sale, or rent. Eliminating her criminality raises her status; criminalizing him lowers his privilege.'[1]

Meanwhile, the theory states, the woman is given support to leave the harmful situation she has found herself in, and targeting demand will have a disciplinary effect on a culture of patriarchal male entitlement: men will be rehabilitated. This should mean that over time, fewer women will be exploited in prostitution, making countries with such a law less attractive destinations for traffickers.

Prostitution is a richly symbolic terrain. It is where our society's anxieties about power, womanhood, and the nation coalesce. For feminist women, the figure of the prostitute often comes to represent the trauma that is inflicted on all women within patriarchy – the ultimate symbol of women's pain, of the violence that women suffer.[2] The client thus becomes the symbol of all violent men: he is the avatar of unadulterated violence against women, the archetypal perpetrator.

We deeply sympathise with this perspective. Our lives too have been shaped by gendered violence, and we understand the political impulse to punish the man who has come to symbolise this trauma. Indeed, we are only too familiar with the specific risk of violence at the hands of clients. And, of course, proponents of the Nordic model are right in identifying prostitution as a deeply unequal transaction – one scarred by patriarchy as well as by white supremacy, poverty, and colonialism. It seems intuitively right to criminalise the men who *are*, in many ways, the living embodiments of these huge power differentials.

Add Scandinavia to this mix and you get an even more potent feminist cocktail. For decades, the countries of Scandinavia have been seen as *the* feminist nations. The Swedish government describes itself as 'the first feminist government in the world', going viral on social media with photos illustrating an all-women line-up at the signing of a bill.[3] In some ways, this self-presentation is reasonable: Sweden, Norway, Iceland, and Denmark regularly top global charts measuring women's rights; abroad, left-wing politicians like Bernie Sanders and Jeremy Corbyn point to them to support their policy proposals and are in turn praised by commentators who see them as carrying the flame for the idea of a more generous, holistic social democracy.[4] Feminists around the world often think of Scandinavia, and Sweden in particular, as a kind of utopia, a place where patriarchy has been largely defeated.[5]

Of course, there are no utopias. People of colour, migrants, transgender people, and people who use drugs are among those whom the generous, feminist Swedish state has a tendency to surveil and police, perceived as they are to fall outside 'Swedishness'.[6] But for those who do not follow those issues closely, and who surmise that Sweden is 'getting it right' on childcare or the pay gap, it seems reasonable to connect Scandinavian prostitution law to wider perceptions of the success of feminism there – and to think it is probably getting it right on sex work, too.*

In other words, many advocates of the 'Nordic model' are driven by straightforwardly progressive concerns: deeply held fears about gendered violence; anger at racism in the sex trade and in society at large; the mostly correct sense that Nordic-style societies are generally better, kinder, more feminist places than somewhere like the United States. We know that many hold these views in good faith. But prostitution law is always ideologically capacious, and this law in particular has sufficient political room for both progressive and regressive strands, which are sometimes in collaboration and sometimes in conflict.

Moreover, there are key differences between the *ideal* 'Nordic Model' laid out by its advocates in policy discussions, and the different versions of the sex-purchase ban in the various places it has been implemented around the world. The easiest way to set aside these ideological and legislative confusions, of course, is to look at the law through a sex worker's eyes.

How Does It Work?

1: The 'Demand'

In the blueprints of the ideal Nordic model, there are four key priorities: the buyer, the seller, 'exit' services and third parties (i.e., traffickers or 'pimps'). Arguably the strongest priority of the Nordic model – as it's envisioned on paper – is to go after the man who pays for sex. In other words, to 'end demand.' It's this intention – the focus on clients – that distinguishes this legal model from other forms of criminalisation, even those which also criminalise the purchase of sex, as in Kenya or South Africa. Elsewhere, the criminalisation of the client takes an ideological backseat to the persecution of the sex worker. Even in the United States, where the police make relatively concerted efforts to arrest clients (for instance, carrying out 'john stings' with

---

* In reality, Sweden has a fairly significant gender pay gap. OECD (2012) , 'Closing the Gender Gap: Act Now'.

female undercover officers), only ten per cent of overall prostitution arrests are of clients.[7] In the Nordic vision of prostitution law, arresting clients is the whole point – the main course, not the side dish. (In practice, the targets of the Nordic Model are less clear-cut, as this chapter will show.)

As we said at the outset, we are concerned about people who sell sex, about how laws and policies around sex work affect them and how to reduce harm to them. So, let's examine what happens to people who sell sex when their clients are criminalised. Think of a woman working on the street: she might have expected to see three or four clients in a couple of hours and head home with the money she needed before one in the morning. But with her clients now criminalised, the stroll is quieter – maybe, instead of seeing her normal two or three before midnight, she's not yet seen anyone. Now suppose someone then approaches her at one in the morning, someone who seems coked-up and aggressive, or who is driving a car with a number plate she was warned by other workers to avoid. She still needs to earn enough money to put food on the table. Her lack of clients so far gives her *less* power to refuse a man she might otherwise turn down.

He might be scared of being seen, which will oblige her to help him stay hidden, perhaps by driving into a darkened park after a quick exchange on the street. Maybe he offers her half her usual rate and refuses to use a condom. If she had already made most of the money she needed tonight, she could insist on business on her own terms, or turn him down completely. But the streets are dead, and it seems like she can either say yes to him or go home with nothing, after hours in the cold. Maybe, trying to make up the shortfall, she stays out working much later than usual and has to walk home through snowy, deserted streets at five o'clock.

This isn't the only effect on her. Think about *who* is still paying for sex. A man who may otherwise have wanted to pay for sex and then go home to his partner and his job might well decide that he now has too much to lose. To be arrested for paying for sex might disgrace him at work and break up his marriage – it seems more sensible to stay home. But there are plenty of men who have less to lose than that. Perhaps he never intended to pay for sex, but was always planning to attack or rob a sex worker – which means breaking pre-existing laws, so why worry about the possibility of a conviction for purchasing sex? Perhaps an arrest for paying for sex *won't* disgrace him at work – he already has multiple convictions for violence against his ex-wife, and his boss doesn't care. The clients who are deterred are disproportionately the 'nicer' clients, or at least those with something to lose. The clients who remain are disproportionately likely to be impulsive, drunk or violent: those with less to lose. (Pro–Nordic Model politician Rhoda Grant even described this dynamic while advocating for its introduction in Scotland, saying, 'While those who currently break the law [i.e., violent abusers] will not see the criminalisation of the purchase of sex as a deterrent, many others will.')[8] Thinking of sex work as always, intrinsically violent, of course, hides the difference between a respectful client and an abusive one.

Everywhere in the world, regardless of the legal model, street-based sex workers use a familiar range of safety strategies.[9] For example, they might work together with a couple of friends, they might take time to assess a client before getting into his car, and they might have a friend write down his car's number plate to signal to him that someone will know who she's with. How does the criminalisation of clients shape or change these safety strategies? Working with a group of friends on the street makes you more visible to the police, which isn't something you can risk if you're hoping to make money. If you're too obviously visible as sex workers, even if you're not worried that you yourself will be arrested, clients won't want to risk approaching you for fear that *they* will be arrested. Again, to get the client's money, you often have to cater to *his* need for safety from arrest – by working alone rather than in a group.

As for having a conversation before getting into his car, that is the time when he is *most* visible to the police as a client, and therefore he will be keen to speed that process up. Instead of having a conversation about services, prices, and condom use while still on the street, he'll ask you to hop into his car and have that conversation while you're already speeding away. Because you need to keep his custom in order to get the money you need, you say yes. But that means you have no chance to reach a verbal agreement about prices and condoms before getting in the car, let alone assess his demeanour or even establish whether he has a friend hiding in the back seat.

These effects compound each other. The sex worker is poorer, so she feels more pressure to accept a client she might otherwise reject; she works later and alone; the nicer clients have stayed away while the more impulsive or unpredictable clients remain; and she has less time to assess him.

In Norway, Silvia, a migrant woman who works on the street, told a reporter: 'Before we did not go far with the customer: we would go to a car park nearby. But now the customer wants to go somewhere isolated because they are afraid ... I don't like it. There is more risk that something bad happens.'[10] In Sweden, Annabel, a street-based worker, says, 'You were still able to get clients after the law. But you had to stand that much longer.'[11] When Vancouver tried criminalising clients, researchers asked sex workers what the effects were. Violet, a street-based worker there, said,

> While they're going around chasing johns away from pulling up beside you, I have to stay out for longer ... Whereas if we weren't harassed we would be able to be more choosy as to where we get in, who we get in with, you know what I mean? Because of being so cold and being harassed I got into a car where I normally wouldn't have.[12]

The Swedish and Norwegian governments' own reports corroborate these sex workers' words. The Swedish National Board of Health and Welfare, for instance, found that 'fear among clients ... makes it harder to use safe meeting places ... meeting places have become more out of the way, such as wooded areas, isolated stairwells and office premises, where clients do not risk discovery.'[13] A 2004 report by the Norwegian Ministry of Justice and Public Security found that

> the Swedish street prostitutes experience a tougher time. They are more frequently exposed to dangerous clients, while the [legitimate] clients are afraid of being arrested ... They have less time to assess the client as the deal takes place very hurriedly due to fear on the part of the client.[14]

Those hit hardest by these worsening conditions are, as always, the most precarious. This is particularly true of homeless street-based sex workers. The Ministry of Justice report found that 'more abuse takes place than previously, as the women cannot afford to say "no" to the clients they have their doubts about', and summarizes the effect of the law thus: 'For those forced to work on the street, life has become much harder ... The law on the purchase of sex has made working as a prostitute harder and more dangerous.'[15]

A social worker in Malmö captures how these dynamics play out particularly strongly for sex workers with substance dependencies, noting that there are

> fewer clients on the streets, and the women still need the money to get the heroin, so the customers are able to offer less money for more ... no condom, for an example ... And if they really do need the money, and they have been standing there the whole night, and they need their fix ... then maybe you say 'Yes.'[16]

For an indoor worker, the most obvious and easiest way for the police to find her clients is by watching *her*. After all, these men are only detectable *as clients* when they visit the flat of someone the police think is a sex worker – clients do not go about their ordinary lives with the word 'punter' emblazoned on their foreheads.

Like her colleague on the street, an indoor sex worker needs to sell sex *much more* than her client 'needs' to buy it. He is indulging in a spot of recreation; she is paying her rent. This means that *she* is pushed to change her way of working in order to keep his custom. She might normally prefer to see clients in her own flat, where she is on her own turf; she can even have a friend quietly looking out for her in the next room. But for the client, going to a sex worker's flat is when he is most at risk of arrest. So he asks her to visit him instead, in his flat or in a hotel room he has rented. Here she is walking into an unfamiliar space.

A Norwegian government report states that, as a result of the law, 'the risk of violence has increased for those who no longer work on the streets ... when [making] a home visit the prostitute does not know what she is coming to'.[17] Instead of *her* friend quietly scrolling on a phone in the next room of her flat and keeping an ear out in case she needs backup, she is faced with a space where the client may, for all she knows, have the rest of his drunk stag party hiding in the bathroom, waiting for the door to click shut behind her.

How do indoor sex workers try to stay safe?[18] Many attempt to screen clients by asking them for their real names, or refusing to take calls from hidden numbers. This means that if the client turns aggressive during the booking, the worker can at least threaten to take his name or phone number to the police. But if a client is criminalised, he may be fearful of the police searching a worker's phone or apartment and identifying him. As a result, he refuses to give basic screening information like his real name, and switches to calling from a hidden number. A man who wants to carry out an assault or robbery will know he can arrange a meeting with a sex worker and be virtually untraceable; the criminalisation of clients gives *him* leverage to refuse to make himself identifiable.[19] In Ireland, sex worker safety organisation Ugly Mugs says it received 1,635 reports from sex workers with concerns about violent and abusive clients in the five months following the sex purchase ban in 2017, a sixty-one per cent increase on the same period in 2016.[20] 'People are … not willing to divulge their details,' said (the late and much missed) sex worker and activist Laura Lee of the introduction of the law in Northern Ireland. 'Everyone suddenly became "John."'[21]

As before, all these effects work in combination. Some clients will stay away, making a sex worker less able to refuse those who remain, even if they seem creepy, aggressive, or try to bargain her down on money or boundaries. This should be easy to understand: anyone whose work depends on getting clients – not just sex workers – will know that when you have fewer clients than you expected, you're in a *weaker* position to turn down clients who are less than ideal. Maybe they're personally abrasive, or asking for work outside your skillset, or not remunerating you fairly. There's a stronger push towards nonetheless accepting them if you're broke.

To try to make up the income she's losing, a sex worker might offer new services – perhaps sex without a condom. A Norwegian government evaluation of the law found that 'prices are lower now than before the introduction of the ban. More travelling, more advertising and somewhat lower prices show that the competition is tougher and the demand is lower nowadays. Men and women in prostitution need to work harder now in order to secure [previous] income levels.'[22] Pause for a minute and empathise with what 'competition is tougher ... men and women in prostitution need to work harder now' means for people who sell sex.

Those who advocate for the Nordic model are correct that the client benefits from a huge power imbalance; what they miss is that client criminalisation *worsens* this power imbalance. This can seem surprising; as human rights lawyer Wendy Lyon writes, 'The criminalisation of only one party to a transaction might intuitively be expected to benefit the other party.'[23] However, this overlooks that crucial fact – which cannot be repeated enough! – that *the sex worker needs to sell sex much more than the client 'needs' to buy it*. This 'asymmetry of need' is essential to understanding the actual impact of the Nordic Model. And it's an effect that intensifies the more precarious the worker is. Think about how desperately a worker might cater to a client if her rent is late or if she's about to go into opioid withdrawal. She'll take on the burden of his need for safety from arrest, which will entail compromising any safety strategies she might otherwise seek to deploy. After all, he is safer from arrest when he is *more* anonymous, and when their rendezvous is *more* clandestine. Wendy Lyon writes that because of this 'need imbalance', 'the seller can ill-afford to seek to extract advantages from the buyer's criminalised status. It is entirely understandable, even predictable, that a sex worker in already desperate straits would negotiate with a client *on his terms* if the only practical alternative is losing the client entirely.'[24] She needs his custom more than he needs to buy sex, right? The Norwegian government itself acknowledges that the situation for sex workers is now a 'buyer's market'.[25]

All of this is inherent to the approach of 'ending demand', which takes much of its basis from simple economics. The idea is that a reduction in demand will lead to a 'correction in the market' whereby, because fewer people want to pay for sex, fewer people will sell it. What this smooth story misses is that the first thing which happens when you reduce demand on any product or service is that the price at which it can be sold goes *down*, and sellers desperately compete to retain a share of a shrinking market. In other words, *the law is working how it is intended to work* when it makes people who sell sex poorer and more precarious. Ann Martin, head of Sweden's anti-trafficking unit, admitted this: 'I think of course the law has negative consequences for women in prostitution but that's also some of the effect that we want to achieve with the law. It shouldn't be as easy as it was before to go out and sell sex.'[26] There is no 'end demand' that does not make people who sell sex poorer – and making people poorer *reduces their power* in interactions with clients. Advocates of the Nordic model are *correct* that most people go into sex work with few (or no) other options. That lack of options is one of the things that makes reducing demand so harmful. When people have few or no other options, they cannot easily 'exit' the sex industry because conditions become harsher.

Critics of the sex industry are sometimes able to recognise this problem in other contexts. Prominent UK anti-prostitution feminist Kat Banyard notes that one way strip-club managers decrease dancers' power with clients is by ensuring that the club is always filled with dancers – 'so there's always heavy competition for custom'.[27] But Banyard strikingly fails to recognise that the same dynamic plays out if you reduce the number of clients willing to pay for sex. As always, this harms the more precarious workers worse. If someone is earning £25,000 a year and their income drops, they might struggle to save or have to move to a cheaper flat, but they'll probably have enough of a buffer to get by. But if someone is earning, say, £7,000 a year, a reduction in their income might push them into crisis. Maybe that means homelessness, or avoiding homelessness by moving back in with a violent ex. Even if they go to a support service – which we'll come to in more detail in a moment – and ask for help with leaving prostitution, that process can take months. During those months, they will be struggling even harder to survive in a sex industry that is now a 'buyer's market'.

Getting close to the poverty line often forces people who sell sex to consider getting the help of a pimp, partner, agent, or manager.

If you have little to no income, splitting half the money from future work is an improvement on no money at all. This is something we've seen in our own communities: in times of low business, such as the summer holidays or after Christmas, sex workers who are scared of going hungry offer to split the profits from any bookings a fellow worker can send their way. This simple dynamic of someone's relative poverty versus the skills or connections of their acquaintance shows how a third party can benefit when business is thin on the ground.

None of this is to say that we think men who pay for sex or who profiteer from another's prostitution are good, or that they have a 'right' to buy sex that should be 'protected' (an accusation often levelled at sex workers by proponents of the Nordic model).[28] It is simply to say that, if you want to reduce prostitution, you need to find a way to do that which doesn't involve making already profoundly marginalised people more precarious. Advocates of 'ending demand' tend to want it both ways: they cite women's poverty as a key driver of the sex industry, but treat poverty as trivial when it comes to thinking about the impact of their own policy 'solutions'. One anti-prostitution organisation, the Women's Support Project, write in support of the Nordic model: 'If men were not prepared to buy sex, then prostitution would not work as a survival behaviour.'[29] When you enact a policy that makes a survival behavior 'not work' any more, some of the people using it to attempt to survive may no longer survive. The UK organisation Nordic Model Now uses a quote from a *fictional* sex worker – made up by a police officer whose job is enforcing the sex buyer law – saying, 'the Nordic model is bad for business, but good for my safety'.[30] This is a notion that only rings true if you don't realise that, as we've seen above, 'business' and 'safety' cannot be separated for marginalised people: *being poorer makes sex workers less safe.*

This is something the feminist movement already understands. It is clear, for example, that the effects of austerity in the UK – which has disproportionately fallen on women – has made it less safe for women to leave abusive relationships. A worker in Women's Aid told a reporter,

At the moment, the big issues for women using our services are around austerity, welfare reform and the housing crisis ... women faced with the choice of going into bed and breakfast [casual nightly accommodation] with children may feel that although their current circumstances are awful, they can at least cook for their child at home.[31]

When women have less access to resources, they are more vulnerable to violent men. This isn't an endorsement of the sex industry. We could be talking about *any* kind of work disproportionately done by marginalised people; it is universally true that simply taking it away will not help the person who is using it to try to survive. People turn to the sex industry as a way of securing the resources they need, and any policy which makes it harder for them to do that will make them less safe – both within the sex industry and in their relationships elsewhere.

2: The Exit Services

So, what happens next? Doesn't the Nordic model include some kind of help?

These initiatives, called 'exiting schemes', are the second strand of the ideal Nordic model envisioned by carceral feminists. Even academic Melissa Farley, a vociferous proponent of criminalising clients, concedes that doing so does more harm than good if these schemes are absent: 'Arresting johns without providing alternatives to prostitution – such as housing, job training, and treatment for the harms of prostitution such as physical and mental health care – can make life more difficult for women in prostitution.'[32] It seems the idea is that when people selling sex see their income decrease, prostitution will no longer be a viable economic strategy and they will be pushed into a programme that finds them alternatives. These exit services are supposed to be integral to the sex purchase ban. Nordic Model Now writes that 'well-funded support and exit services are vital ... and the Nordic Model is the only legislation that prioritises this approach in assisting women to rebuild their lives'.[33]

Such a scheme could take many forms – most obviously direct economic support, such as help with accessing benefits or other employment. It could also mean help regularising someone's immigration status so they can get a job in the mainstream economy. It could mean prescription drugs, counselling or other healthcare. It could mean access to childcare, education, housing – anything that addresses or alleviates the factors surrounding the person's entry into sex work in the first place.

The very name 'exit scheme' is problematic; it reveals a shaming focus not on where a person is trying to get *to*, but where they are coming *from*. In other contexts, such schemes might be called 'pathways to new employment' schemes or 'career development' schemes. For prostitutes the focus is firmly on what must be left behind.

Effective and non-judgmental support schemes *are* a good thing – all kinds of people need assistance with benefits, bureaucracy, childcare or new skill acquisition. Unfortunately, projects that aim to shift sex workers out of prostitution often are ineffective and judgmental.[34] Worse, some of them even criminalise sex workers, as in Kent's 'Safe Exit' programme, discussed in chapter four. As such, the term *exiting scheme* carries some baggage for sex workers. But sex worker advocacy is not simply about making sex work safer: it is also about removing the barriers to leaving it behind. Any action that, without judgment, seeks to give sex workers *more* or *better* options is therefore both an 'exiting scheme' *and* a sex workers' rights goal, and sex worker activists are already working on such projects all over the world.*

At the state level, however, initiatives like these need cash, and lots of it: enough to begin to replace prostitution as the key form of economic support in the lives of people like Silvia, Annabel, and Violet – if that's what they want. People who sell sex often have a range of complex needs, and holistic support cannot be done on the cheap.

---

* For instance, the sex worker led organisation Pow-Wow, in Zimbabwe, runs an 'income supplementation' project that helps sex workers find other sources of income alongside sex work. NSWP, 'Pow Wow', 2018, nswp.org/featured/pow-wow. The X:talk project in London helps migrant sex workers learn English language skills, which helps them both to negotiate better conditions in sex work and potentially to find alternative work. More information is available at xtalkproject.net.

This should be something that sex workers and anti-prostitution progressives can agree on – indeed, such advocates often rightly emphasise the fact that leaving prostitution, even for people who want to do so, is a complex process that takes time and support.[35]

In a sense, if you want Silvia, Annabel, and Violet not to be prostitutes, there *is* an easy solution. If Silvia is earning £200 a week from a couple of nights of street-based sex work, just give her the £200 a week she needs. (This, it should be emphasised, is not exactly the same as finding Silvia a different job which pays her £200 a week. Earning £200 relatively quickly, in two nights of sex work, is a different proposition to earning £200 doing shift-work on the minimum wage – even more so if you're paying for childcare or if you have a disability. Silvia may have her own reasons to be unable or unwilling to take a minimum wage job, or indeed any other job offered to her by someone who lacks an understanding of her specific needs. 'Help' that demands that the recipient just *get a job* rapidly becomes punitive, as anyone navigating Britain's fraying social safety net can attest.) People sell sex to get resources. If you ensure they have the resources they need, they will choose to do something else with their time.

The Nordic model's good reputation for exit services does not hold up under scrutiny. In 2005, a report by the Swedish government found that 'criminalisation cannot be anything but a compliment in the process of reducing prostitution and cannot in any way replace social initiatives. Despite this intention, *no extra funds have gone to social services* ... while the police received additional funds for this purpose on repeated occasions' (emphasis added).[36] A left-wing politician raised concerns in the Swedish parliament that 'in Stockholm there are Prostitution Centres, which work with the treatment of people who have or have been in prostitution ... [the centres'] resources are small'.[37]

It is hard to believe claims that the Nordic states see sex workers as victims who deserve care when a rapist can get a lower sentence 'because his victims were prostitutes'.[38] And no one seems to have given the Swedish police the memo that prostitutes are supposed to be supported. Swedish Detective Superintendent Jonas Trolle memorably told a reporter, 'It should be difficult to be a prostitute in our society – so even though we don't put prostitutes in jail [sic], we make life difficult for them.'[39]

One policy worker from the Swedish women's NGO sector told a researcher, 'If [the prostitution law] was supposed to help those women, then you would also have a huge programme, a social programme for them, which was never introduced.'[40] A senior government advisor on prostitution painted a similar picture, noting,

> Discourse at the political level is always more important than doing something for people within this category on the ground ... The government should have known that they've done nothing, absolutely nothing to improve social services for people who sell sex, and they haven't given a penny to the municipalities. Of course it was expensive ... it's less expensive, of course, to export and promote the law through conferences and [screening documentaries].[41]

Sex worker communities see through these shortcuts. Canadian activist collective Stop The Arrests (STA) says that sex workers 'are forced via the courts to participate in programming to help them move away from "poor life choices" ... it tends to place the focus on individual rather than societal change. Money talks and bullshit walks!'[42]

The services that do exist are imbued with hostility to sex workers, in which distributing condoms or other harm-reduction materials is seen as encouraging sex work. 'Maybe some young girls ... they find this [safety resource] on the internet, and say "Ah, maybe it could be really safe, because I have this handbook"', comments the Swedish National Coordinator Against Trafficking and Prostitution, adding snidely, 'If they make so much money, maybe they could buy their own condoms.'[43] One social worker in the Stockholm Prostitution Unit comments: 'I think it might take longer to do something about your problems [i.e., prostitution] if you get helped during the time.'[44]

Lisa, a sex worker in Sweden, reported that the Stockholm Prostitution Unit wouldn't help her *until* she had quit prostitution:

> The [social worker] told me she was going to help me, to write [a note authorising sickness benefits] ... so she said, 'If you are stopping

prostitution for three months, and you don't do anything for three months, then I will write that.' ... So I was angry, because if I am not working in sex work, how am I going to get money? I need first money, then I can stop.[45]

In Ireland, reports that asylum-seeking women were selling sex sparked alarm from the justice minister Frances Fitzgerald and became fodder for her campaign to introduce Nordic model–style legislation. Fitzgerald commented, 'I did find and I do find those reports shocking. I certainly don't want to see any woman in Ireland feeling that the only option for her is prostitution in order to look after her family.'[46] People who are seeking asylum in Ireland – a process which can often last for many years – receive an 'allowance' from the state. At the time the reports regarding prostitution emerged, this allowance was just nineteen euros a week. When the draft bill to criminalise clients in Ireland was published, Wendy Lyon wrote,

There is no reversal of the cuts to social welfare and child benefit which have undoubtedly pushed more women into prostitution; no increase in the €19 per week given to women in the asylum system; no additional funds for education, training or drug-treatment programmes that might open up other options.[47]

At the time of writing, the allowance that people seeking asylum receive from the Irish state has increased – to just €21.60 a week.[48] When people are pushed into prostitution by poverty, the response of the Nordic model is not to alleviate their poverty, but to try to take away their survival strategies.

Even if these services were both well funded *and* non-judgmental, pushing sex workers into them by making the sex industry a harsher place is still cruel. Even if they want to, it is the most marginal sex workers who will generally take the longest time to get in touch with services and to change jobs. If you have a drug dependency or poor mental health and you struggle to keep appointments, then you'll struggle to access services. If you're an undocumented person who worries that making yourself visible to services means you'll be deported, or a mother who fears that outing yourself as a prostitute to social workers means you'll risk losing child custody, then – *even if* these worries turn out to be unfounded – you might hold on as long as you can before taking the risk of approaching services. The complexity of such situations means it may take several months – or longer – to exit. And, in the meantime, you'll still be working in a sex industry that has been made deliberately harsher. But all this is hypothetical, because even the exit services in Sweden – *the epicentre of the Nordic model* – aren't meeting the needs of those who want to leave sex work.

3: The Seller

The third key principle of the Nordic model is supposed to be decriminalising prostitutes. This feature is thrust forward time and again by its supporters. Banyard describes the way the Nordic model 'criminalises sex buying and third-party profiteering, but it completely decriminalises selling sex.'[49] British Member of Parliament Thangam Debbonaire says 'Nordic Model supporters have always been clear. Full decriminalisation of supply, criminalisation of demand.'[50]

Again, the intentions, on the whole, are perhaps good. However, in practice, in every country that has Nordic-style laws, much criminalisation of sex workers has been *retained*. There are municipal laws against soliciting, the criminalisation of sex workers who share a flat, targeted evictions of sex workers, and the aggressive use of prostitution law and immigration law in concert to deport sex workers.

In France, supporters trumpeted the success of the Nordic model a year in, with the claim that nearly a thousand 'johns' had been arrested and 'zero prostituted persons'.[51] However, Wendy Lyon found a somewhat different story. Only the *national* law against soliciting has been repealed. There are still various *municipal* 'anti-prostitution decrees' that lead to continued arrests of street-based sex workers.[52] Not quite 'zero arrests' for 'prostituted persons', then.

When Ireland implemented the Nordic model, ministers rejected a provision that would have allowed sex workers to keep the money they had on them when their client was arrested. Instead, when a client is arrested, the police take all of her cash as 'proceeds of crime'.[53] This is, it should be obvious, a de facto fine for sex workers. In Norway, street-based sex workers were still being fined several years after they had allegedly been 'decriminalised'. Police routinely evict sex workers if they find out where they live, and under Norwegian law, refusing to give your address to a police officer when they ask is punishable with a fine. If the worker discloses her address, she will be evicted (generally on the same day); if she does not, she will be fined.[54]

Black women are disproportionately targeted by such enforcement. Tina, a Nigerian street sex worker in Norway, comments, 'When you are Black, they take the Black women and leave the white man.'[55] Esther, a Black sex worker working in Norway, says she had seen a significant shift:

> From 2008 to 2009, police would ask how you were doing. Since 2011, they have clamped down. Now they come and it's like [she hits the table] bam, bam, bam! They are much worse to Nigerians than Romanians and Bulgarians. Last year [2014] was the worst. Since September last year, it has been war – they don't want to see a Black face.[56]

Nigerian street worker Eunice told Amnesty, 'Customers know that police will react if white girls are hurt. They know they won't do anything to help Black women.'[57]

'There is absolutely no shadow of a doubt that what is going on in Norway is having the most detrimental impact on the most marginalized sex workers,' says Catherine Murphy from Amnesty International. 'The people pursued by the police the most, the most at risk for violence, the ones subject to being made homeless or deported. The impact is being felt most strongly for those women.'[58]

The over-policing of marginalised groups is not a problem created solely by the Nordic Model of course. Police forces all around the world already target certain populations for bullying, blackmail, theft and assault. But their power to do so is cultivated *through the laws they* enforce and the legitimacy those laws lend to their office. Anti-prostitution laws bolster the authority of police to enter into the lives of prostitutes, on the grounds of disrupting their survival.

Sydney, an Indigenous sex worker from Canada, demonstrates the opportunistic mindset of cops who exploit any chance they get to harass sex workers on the street. She recounts, 'I had a cigarette in my hand and it was burning out and they were like, "What are you going to do, throw that on the ground? If you do, we are going to make you pick up all the cigarette butts around here."'[59] Jenn Clamen, from Montreal-based sex workers' rights group Stella points out 'when we introduce police and law enforcement as "saviours" – which is what the Nordic regime attempts to do for sex workers – we give police another tool in their arsenal to attack these communities.'[60]

The Criminalisation of Indoor Workers

In almost every jurisdiction where the Nordic model operates, sex workers sharing flats are criminalised. In Oslo, Norway, a sex working woman was prosecuted as a brothel-keeper for sharing her flat with two friends – even though the court acknowledged that her primary motive was safety.[61] Police in Sweden stake out flats to 'catch' pairs of sex workers.[62] In Northern Ireland, the first arrests made when the Nordic model was implemented was one client – and three sex working women, who were arrested for brothel-keeping as they were found, during the raid ostensibly aimed at catching the client, to be sharing a flat.[63]

The Republic of Ireland implemented the Nordic model in March 2017 – and in July 2017, two migrant women were convicted of prostitution offences in the small town of Tralee in County Kerry. Florina, who was renting a house, was convicted of allowing the house to be used for prostitution, although the court accepted that she did not benefit 'materially or financially' from the set-up. Her friend Mihaiela was charged under the brothel-keeping law with 'using the same address for prostitution' and was convicted and fined.[64] Advocates of the Nordic model might think that Florina, the main tenant, deserved to be prosecuted as a brothel-keeper, although prosecuting a migrant woman for a flat-share from which she was not benefitting financially seems a harsh application of the law. But it is hard to see on what basis such an advocate could argue that Mihaiela should be prosecuted.

Some prominent Nordic-model advocates deride the idea that sex workers might want to work together. A senior human rights advisor at the Carter Center, for example, claimed that 'working together for safety' is just a 'code for running a brothel' or 'pimping', adding that 'pimps call themselves sex workers, so that's convenient'.[65]

In reality, sex workers sharing an apartment is very normal. If you have ever had a housemate to cut housing costs – or to enjoy their company – you should empathise with why sex workers might want to share working flats. (There is something intensely dehumanising about the implication that sex workers are so alien that these normal, human considerations do not apply to us.) It is also an obvious safety measure – one used by many other kinds of workers. Even some advocates for the Nordic model acknowledge having shared flats in this way during the time that they were selling sex. Prominent campaigner Rachel Moran writes in her memoir that, 'If I'd get a request for a call-in … I'd use a bedroom in the brothel of one of the women I was associating with at that time. I'd pay them a fee for the use of the room, which was common practice. *I'd made money myself that way when I had my own apartment*' (emphasis ours).[66]

Moran has been one of the most active campaigners for the Nordic model across the globe for many years: she has spoken with politicians and addressed the United Nations; her story is cited by other advocates as *the* illustration as to why the Nordic is needed. In such a fraught and adversarial context, Moran's off-hand acknowledgement that not only did she share a flat with other workers, but she 'made money … that way' reads strangely. Any current sex worker who made such a comment would be damned by Moran – and the law she helped bring in – as a pimp. We do not want to engage in a similar smear. Moran's way of working seems legitimate and unremarkable; after all, there is an 'opportunity cost' to letting another worker see a client in your room, when you yourself could have been using the room to work in. Outside overheated sex industry debates, it would not seem alarming or note-worthy to ask a friend for a small financial contribution towards your bills if they are using your space. What is painful, of course, is the hypocrisy: the Irish law that Moran spent years campaigning for penalises women doing exactly what she describes herself doing – and indeed women behaving 'more sympathetically', such as those who took no financial contribution and simply allowed a friend to share their space. (The Nordic model in Ireland doubled the penalties for 'brothel-keeping' from a six-month jail sentence to a year.) When questioned on this hypocrisy, Moran declined to give a clear answer as to whether she felt that a prosecution for brothel-keeping would have helped her at this time in her life.[67] Of course, it is not just Moran's question to answer: all advocates of the Nordic model should perhaps explain whether they think the prosecution of Moran as a brothel-keeper would have been a positive thing for her or for society at large – and if not, why they are happy to push for laws under which so many other sex workers are prosecuted just for doing the same as she did.

Examples abound. Even selling sex in 'duos' – i.e., advertising threesomes – can put sex workers afoul of brothel-keeping laws: sex workers David and Celia, a married couple, were convicted of brothel-keeping charges in Ireland in May 2018 for working together in this way. The two narrowly avoided jail and were each fined €600.[68] And there's seventy-three-year-old Terezinha, prosecuted for brothel-keeping in Ireland in July 2017. The court accepted that no coercion was taking place. Terezinha was simply renting a flat from which she herself could sell sex and was sharing it with another sex working woman. Terezinha was visibly distressed during the court case and spoke via a court interpreter. She was selling sex out of desperation in order to pay her son's medical bills. She had been in Ireland for four days and had seen only one client, making eighty euros. The court took the eighty euros as a fine, and the judge 'ordered that the money … could be given to an organisation that helps women involved in the sex trade'.[69]

Evictions

Police operating under Nordic-model legislation view disrupting commercial sex as good in itself and frequently deploy 'be cruel to be kind' strategies against sex workers. In Sweden, landlords who rent property to sex workers can be criminalised for 'promoting' prostitution, with obvious consequences for sex workers' increased precarity and risk of homelessness. The law directly pushes for the eviction of sex worker tenants: 'If [the landlord] does not do what is reasonably required for *the termination of the tenancy*, he or she will [be] considered to have promoted the business' (emphasis ours).[70]

The Norwegian police even had a specific operation to evict sex workers. They would tell a landlord that they suspected a specific tenant to be a sex worker and invite the landlord to either evict the tenant or face prosecution themselves. The tenants were evicted. As if to deliberately dispel any doubt as to what this policing strategy was aiming for, the police gave it the name: 'Operation Homeless'.[71]

The financial outlay involved in being evicted is often much greater than the fines given to buyers caught paying for sex. An evicted sex worker will lose her deposit; if she has paid that month's rent already, she will lose that too. It should be obvious to any empathetic person that being suddenly made homeless and losing a large amount of money will not help anyone out of prostitution. Such measures sit uneasily with the claim that Nordic model–style legislation treats prostitutes as victims of violence. Who could think that women experiencing violence should be evicted?

Mercy, a Black sex working woman in Norway, was evicted this way three times between 2013 and 2014.[72] On one occasion, she was effectively 'evicted' while she was out at the shops: the landlord changed the locks. She had to beg to be allowed to collect her possessions, telling Amnesty, 'I had to wait a week with no clothes or money or anything.'[73] Another sex worker, Mary, says, 'Sometimes they would give us just a few minutes to get out … We would lose the money that we had paid.'[74] Eunice says, 'I have been given minutes to leave my apartment. You don't have time to get all your things. [I had to go and] sleep in the train station.'[75] Esther says, 'The police gave us twenty minutes to get out. We were cooking soup at the time and we had to take the pot out in the street with us.'[76] In 2014, nine Black sex workers reported to the Oslo police that they had been raped and assaulted by a man armed with a machete who had posed as a police officer. A few days after their report, their landlord, alerted by the police that his tenants were sex workers, evicted them.[77] Amnesty spoke to dozens of women evicted in this way, and found that all but one were given a day – or *less* – to leave their apartments. Every single one was Black.[78] Operation Homeless is no longer a specific operation – not because the police realised it was horrifying, but because the work of evicting mostly Black sex working women has been 'mainstreamed' into the work of Oslo police.[79]

Deportations

Deportations are intrinsically violent, but the deportation of sex workers from countries that have implemented the Nordic model is often particularly brutal. In Canada, sex worker group Butterfly says that migrant women are frequently detained indefinitely by immigration enforcement. Some spend weeks or even months being subjected to 'inhuman and degrading treatment, false allegations, and false evidence being used to keep them detained' before being deported.[80] One sex worker named Cookie said, 'The first night was incredibly cold since I only had my vest while sleeping on a board. I thought to myself, "I have no clothes and I have no food, what did I do wrong?" For a full week, I was not allowed to shower or change my clothes.' Butterfly reports that another migrant sex worker stayed with a friend after escaping domestic abuse, and was then attacked by a client in the flat they both shared. When the police arrived, they immediately arrested her friend on suspicion of trafficking her, and arrested her on suspicion of working illegally. Both of the women were deported.[81]

Police in Nordic countries routinely use sex workers' reports of violence to deport them. One woman, whom the police had identified as a sex worker after she reported an incident of violence that gave her a serious head injury, was deported from Oslo so rapidly that the injury made it difficult to travel.[82]

In 2014, three Nigerian sex workers in Oslo were attacked and robbed in their home at gunpoint. The women went to an emergency shelter to recover, but when they returned to their home a few days later, they were arrested and deported.[83] They had valid visas and had not overstayed them. To deport people who come to your attention as *victims of a violent crime* is an incredibly aggressive enforcement approach, not one that should be considered normal or legitimate. When a case came to light in 2017 of a woman in London who had been threatened with immigration enforcement after reporting a rape, there was – rightly – a national outcry.[84] Yet Nordic prostitution policy, where such cases are routine, is held up as aspirational and feminist.

In our view, nobody deserves to be deported. But the police break even their *own* rules by deporting sex workers who have a legal right to be in the country. Swedish authorities routinely deport migrant women from other EU nations on the grounds that sex work constitutes 'a threat to public order and security' or a 'a dishonest means of support'.[85]

It is no coincidence that so many of the sex workers deported from Scandinavia are Black women. The Nordic model emerged in response to racist anxieties about the migration of Black sex workers, particularly to Norway, who were depicted through the stigmatising trope of the sexually aggressive Black woman.[86] Oslo sex worker outreach organisation Pro Sentret notes that when the law was drafted,

> There was lots of discussion about how 'the streets had become immoral'. Most of the debate was about the very visible Nigerian women … There were politicians talking about how terrible it was for them to be approached by these women. The women were treated like they were garbage that needed to be cleaned away. The media stories were about 'Black whores' causing 'immorality in the streets'. That was the main focus.[87]

The criminalisation of sex workers for sharing flats, the use of fines and evictions against sex workers, and the extremely aggressive use of deportations are incompatible with the claim that the Nordic model 'totally decriminalises' sellers. It retains, adds, and intensifies numerous tools with which to harass, prosecute, arrest or harm sex workers through criminal law or civil measures. In conveying to the police that disrupting commercial sex is their job, the law pushes the police to use these tools against sellers – which they do with particular alacrity when the seller is Black.

The effect, of course, is that the seller has a good reason to hide from the police, making Nordic cops' endless comments about how easy it still is to find sex workers ('if the punter can find prostituted

women, so can the police')[88] more chilling than jocular. It throws into
a harsh light the rhetorical question that we hear a lot as activists.
'How can a prostitute in Sweden be in danger', we're asked by cops
and politicians and campaigners alike, 'when all she has to do is pick
up the phone, even if the punter is rude to her, and the police will
arrest him because he is already committing a crime?'[89] Such a question must be rhetorical, because clearly these campaigners have never
paused to hear sex workers' answers.

The answer, of course, is that a sex worker working under the
Nordic Model still has a lot to fear. If she's a migrant – even one
with a visa – she can be arrested and taken to a deportation centre
today. If her name is on the tenancy of a flat she shares, she can be
prosecuted. Would you call the police if doing so would make you
homeless today, or open you up to prosecution? Dorothy, a migrant
sex worker in Canada, spoke of how this fear shaped her behaviour;
'They [the robbers] treated us like a money machine. We were robbed
four times in one week … We could not call the police, otherwise, we
would have had more trouble. I told the police about this [after they
eventually arrested and detained me], but they did not care.'[90]

When people who sell sex have desperate, urgent reasons to hide
from the police, we are profoundly vulnerable to violent men. Such
men know that they can attack us, rob us, or assault us – and because
contacting the cops means we'll risk being made homeless on *top* of
being robbed at gunpoint, we won't contact the cops. Sex workers
under such a system are sitting ducks.

4. The Pimp and the Trafficker

As we noted when we discussed demand, third parties like managers
benefit when sex workers' lives become more difficult. For instance,
where sex workers face legal obstacles to tenancy – as is the case
under the Nordic model – it makes sense to get another person to
be a 'go-between' with the landlord. Such a relationship is one of
hugely uneven power: if the 'go-between' requests three hundred
pounds a month to do this, the sex worker is stuck having to pay
him *as well as the landlord*, and if she won't or can't, he can easily
get her evicted. The Norwegian government writes that in Sweden,

prostitutes' 'dependence on pimps has probably increased. Someone is needed in the background to arrange transport and new flats so that the women's activity is more difficult to discover'.[91]

The victims of exploitation and sex trafficking are a key concern for many feminists, including sex worker activists. There are women in abusive relationships who have been coerced into prostitution by their partner. There are those working in prostitution who have been coerced into it by people who promised them different work, and to whom they pay some or all of their earnings from sex work – usually to pay back a debt for crossing the border.

Does the Nordic approach make the situation better for women like these? Bear in mind that there is no simple binary divide between sex workers and those you would consider trafficked. All of these people are using the safety strategies we have outlined in this book, when they can. All, for whatever reason, are seeking to make money – whether to buy drugs, placate a violent partner or abusive manager, give to a landlord or send to a dependent family member. Or indeed to pay off a people smuggler.[*] Policies which make a prostitute's life harder *will make the lives of those you would consider trafficked harder, too.* Think back to the Norwegian government report cited earlier in this chapter – the one that said the sex buyer law meant that people in prostitution now had to 'work harder'. That applies to everyone selling sex in Norway; there isn't an exemption for those in the most exploitative situations. Another Norwegian government report into the sex buyer law states this even more bluntly: the worst harms,

---

[*] We have used the phrase 'people you would consider trafficked' to reflect how fluid and subjective such a designation can be. As per chapter 3, governments tend to use the term trafficking not to reflect actual harm, but in order to give a progressive gloss to anti-migrant and anti-prostitution policing. Because the designation of trafficked person is supposed to bring with it some entitlement to support from the state, those that governments deem trafficked are a tiny proportion of those harmed within state-led systems such as border policing. For anti-prostitution campaigners, the designation of trafficking is one that seems to reflect those who they feel sympathy with, versus those who such campaigners find less sympathetic – perhaps because the person in question is advocating for sex workers' rights rather than carceral solutions – excluded from terms like *trafficked person* regardless of their experiences.

it notes, accrue to '"addicts, the mentally ill, and people from other countries" – the forced prostitutes'.[92] And if an exploited migrant sex worker goes to the police under the Nordic model, as under other models, she will be deported with her debt unpaid. As a report to the Swedish parliament noted, when women are 'discovered by police' and found to 'have been missing a legal basis for their stay', they will 'often ... have been immediately [deported] without the police attempting to investigate under what conditions they have come and stayed in ... this means that significant information about trafficking in human beings has been lost.'[93]

If such a woman tries to seek new employment through exit services, she may be told she needs to quit sex work before they can help her. She is likely to be fearful of approaching exit services at all, for fear that revealing herself to anybody 'official' will lead to her deportation. So she must continue to sell sex – whether under duress or entirely of her own volition – all the while the number of clients shrinking, the shifts getting longer, and work growing more dangerous.

Would all this be worthwhile if the market for commercial sex in Nordic countries is smaller? *Fewer* women will be exploited in prostitution and even trafficked, right? The problem with this idea is that criminal law is not a key determinant of the size of the sex industry in any given country. Look at the United States. If criminalisation was the key factor in the size of a country's sex industry, the US would have a tiny sex industry. As chapter 5 details, in many states, penalties for purchasing sex far exceed those in Scandinavia – and of course sex workers themselves, along with managers, landlords, taxi drivers, and colleagues, can all be swept up into prosecution. Yet the US has a *huge* sex industry. That's because the key determinant is not criminal law but *poverty* and people's access to resources. When a country has no social safety net, or when the social safety net excludes some, people struggling to avoid homelessness or to pay for healthcare might well sell sex in order to get housing or medication. People who are undocumented struggle to enter the mainstream labour market or to assert any labour rights. In these contexts, some people sell sex – often under conditions that are, to a greater or lesser degree, exploitative or abusive. But the solution isn't to criminalise commercial sex; if it was, the US would have zero trafficking. Instead, it is to ensure that people have access to the resources that they need, including the right to safe migration and the right for migrants to work and assert labour rights without fearing deportation.

In fact, Swedish policymakers aren't at all clear on what the law has achieved. Claims that levels of sex work have declined are generally misleading, as they are usually based only on levels of street-based sex work.[94] Street work in Stockholm did indeed decline briefly after 1999, but then went back up again – and the law probably merely speeded a transition to indoor work that was already being facilitated by the internet.[95] 'Today it is impossible to run a brothel in Sweden', boasts a cop to anti-prostitution campaigner Janice Raymond, who uncritically repeats him.[96] But, according to police, the number of brothels in Stockholm has increased sharply. In 2009, they estimated there were ninety Thai 'massage parlours' (which offer sex) in the city; by 2013, the number was 250.[97] Swedish politicians complained of the sex industry's resilience, noting in 2003 that street prostitution in one county had more than doubled.* Contrary to the claims of 'abolition-ism', Swedish politicians argue, 'We have never thought that you could eradicate prostitution with it, but [the *sexköpslagen*] is an important signal of what is acceptable in a society and not.'[98] Not exactly the 'existential threat' to the sex trade that advocates claim, then.[99]

Can Anybody Hear Us?

All over the world, it is routine for anti-prostitution policing to involve evicting sex workers, prosecuting them, and deporting them. Only in the Nordic countries, however, is this imagined as a *feminist* achievement.† For Sweden particularly, cleansing the nation of

---

* Swedish Parliament, 'Förbud mot försäljning av sexuella tjänster' [Prohibition of the sale of sexual services], Motion 2002/03:Ju284, riksdagen.se.

† 'The crude measurement of success that Norway is applying to its anti-trafficking work – namely, an overall reduction in the commercial sex market – means that Norway can in effect claim success for deporting traf-ficking victims to other countries'. Amnesty International, 'The Human Cost

undesirables as a form of social improvement has long been part of national identity. In the early twentieth century, the political theory of *folkhemmet* ('the people's home') was established to conceptualize the ideal Swedish society and its benevolent welfare state. The basis for this idea is that, like a small family household, Swedish citizens contribute and in turn are benignly looked after by the state, which acts as a 'good parent', steering its offspring away from misbehaviour and corruption.[100] Unsurprisingly, the role of the prostitute in *folkhemmet* is an antagonistic one. Who but a prostitute could more archetypally threaten the family hearth? Other groups, too, are seen as similarly disruptive to Swedish familial normativity: people who use drugs, people with HIV, transgender people. How this 'national family' has historically responded to these groups paints a picture of Swedish control.

In the name of *folkhemmet's* eugenicist commitment to 'social hygiene', 21,000 people were forcibly sterilised before 1975. Ninety per cent of those sterilised were women who were deemed to be 'inferior, anti-social, dangerously hypersexual … promiscuous or feebleminded'.[101] During the 1990s, the Swedish state incarcerated people living with HIV without trial, some of them for years – ninety per cent were sex workers and drug users.[102] This legacy lives on in Swedish governance. In 2009, a Left Party politician noted that these punitive responses to HIV played a part in the social construction of 'the nice clean Sweden'.[103] In order to legally reassign their gender, trans people were subject to compulsory sterilisation until 2013.[104] Even the presence of drugs in the body is criminalised.[105] This is a far harsher anti-drug law than any other European country has, which goes some way towards explaining Sweden's devastating number of drug deaths – the second-worst in Europe.[106] Ultimately, only Sweden's 'ideal', normative citizens – healthy, productive people of Nordic stock – are those who can be deemed responsible and rational, looking after themselves in a way that is independent but in accord with family rules.

---

of "Crushing" the Market: Criminalization of Sex Work in Norway', report, EUR/36/4024/2016, 26 May 2016, 11–12.

Protecting the Brand

For anti-prostitution feminists beguiled by the idea of the 'people's home' – a utopia of social order – Sweden's prostitution law represents the dream. Reality cannot be allowed to intrude. We hear a litany of praises exalting Sweden's 'decriminalisation' of 'prostituted people.' The UK feminist group Object says, 'the "Nordic model" completely decriminalises those who sell sex acts whilst offering support services to exit prostitution', while Dr Meagan Tyler from the Nordic Model Information Network says the law, 'basically hinges on, essentially, a legal framework where all prostituted persons are decriminalised, so there's no criminal sanction against anyone in prostitution, but sex buying, pimping and brothel keeping are all criminalised.'[107]

When someone raised 'Operation Homeless' in the comments section of her website, prolific anti-prostitution feminist Meghan Murphy was confused:

> Can you at least explain … how and why the police are supposedly 'seeking out and harassing sex workers' and what that has to do with the Nordic model? It seems the articles you've provided have something to do with something called 'Operation Homeless' – I don't know what that is and I don't understand how it relates to the Nordic model.[108]

Murphy has penned literally hundreds of articles *advocating for the Nordic model* over a period of years. For her to not know about Operation Homeless betrays a notable – and typical – lack of feminist curiosity about sex workers' experiences under the system they are advocating for. Similar examples abound. In her book *Pimp State*, which also advocates for the Nordic model, Banyard writes, 'Securing the Sex Buyer Law isn't a case of job done for campaigners. Instead, the task turns to prising open the full potential of the law, which sometimes includes pressing for amendments in the legislation itself.'[109] At this point, the reader might wonder if *Pimp State* will acknowledge Operation Homeless, prosecutions, deportations, or other abuses that sex workers suffer in Nordic nations. Banyard instead continues, 'In Sweden, for instance, the maximum possible penalty for paying for sex was increased in 2011 from six months to one year's imprisonment'. These sorts of issues – that the law has sometimes not been enforced enough against clients or that the penalties were too low – are the *only* criticisms of the law Banyard raises.

Another anti-prostitution activist told an audience of activists and politicians, 'Of course under the Nordic model no one selling sex is criminalised and yet we're told constantly that [they] are criminalised de facto, *and I'm not sure what that means*. I mean you're either criminalised for selling sex or you're not' (emphasis ours).[110] When Amnesty's report came out – full of the voices of women like Mercy, Mary, Esther, and Eunice speaking of criminalisation, eviction, and deportation – UK campaign group Nordic Model Now simply commented, 'The Nordic model works and should keep on keeping on.'[111]

The *sexköpslagen* brand is closely linked to ideas of innovative social democracy. As a result, when other countries implement prostitution laws based on those of Sweden, they tap into the same feminist cachet – even when such pats on the back are far from deserved.

In Canada, Bill C-36 – or the Protection of Communities and Exploited Persons Act (PCEPA) – was introduced in 2014. The law (which criminalised clients and advertising, while retaining most of the existing penalties for prostitutes)* brought an array of political flavours to the fore, from regressively hostile to progressively poetic.

---

* Canada's old legal regime of criminalisation (similar to current UK law) was dismantled when the Supreme Court of Canada struck down three of the major prostitution provisions, on the grounds that they violated the human rights of safety and liberty for sex workers. The judges were, in part, influenced by the serial murders in Vancouver, BC, whose victims were predominantly Indigenous and targeted for violence because the criminal law in the old regime contributed to their vulnerability. However, instead of prioritising safety, in line with the Supreme Court's judgment, the Conservative government added a slew of additional criminalisations with Bill C-36. This Bill included penalties for 'communicating for the purpose of selling sexual services in a public place', which continues to criminalise sex workers themselves. See *Canada (Attorney General) v Bedford* 2013 SCC 72, Supreme Court Judgment, scc-csc.lexum.com; A. Nanda, 'From Bedford to the MWCI, Chronicling the Legal Consequences of Pickton', *The Court*, 8 January 2014, thecourt.ca; The Canadian Press, 'Controversial prostitution law introduced on day of action on violence against women', *The Star*, 3 December 2014, thestar.com.

Conservative MP Joy Smith spoke with heartfelt compassion of a young abuse survivor who had inspired her fight to bring the bill about: a 'living, breathing, beautiful human being, with a soul'.[112] Truly an admirable sentiment (it's never a bad time, of course, to be reminded that prostitutes have souls), especially when compared with the words of Conservative colleague Donald Plett, who said, 'we don't want to make life safe for prostitutes – we want to do away with prostitution. That's the intent of the bill.'[113]

Other proponents of C-36 framed the issue as one of 'community harms' such as noise, impeding traffic, harassment of residents, 'unsanitary behaviours', and the encroachment of sex workers into the spaces of schoolchildren.[114] Again, 'end demand' reveals itself to be roomy enough for multiple political ideologies. In the same debate, Smith again asserted her feminist credentials: 'This bill is … historic and it's progressive. For the first time in Canada's history, women trafficked into prostitution will not be treated as nuisances, they'll be treated with dignity.'[115]

Shortly after that, eleven migrant sex workers were arrested in Ottawa and deported.[116] For all that feminists say they prioritize tackling violence against victims – addressing the hurt caused *to us* by the buying of sex – it is striking how frequently this mask slips. When it does, we see yet again that the goal of 'doing away' with sex workers and the spectre of 'harm to the community' drive these policies. For those who have known violence in the sex trade, the doublespeak of these politics is clear.

As for the laws' vaunted disciplinary effect on male sexual entitlement, well. As evidence emerges of harms to sex workers and little or no reduction in the size of the sex industry, anti-prostitution feminists keen to 'protect the brand' of the Nordic model increasingly shift to citing changes in social attitudes towards prostitution as a key metric of the law's success. When the law was first implemented, most Swedes did not support it. Nearly twenty years on, a large majority of the population does. As Banyard writes, 'That attitude shift is at the heart of the Sex Buyer Law. Its presence on the statute book, and its enforcement on the ground, is about society collectively drawing a line in the sand.'[117] The suggestion is, of course, that the effect of the law has been to set a new and more feminist norm: Swedes no longer think it is acceptable to 'buy a woman for sex'.

In making this argument, advocates of the Nordic model make a telling omission: the same survey that shows many more Swedes now think it unacceptable to *pay* for sex *also* shows that many more Swedes now think it unacceptable to *sell* sex, too. A majority of Swedes, particularly women, would like to see prostitutes fined or jailed.[118] The 'line in the sand' that Banyard and others are so keen to celebrate looks much less feminist when it is drawn to penalise not only the client *but the prostitute, too.* As retired academic Robert Fullinwider writes, 'The shift in opinion to a strong majority favoring criminalizing all facets of prostitution suggests the sex purchase ban has implanted a norm, to be sure, but ... it may not be a norm feminists should take comfort in.'[119]

Patriarchy, Police, and the State

Sex worker activists often note that anti-prostitution rhetoric is a welcoming place for male-feminist grandstanding. Anti-prostitution politics serve the desire of the 'good guys' to bolster their own manhood, and ostensibly feminist-adjacent campaigning can be fuelled by some pretty chauvinist ideas. As one Swedish prosecutor told an audience,

> A real man should manage to get his women, get his due of sex, by powers of seduction and mutual consent, and for love, or mutual enjoyment, or procreation, or for passing the time of day; not for money. Going to prostitutes was cheating, it was degrading, it was contemptible, beyond the pale. Whores were for losers.[120]

This view of 'real men'; the jab at 'whores' – let alone the idea that a 'real man' should 'get his due' of sex and women – are hardly testament to the feminist credentials of Swedish policymakers.

Lionising the police does much to establish these politics as a friendly environment for other self-identified 'feminist men'. If the police are going to deliver justice for poor, abused women, they can be held aloft as a symbol of heroic masculinity, a portal through which others can enter. While they project themselves into the figure of the 'heroic' police officer, male anti-prostitution campaigners can use these politics to superficially distance themselves from other kinds of masculinity. ('Whores were for losers.') The politician who proposed the law in Sweden specifically notes the feminist credentials of his countrymen, claiming that the law went forward because 'Swedish men had different view[s] on prostitution than men from other parts of the world.'[121] Journalist and feted anti-prostitution campaigner Nicholas Kristof revealed a rather strange view of sex when he bemoaned American 'promiscuity' in the *New York Times* while claiming that Indian men have a cultural tendency to pay for sex with fourteen-year-olds.[122] Such condemnations dwell heavily on the morals of individual – often racialised – 'bad guys'.

By advocating 'end demand' laws, men relocate the blame for patriarchy onto more obviously monstrous men and feel superior in calling out those *other* men's violations or objectifying treatment of women. The hypocrisy is, of course, that the anti-prostitution movement is at times deeply violating and objectifying to sex workers. Anti-prostitution feminism is a place where men can participate in flinging slurs like *holes, whores, orifices,* and *cum dumpsters* at sex workers – and call it feminist analysis.[123] It's a place where men who consider themselves feminist-aligned can patronise and dismiss prostitute women, as men have done for centuries. It's a place where a police officer can rifle through the bathroom bin at a sex worker's flat, retrieve blood-soaked tampons, publish photographs of them in his memoir (with a touching dedication to sex workers he has met in his work: 'This is my attempt to describe your reality'), and still be treated like a feminist activist.[124] As sex worker Charlotte Shane observes, anti-prostitution feminism makes it progressive for men to dwell incessantly on violent, coercive sex and abject bodies while at the same time enjoying praise and even Pulitzer Prizes.[125]

Meanwhile, anti-prostitution feminists hone in on the abuse and exploitation of 'pimps and punters' while overlooking – or tacitly supporting – similar abuses by police, landlords, and immigration officers. You will search a long time if you are looking for any comment on the arrest, confiscation of money, or brutal deportation of sex workers that occur in jurisdictions with 'Nordic model' branding. Journalist Joan Smith travelled to Sweden in 2013 to report on the *sexköpslagen* and asked the police whether prostitution had become more dangerous for women. She confidently reports that 'all the Swedish police officers I spoke to insisted this was a myth'.[126] Her piece opens and concludes with an officer in a police car, watching sex workers through the window. It would be hard to think of a better way to encapsulate carceral feminism than this: a perspective that opens and closes with shadowing a police officer, sitting in his seat, literally sharing his position and reproducing his gaze. It is clear in whose shoes Smith is walking – and it isn't those of the distant, apparently-voiceless women.

The power difference between men and women is one kind of structural imbalance; the power difference between sex workers and the police is another. Swedish feminist commentator Gunilla Ekberg writes, 'Those who are pro-prostitution of course ignore power differences between men and women' – but carceral feminists are deeply invested in both ignoring and reinforcing the power differences between the police and prostitutes.[127] In attempting to eradicate the gendered inequality that they rightly see in the purchase of sex, they intentionally or accidentally strengthen the state's power to harm prostitutes – which is, of course, itself a deeply patriarchal dynamic. You might think that this leaves us, as feminists, at an impasse: if challenging the patriarchal sex industry strengthens the patriarchal state, then it is hard to see how we can proceed. In fact, of course, it is easy to imagine a world wherein no man is able to pay for sex – simply because everyone who might have needed to sell it *already has the resources that they need*. We can work towards a more feminist world by making women less poor – but not through bolstering the patriarchal power of the carceral state.

Ignoring or bolstering state power allows the experiences of people like Mercy, Mary, Tina, Eunice, and Esther to fall through the cracks. Mainstream feminism maintains a profound uninterest in the experiences of women like them – the direct state violence (fines, evictions, and deportations) and the violence they suffer because the state fails to protect them. When journalists write that the Nordic model 'decriminalises women who sell sex' and campaigning organisations repeat the claim that Sweden's law 'completely decriminalises all those who are prostituted', it's hard to draw any other conclusion than mainstream feminism *simply doesn't count* the criminalisation or deportation of mostly Black migrant sex workers in Nordic countries.[128]

As we wrote in the chapter on borders, deportations are a violation of human rights: people are ripped from their families and friends simply because of where they happened to have been born. Yet even within the left, the injustice of deportation can sometimes prove a slippery topic to keep on the table.[129] Despite claims to radicalism, an analysis of borders rarely features in anti-prostitution advocacy. A generous assessment of this would suggest that, for some, borders and immigration seem too permanent or unchangeable to reckon with – that they will never go away.

As sex workers and feminists, we do not accept that borders and their enforcement are inevitable or immutable. We too are working towards a radical feminism that can abolish borders, capitalism, *and* the sex industry *without causing harm to sex workers*. Just as it is a bad cliché to claim that a future without commercial sex is a futile endeavour because 'the sex industry will always be there' or it's 'the world's oldest profession', it is also a feeble excuse to dismiss border abolition simply because it is difficult to change.

In this chapter, we have tried to speak to both the 'ideal' Nordic model, and the Nordic model as it really exists. The Nordic model as it really exists includes harm to sex workers, and when its advocates refuse to acknowledge or to try to fix these harms they reveal their ultimate disregard for the safety of people who sell sex. But even if these problems – the deportations, the evictions, the fines – were fixed, the 'ideal Nordic model' would still harm people who sell sex, and harm the most marginalised the worst. That is because any policy that makes sex workers poorer will also tend to make them less safe. As Thai sex worker collective Empower have pointed out, criminalisation is about what can be *taken away* from sex workers. If you care about the most marginalised people in society, why not start from thinking about what can be *given* to them?[130]

7

Charmed Circle: Germany, Netherlands, and Nevada

Regulationism: A legal model that heavily regulates a legal strand of the sex industry while continuing to criminalise workers who can't or won't comply with various bureaucratic requirements, such as mandatory health testing, employment in certain venues, or registering publicly as a prostitute. Also called: legalisation, licensing, *Prostitutionsgesetz*.

> 'This law won't protect sex workers. It is just about control.'
>
> – Sex worker in Germany[1]

Many people are familiar with the terms *legalisation* and *decriminalisation*, yet without realising that these words refer to distinctly different things.

Under legalisation, *some* sex work, in *some* contexts, is legal. This legal sex work is heavily regulated by the state – generally not in a way that prioritises the welfare of workers. This is, in part, because a mindset that advocates for legalising sex work tends to see prostitutes not as workers but as anxiety-inducing vectors of disease or symbols of disorder who must be controlled. Often, to legalise means to implement new laws related specifically to sex work, including new criminal penalties, rather than repealing the existing ones.

By comparison, decriminalisation – which we'll come to in more detail in the next chapter – describes a situation where sex work is legal *as the default position*. With legalistion, only some sex work, in only some contexts, is legal, whereas with decriminalisation, prostitution is, as a starting point, not a crime. The regulations that exist under decriminalisation tend to prioritise the welfare of people who sell sex – in part because a mindset that advocates for decriminalisation tends to see sex workers as *workers*, and from that flows a concern for workers' rights.

To feminist sceptics, legalisation – the idea of the government giving licenses to brothels or creating special zones for street work – rolls out the red carpet for patriarchy. What kind of message does it send when the state formalises prostitution? What effect does a legally ratified sex trade have on male sexual entitlement? Are the exploited bodies of women working in these places becoming damaged from overuse? Anti-prostitution campaigners have long objected to any form of legalisation, highlighting the effect of global 'brothelisation' on the well-being of 'prostituted women'.[2]

Although diverse nations have legalised their sex industry (including Bangladesh, Austria, Senegal, Latvia, Tunisia, Hungary, Peru, Venezuela, Chile, parts of Australia, and some counties in the US state of Nevada), much feminist discussion focuses on the regulatory models of Europe – particularly Germany and the Netherlands – which are often described in terms such as 'a free-for-all', 'relaxed', 'an open house', and 'liberal'.[3]

Liberal support for regulationism is linked to the notion that prostitution is something innate, perennial, inevitable – the dirty job that *someone* has got to do. This has deep roots: Christian theologians, for instance, have argued that commercial sex is an outlet for sexual impulses that would otherwise result in worse sins.[4] The patriarchal double standard praises men for having multiple sexual partners but shames and condemns women for the same. Mathematically, the only way for men to practice promiscuity while allowing the majority of women to remain 'respectable' is for a small number of women to be extremely sexually active. An 1897 editorial in a Johannesburg newspaper stated it more explicitly: 'The virtue of the *monde* is assured by the *demi-monde*.'[5] That is, patriarchal sexual norms render sex work not only economically viable but in some sense *necessary* – whether for the benefit of the individual client or for the benefit of society.

Then there are those who see in sex work a greater capitalist purpose. This logic suggests that with an entrepreneurial outlook, there is hope for the sex industry – which, much like the cannabis market, is a wild frontier that simply needs the firm guiding hand of a rich grown-up. These industries, in the hands of the right people, can become a boon for all who would benefit from tourism, taxation, and regulation, making the rich richer and the sex workers who share their vision more visibly legitimate as professionals. This ideology also sometimes sees the rights of workers as interchangeable with the rights of managers in sex work, the logic being that the latter are criminalised also.*

To the exasperation of sex working feminists, we are often accused of being invested in these same values. When we make clear that we're asking for the *decriminalisation* of sex work, we are persistently misunderstood to mean *legalisation* and are maligned as liberals, capitalists, or men's-rights activists interested in securing the unimpeded primacy of male sexuality. If the decriminalisation of prostitution is falsely characterised as legalisation and the two are semantically bound together, then advocates for prohibition can blame both policies for the failures of one.

Contrary to its false reputation as a benign sex fun-fair, a regulationist legalisation approach to prostitution is not friendly for sex workers. Regulationist laws manifest in wildly different ways as countries on every continent anxiously try to eliminate selectively, through criminal law, what they consider to be the most pernicious aspects of prostitution. As a whole, these approaches speak clearly to a set of cross-cultural fears that will by now be familiar to the reader – the fear of the visibly queer or diseased body; the fear of migrancy; the fear of sexualised social contamination; the fear of disorderly, unsupervised women roaming freely in society or commanding economic power by organising their work among themselves.

---

* We share the criticism levelled by anti-prostitution feminists at the disgraced International Union of Sex Workers (IUSW) for its decision to allow managers to organise alongside sex workers. This decision makes sense within a politics that is narrowly directed against the power of the state, since managers also face criminalisation. It neglects, however, the fact that managers (in any industry) have power over their workers and can use that power to exploit them. The fundamental purpose of unionisation is to shift the balance of power back to workers, and this cannot be achieved if managers are allowed to organise alongside them.

The 'Charmed' Circle

Paradoxically, to legalise sex work is not necessarily to make the work legal. Rather, it creates a two-tiered system where some is legal and much is not. In Nevada, for example, ten out of seventeen rural counties permit licensed brothels, and no sex work can legally take place in any other areas (including the biggest city, Las Vegas). In the Netherlands, people sell sex legally in brothels and sex clubs, red-light-district windows, *tippelzones* (street sex work zones), sex cinemas, and massage parlours, and these are licensed at the municipal level. Elsewhere, it's still illegal.

Since legalisation in the Netherlands, more than forty per cent of these venues have lost their licence, leaving sex workers fewer places to work legally.[6] In Germany, the Prostitutes Protection Act of 2017 stipulates that all sex workers must be registered and issued with a sex worker ID card. Some of the conditions for receiving this card include testing for pregnancy, STIs, and drug use, as well as mandatory counselling.[7]

Nevada, the Netherlands, and Germany are typical of places that impose rules on how the sex industry may operate. The most precarious sex workers cannot comply and so must work illegally, forming a vulnerable, criminalised 'underclass'.

Trans women, for example, are barred from work in the state-run brothels of Turkey.[8] Many sex workers in Germany live far from the narrowly designated 'prostitution zones', and so work outside them.[9] Many Australian sex workers cannot risk losing their privacy by adding their names to the government's official register of prostitutes.[10] Those in Nevada with a criminal record – often for survival crimes like shoplifting – cannot work in the legal brothels.[11] Sex workers close to the poverty line have no means to pay the rent on a Dutch red-light window (about €80 to €160 per shift, payable in advance).[12] In Senegal, sex workers living with HIV cannot produce a health certificate for the police and so cannot work legally; they are known as *les clandestines*.[13] Married women in Greece are barred from work in state-regulated brothels.[14] Undocumented migrants cannot work in *any* legalised jurisdiction.

For these people, the idea of a 'legalised' framework is meaning-less: the state has drawn a charmed circle and they are not standing inside it. With such significant barriers to overcome, legal status is unobtainable for the vast majority of people, and in most places the amount of illegal, unregulated sex trade far exceeds that of the legal sex industry.

In Germany, a migrant, trans street worker commented on the 2017 implementation of the Prostitute Protection Act, saying; 'I have … no health insurance and often no place to sleep. Now I should get registered? How should that work?'[15] Dee, a migrant sex worker in Austria, says,

> I am powerless here. I don't get a wage slip. I can't take out any credit or loans. I can't lease a car. I pay the tax office, I pay social security, but I won't get a pension. I don't get anything. I also don't get unem-ployment benefits … I can't do anything in my name.[16]

The Dutch sex workers' rights organisation De Rode Draad describes the previous Dutch system of *gedoogbeleid* (policy of tolerance) towards sex workers: 'Formerly these [migrant] women's work was tolerated in the same way as other sex workers' [work]. With the legalisation of one group of women, the work of another group of women now becomes illegal.'[17]

This two-tiered pattern is a universal feature – and failing – of the laws we refer to as *legalisation* or *regulationism*, which is that they tend to empower the worst profiteers. A frequent feature of legalised regimes is that working for a manager is legal, whereas working independently, either on your own or with friends, is fully or partially criminalised. The result is that legalisation *pushes sex workers into working for managers,* and grants managers addi-tional power over workers. As former brothel worker Mariko writes, 'The legal brothels wave their legal status as their carrot so that you feel like *you need them* to make that money.'[18] If your options are to keep working for a manager or to go independent and risk arrest, you may be compelled to accept substandard or even abusive workplace conditions. Former brothel worker Amy Walker says of her time in Melbourne brothels, 'It's in the best interest of the brothel owners for the women to be insecure, uncomfortable and competitive.'[19]

Sex workers have told us that they have known brothel managers in Nevada to tip off the police about independent workers nearby, since these workers represent a threat to their business that can be 'solved' by having them arrested.[20]

Legalisation exacerbates the existing vulnerabilities of sex workers. After the introduction of the Prostitutes Protection Act, a parasite industry immediately sprung up to offer services to struggling sex workers; for example, providing dummy addresses and post forwarding, or helping with German-language application forms. This, of course, allows predators to easily identify sex workers who might be targeted for exploitation: the ones who are uncertain of their rights or close to the breadline.[21] A street-working migrant in Germany says,

> My boyfriend is handling the bureaucracy for me. I try to understand what he does, so that I won't be too dependent on him, but I haven't succeeded yet. Due to the increased complexity of having to register under the Prostitutes Protection Act, I will understand things even less, and those of my colleagues who work with pimps will become even more dependent on them.[22]

Those who have to work illegally under a 'legalised' regime remain subject to many of the harms of clear-cut criminalisation. Their interests and those of the police are still in opposition.[23] In Germany, police now have the power to enter any prostitution venue at any time.[24] As in any criminalised system, when the police act as the de facto regulators of sex work, it not only provides fertile ground for police corruption but blocks those who are in breach of regulations (often the vulnerable street workers most at risk of violence) from accessing police assistance when needed. Many will not report an incident of rape or assault at work, because they may well be opportunistically targeted by the attendant police officer for a charge or other penalty regarding their unauthorised work. During the trial for serial rapist and murderer Adrian Bayley, it emerged that at least ten of his rape victims in Victoria, Australia – where sex work is regulated – were sex workers who had refused to give evidence because of distrust and fear of the police.[25]

As for those sex workers who *can* work legally, regulationism treats them like tearaway adolescents grounded by fretful parents. This results in measures to confine the worker to the four walls of the brothel. Under legalisation in Western Australia in the 1970s and 1980s, sex working women were

> not allowed to have relatives within a 500-kilometre radius, could not have their brothers to visit, were not permitted to have stable relationships with local people and they were restricted to certain areas of the town ... access to the swimming pool was restricted. The women must live in ... the brothels.[26]

In present-day Nevada, legal sex workers are generally issued a curfew for the duration of their contract and must live on the premises. 'Girls do leave all the time, to go to town, to get their nails done', says George Flint, who works as a lobbyist for the brothel bosses in Nevada, 'but I'm a huge fan of girls staying on-premises. Without the controlled environment that the brothel provides, they may turn tricks outside without safety things' (i.e., condoms).[27] If gone for longer than twenty-four hours, workers must pay to be screened for STIs – a useless precaution, given that infection from recreational sex wouldn't show up within two weeks anyway, but one designed to be a financial and social deterrent from straying too long from the 'safety' of the institutional hearth. On the streets of legalised Europe, sex workers may be confined to boxes or shelters and permitted to work legally only within a specific zone.

As well as being hemmed in, sex workers may also be cast out or pushed to the edges, out of sight. Zoning measures which place sex working venues far from the community, in locations such as industrial parks, isolate women and enable violent assailants to target them. In one town in rural Nevada, local ordinance dictates that when a woman stops working at a legalised brothel, she must 'leave town on the next available mode of transportation'. Susan Lopez, director of the Las Vegas Sex Workers' Outreach Project, says 'Sometimes it feels like they just want to keep the "dirty whores" out of the city so that they don't infect the public.'[28]

The 'infectious' body of the prostitute is present in any conversation about regulating sex work, and the discourse around public health makes the harms of regulation more difficult to discern. Oppressive control of people's bodies seems somehow more reasonable when it implicates the health of the whole nation. Why shouldn't sex workers be obliged to submit to health checks? Who could possibly suffer under such laws?

These often-well-meaning observations fail to take into account that whatever is made obligatory automatically produces a co-existent violation of that rule. This is, ironically, profoundly ineffective at protecting public health: should a sex worker be found to have an infection and face punishment, they are given an incentive to evade similar tests in the future. Similarly, those poor enough to be persuaded in a moment of need to agree to condomless sex for extra money are likely to avoid health services in order to avoid criminalisation.[29]

In Senegal, police actively target registered sex workers for extortion or sexual coercion, which is one reason so few choose to register.[30] And in many nations, test results are made available to law enforcement – meaning that HIV-positive workers risk being charged under HIV non-disclosure laws if they are found to be working. Again, this gives sex workers who suspect they may be HIV-positive a huge incentive to *avoid* healthcare services.

We unequivocally support free and easy-to-access healthcare. All over the world, from Cape Town to Glasgow, sex workers campaign for better health services and even set them up, on shoe-string budgets.* But *mandatory* testing is a violation of human rights. Everybody deserves medical privacy and medical autonomy, and mandatory testing violates those core human rights. These policies show sex workers that 'public health' doesn't include preserving *their* bodily autonomy and privacy, and encourages them to deploy savvy

---

* For instance, Umbrella Lane is a sex worker run charity in Glasgow, Scotland, that provides free safer-sex supplies and trains health workers to offer non-stigmatising advice and health services to sex workers. Their website is umbrellalane.co.uk.

evasion strategies in times of infection if they need to put bread on the table.

In 2008, a male sex worker in Australia was convicted of working while HIV-positive and was outed and shamed in the press. (There was no evidence he ever worked unsafely or transmitted the infection.) The media furore meant that the average number of sex workers getting tested in the area per fortnight dropped from thirty to less than two.[31] No one wanted to risk being told that they too were living with HIV – and could become a target for the same furore. Interventions in the name of 'public health' have the opposite effect if they drive sex workers away from healthcare.

Even when it comes to sex workers with no infections, sexual-health certification creates a false sense of security. Not all infections show up on the tests straight away, so any clear result only refers to what you were doing a couple of weeks ago.[32] Inappropriately punitive screening wastes public funds and occupies a huge amount of resources – resources that could be devoted to public-health measures that *actually work*. One public-health professional spoke almost with pride of this superstitious approach in 2006: 'We test these people so often, it's almost like we over-test them.'[33]

Who Benefits?

Far from advocating *for* regulationism, we stand firmly in opposition to it, alongside other feminists. There can be no doubt that this legal framework is not designed to benefit the worker – it lines the pockets of non-prostitute men, most notably those who manage or facilitate prostitution. As the sex worker community blog *Tits and Sass* puts it, 'Legalization serves the man.'[34] Academics Hendrik Wagenaar and Sietske Altink point out that many city authorities in the Netherlands decided to 'cap' the number of brothels at the number that existed when legalisation came into effect. This paved the way for an 'oligopoly' of powerful and ruthless brothel owners to control the market.[35] Employees suffer in the workplace when wealthy capitalists feel comfortable depriving their employees of decent working conditions. In this, the legalised sex industry is not unlike the 'disruptive' startup

Uber, where increasingly precarious workers are heavily regulated by the company they work for, with no rights.

Much feminist analysis of regulationism amounts to flawed and racialised panic about 'trafficking explosions', while complexity is lost in these conversations. The two-tier mechanism is simply another iteration of the exploitative mesh that traps so many migrants when they cross borders and must choose between poverty and illegal work. Criminalised working spaces are inherently vulnerable for the worker, and if migrants are barred by their immigration status from other forms of work, they are primed for exploitation at the hands of third parties in the illicit economy.

Traffickers, pimps, and clients alone do not produce all that is harmful in the sex industry. Any robust analysis of the failings of legalisation would be incomplete without recognising the role the state plays. Under legalisation, police and the criminal justice system still draw the same paycheques from prostitution they do elsewhere in the world, through fines and confiscating cash.

Regulating prostitution allows the state to have its cake and eat it too. On the one hand, it can punish unacceptable sex workers and seize their money. On the other hand, it enjoys the financial perks of a legal sex industry: business taxes on licensed brothels, income from tourism, and a reputation as a fantastic lads' holiday destination.[36]

In the debate, there is often an uncomfortable clash of 'sex workers' rights' and 'consumer rights', with these discussions uncritically framing the sex buyer as someone with a need for (or even a right to) sex. Regulationism says that the sex worker's body must be regulated *for the good of the client*, rather than entrusting that workers will oversee healthcare for themselves.

Crediting the sex worker with the same trust bestowed on the client is incompatible with a perspective that sees 'selling one's body' as a form of self-harm. In this worldview, sex workers represent aberrant bodies who must have medical intervention thrust upon them whether they want it or not.

Fighting the Power

'All prostitution is evil', German author and anti-prostitution feminist Alice Schwarzer said as she opened a conference-panel debate in
Berlin in 2013. Unfurling banners and opening red umbrellas, fifty
sex workers disrupted the event, hoping to draw attention to their
first-hand experience of the topic at hand. Their flyers read, 'Appeal
to Strengthen the Rights of Sex Workers and to Improve Their Living
and Working Conditions'. Schwarzer, undeterred, spoke over them
into the mic: 'Fold up your little umbrellas. You get your turn later.
First we will speak now.'[37]

Germany's ironically named Prostitutes Protection Act was
vehemently opposed by sex worker led organisations before its
implementation in 2016. Since then they have made repeated calls
for the law to be repealed on human rights grounds. As German sex
worker group Hydra e.V. puts it, 'We reject it politically … [it] will
drastically change the living and working conditions of people who
do sex work.'[38]

Media coverage of Germany's sex industry is often saturated with
panic. The idea of 'flat-rate brothels' in 'the bordello of Europe'
garners particular distaste, with little attention given to how this
iteration of commercial sex might alter workers' experiences.[39] Some
flat-rate brothels – where a client pays a one-time entrance charge
and can see multiple workers – pay a guaranteed hourly wage rather
than a client-based commission, meaning that while conditions are
inevitably variable, these jobs can represent a stable income compared to most forms of sex work.[40]

Sex workers in the Netherlands face similar struggles. In 2015,
the mayor of Amsterdam made efforts to stamp out prostitution.
This included planning to close nearly a hundred workplaces and
eroding privacy rights by collecting data on sex workers' mental
health.[*] On Labour Day, after eighteen red-light windows were

---

* In a letter to the Dutch minister of justice, the mayor wrote, 'To test the
degree of a sex worker's self-reliance, it is necessary to gain an insight into his
or her physical and mental health. This to detect possible risks early on. To gain
this insight, it is necessary to process personal data of sex workers.' E.E. van der

closed down (with nearly eighty more set to follow), the workers who'd been made redundant took the city council to court. To draw attention to their case, they occupied one of the closed windows for a day, and later in the year more than 200 people marched through the streets to demand sex workers be given more power in policy discussions.[41]

In the UK, the strip-club industry is, in a sense, legalised in similar ways. Strip-club licensing is tightly regulated by local councils and extremely expensive. This came about in the 2010s in large part because anti–sex work feminists objected to permissive licensing – particularly in terms of what the existence of strip clubs symbolised for non-stripper women. Clubs now have to pay thirty thousand pounds annually for a licence. The clubs started to use 'house fee' systems and on-the-spot employee fines as a way to recoup the money they were newly losing to the licence fees, leading them to over-staff the clubs and forcing the dancers to share fewer customers for less money.[42] In 2014, after a series of protests by a coalition of feminists and local residents, a strip club in London had its opening hours cut by the local council, who gloated about the '676 hours a year less objectification of women'.[43] There was little interest in how 676 less hours of wages a year might feel for the club's staff, none of whom were included in the campaigning.

Time and again, sex workers watch as mainstream feminist intervention and commentary neglects workplace power relations and the need to earn a living. In these analyses, forced health examinations are nothing to worry about, and making sex workers carry an ID around that reveals their real name to potential predators is fine. Schwarzer, despite identifying as an 'abolitionist', supports forced health checks and compulsory registration, while leading feminist Julie Bindel criticises regulationism as a legal model but suggests that the promise of registering prostitutes is one of its few redeeming features.[44]

Laan, Mayor of Amsterdam, 'Letter to the Minister of Security and Justice I.W. Opstelten', 23 February 2015, archived and available in Dutch and English at researchprojectkorea.files.wordpress.com; F. Anna, 'Mayor Amsterdam wants to violate privacy rights sexworkers', Behind the Red Light District, 31 March 2015, behindtheredlightdistrict.blogspot.com.

Many anti-prostitution feminists envision state interference uncritically, as harmless for women or even as a form of protection. Writer Kat Banyard approvingly quotes a woman who tells her:

> If it hadn't been legal I wouldn't have done it ... as I wouldn't rob an old lady or as I won't steal at the shop or something like that. I wouldn't have made this decision if it wouldn't have been so easy and legal. I really had wished that it wasn't legal and that the state – in Germany, you know we call the state 'the father' – and I really had the wish that the father had protected me from that with a good law.[45]

Setting aside the implication that a prostitute should be criminalised in the same way as someone who robs an old lady (a strange implication to find in an ostensibly feminist text), for women to ask the 'father state' for protection from what we might perceive to be our own 'bad decisions' is about as explicit an appeal to patriarchy as you can get. The word *patriarchy* literally translates to 'rule by the fathers' – or the 'father state', one might say.

Though these politics are incredibly frustrating and harmful to sex workers, it isn't hard to see how they happen. Regulationism represents an understandable nightmare: that we are headed for a hyper-capitalist sexual dystopia where men profiteering from women's prostitution is a legitimised, unstoppable industry and women's bodies are cogs in the machine.

We don't disagree that legalisation is bad. In fact, what we'd like very much to do is lead a more robust conversation with people like Bindel, Banyard, and Schwarzer about *why* and *how* exactly it is bad and what the alternatives are. To regulate and control sex workers – with the threat of punishment if they don't comply – is to abandon the poorest and most vulnerable to the shadows. To these workers, legalisation *is* criminalisation, since the ability to work within the law is in practice beyond them. It's tempting to imagine drunken, aggressive stag parties stumbling out of bars in Hamburg's Reeperbahn or Amsterdam's De Wallen red-light districts and think that only additional restrictions, penalties, and punishments will help. But penalties, however they manifest, only make the sex industry more dangerous for sex workers. Penalties mean taking power from workers and giving it to the police, employers, or clients.

Next, we will explore the ways in which *lifting* these laws – rather than adding more – can benefit workers.

8

No Silver Bullet: Aotearoa (New Zealand)

Full Decriminalisation: A legal model that decriminalises the sex worker, the client, and third parties such as managers, drivers, and landlords and regulates the sex industry through labour law.

> A few days after decriminalisation had passed, I attended Auckland district court with a Fa'afafine[1] street sex worker who was the last person picked up for soliciting, on the eve of the third reading of the PRA [Prostitution Reform Act]. The judge looked at her charge sheet and declared, 'Madam, you are no longer a criminal. Your offences no longer exist today. Prostitution is decriminalised. You are free to go'.
>
> – Annah Pickering, New Zealand Prostitutes' Collective (NZPC)[2]

As should be abundantly clear by now, most of the world's prostitution law is not fit for purpose. Criminalising sex work isn't working. At its core, exchanging sex for money – like migrancy, drug use, and abortion – is a legitimate and pragmatic human response to specific needs. Prohibiting it produces evasiveness and risk-taking among sex workers, driving them into the margins and exposing them to even more harm.

Many feminists present the Nordic model as 'the answer' to 'the problem', often without a critical assessment of its flaws ('Sweden's Prostitution Solution: Why Hasn't Anyone Tried This Before?'),[3] but no single piece of legislative reform – no matter its approach – can be a silver bullet for the many problems sex workers face.

The sex workers' rights movement, too, often appears to clutch at magical solutions. The movement is at pains to express in the simplest of terms that what sex workers *want* – and urgently *need* – is decriminalisation. Sex workers brandish the example of New

Zealand,* where the Prostitution Reform Act of 2003 (PRA) decriminalised sex work, as a talisman against the Nordic model: *Not that law, this one.* The logic is sound enough; if the problem is criminalisation, then it seems the answer must be *de*criminalisation.

Readers of this book, too, would be forgiven for hoping that this chapter might produce a watertight solution, a panacea where the dangers of prostitution can be swept away. For that to happen, however, it would have to actually *be* one singular problem rather than a matrix of oppressions that act together.

The example we have of decriminalisation in practice is New Zealand. This *incomplete* achievement of full decriminalisation – we'll come back to this caveat – is the closest we have come to ideal sex work laws. New Zealand has discarded penalties for street work and brothel-keeping, allowing collectives of sex workers to work together, or in managed brothels. Employers are accountable to sex workers through labour law. This framework has won praise from women's-rights organisations, human rights organisations, and international bodies like Amnesty International, Human Rights Watch, UNAIDS, and the World Health Organisation.[4]

Ultimately, as we've indicated, New Zealand does not far enough. While this is unquestionably landmark progress for sex workers' rights, some of the most marginalised sex workers in these jurisdictions are still left behind, unable to enjoy full access to the freedoms granted to other workers when the new legislation was passed.[5] Although the stigma of being a prostitute has lessened, a legal change in place for under twenty years has yet to undo the damage of the millennia that came before it. Some police power has been taken away, but sex workers still have little reason to trust the cops, whose job at a structural level continues to be to harass, surveil, and incarcerate the vulnerable, the poor, and the 'troublesome.' Successive right-wing governments have imposed austerity measures, and Māori, trans, youth and homeless populations are still over-policed and underprotected.[6] Border laws mean that undocumented migrants must

---

* New Zealand is the name coined by European explorers and colonists (*Pākehā*), whereas Aotearoa is the name used by Indigenous Māori people.

keep working illegally, and the failed war on drugs rumbles on. This all shapes a context where, tragically, the murder of sex workers has not ended.[7]

The Global Alliance Against Traffic in Women (GAATW) describes the New Zealand model as 'contradictory':

> On the one hand, the decriminalisation of sex work is a protective factor against the exploitation of sex workers, since they have the right to challenge exploitation. However, the policy which prohibits migrant sex work means that not all sex workers fully benefit from decriminalisation ... [It] is vital that [the benefits are] further strengthened by ... extending rights to migrant sex workers who are holders of temporary permits.[8]

Nonetheless, the sex workers' rights movement is clear in its demand for decriminalisation, with the New Zealand model as a *starting point*.* While there is much to say about what could be improved upon in New Zealand, none of it detracts from the evidence that *criminalisation* – of work, workplaces, clients – harms sex workers and must be lifted. The problems of the New Zealand model lie in the fact that some elements of criminalisation (such as the criminalisation of drugs, migration, and migrant sex work) remain, thus maintaining some of the harms present in any criminalised nation. This draws criticism from the anti-prostitution movement but, clearly, the solution to the problem of the remaining vestiges of *criminalisation* is not to retreat from *de*criminalisation.

With the privilege of uninterrupted space afforded to us in this chapter – so rarely afforded to sex working feminists attempting to discuss legal reform – we can explore what is *effective* in reducing harms in these iterations of decriminalisation. We can examine the usefulness of claiming these countries as a benchmark for nations where commercial sex, culture, economy and population may look

---

* Because New Zealand decriminalised sex work in a single legal change, the terms *New Zealand model* and *decriminalisation* are often used interchangeably. We want to separate these ideas: the New Zealand model is *one example,* while decriminalisation is *the wider concept*, which could be implemented differently in different places.

very different. We can speak to a future where the full decriminalisation of sex work benefits sex workers around the world.

'It's Work, It's Working'[9]

What is decriminalisation? Decriminalising prostitution is a process of overturning criminal laws (for example, soliciting) and administrative or civil orders (for example, ASBOs) that punitively target street work, collective work, employed work, advertising, and so on. These are the laws designed to punish workers and eradicate workplaces. In a decriminalised system, the sale, purchase, and facilitation of commercial sex has largely been shifted out of the realm of criminal law and into the framework of commercial and labour law. The purchase and facilitation of sexual services remain subject to the same reasonable laws on coercion, exploitation, bullying, assault, and rape that apply in other contexts.

In New Zealand, street-based sex workers can work with groups of friends, in brightly lit, central areas of their choosing, without fear that they or their clients will be arrested. Public-health researcher Lynzi Armstrong has found that 'sex workers now feel more able to work ... in well-lit, safer places'. Sex worker Claire says that prior to decriminalisation 'we were in the darkest places ... just real shady' and contrasts this to the present, where 'it changed ... a lot of us had to hide before then'.[10] Armstrong writes, that for street-based workers, the 'screening process [of clients] is ... less complex in a decriminalised context'.[11]

Ninety per cent of street-based sex workers interviewed for a review of the PRA commissioned by the New Zealand Ministry of Justice told researchers that they felt the law meant they had employment rights.[12] Another ninety per cent felt they had occupational health and safety rights. Impressively, ninety-six per cent said they felt they had legal rights. (These high numbers are all the more impressive because they may well be better than for workers in other kinds of precarious labour. Call-centre work, for example, is 'designed in a way that strips workers of their rights'.)[13]

Catherine Healy, the national coordinator and a founding member of the New Zealand Prostitutes' Collective, speaks to this enhanced sense of power for the worker:

> Decriminalisation means that people have a higher expectation of things working well and working properly ... an expectation that things can be put right ... 'Who can I tell?' is the first response instead of what we used to hear [before decriminalisation], like, 'Well, there's nothing we can do about it.'[14]

Indoor sex workers can work with friends from a shared flat as an informal co-operative without having to jump through bureaucratic hoops or fear raids or arrest. Both indoor and outdoor workers can communicate clearly and directly with clients regarding services, condom use, and money, without having to rush or use euphemisms.* As one worker said, 'I tell them from the start what they can and can't do, really'. Managers are accountable to labour laws designed to protect sex workers, and reporting a manager will not mean the loss of an entire workplace and job. Assaulting or abusing a sex worker – as an employer or as a client – remains criminalised (as does the assault or abuse of any worker), but the *work* of sex work is instead governed by the same labour laws and employment protections that apply to many other workplaces.

Sometimes people aren't sure what employment protections might look like in the context of sex work. The idea of labour protections in brothels seems alien and strange, occasionally even risible. (Indeed, one conservative commentator objected to the term *sex worker* precisely on the grounds that it 'suggests there's a union, pension fund' – an absurd definition of a worker given that many workplaces lack union representation, and, increasingly, a pension pot.)[15] Needless to say, sex workers don't find laughable the notion

---

* For example, under a fully criminalised regime like the US, a sex worker may describe her services in an ad as 'intimate full-body massage'. In different contexts this euphemism may mean full intercourse, French kissing, or oral sex with no condom. Abusive clients will often exploit this ambiguity by pressing for an activity (such as unprotected intercourse) that the provider is not happy to do, claiming that it was implied to be on offer.

that they should have access to workplace protections and security. Some examples of labour rights that sex workers expect within a decriminalised context include protection from sexual harassment at work, adequate breaks on shifts and between shifts, a requirement for management to supply safer sex materials (and to back up workers in insisting on safer sex with clients), provisions barring workplace discrimination, and the right for sex workers to refuse clients and to receive support from their managers in doing so. Surveys have found that sex workers in all sectors feel more able to refuse clients since passage of the PRA, and workers in the managed sector are now far more likely to have actually done so.[16] Are these laughable? Vicky, a managed sex worker in Wellington, says, 'From what I hear from women ... who worked before the law changed, it's a lot better for us, and it's a lot more open, and girls aren't having to fight their own battles every night between clients and employers.'[17]

It is worth remembering that there is an intrinsic class tension in all workplaces – between the interests of managers or owners, and the interests of workers. The structural role of managers and owners is to extract as much profit as possible from the labour of employees. In theory, decriminalisation brought sex workers' workplaces in New Zealand up to the legal level of other workplaces in terms of workers' access to rights and safety. This is not to say, however, that decriminalisation has eliminated exploitation, any more than other workplaces (for example, restaurants or construction companies) are free of exploitation simply because they are not criminalised. Decriminalisation cannot wash away class conflict between the interests of management and employees; instead, it aims to mitigate the *intense* workplace exploitation that is propped up and fuelled by criminalisation.

To be able to work indoors with friends without fearing arrest *adds to a worker's power in their relationship with their manager.* Ultimately, if they need to, the worker can leave and work with friends. This power is reflected in the data: since New Zealand implemented decriminalisation, fewer people are working for managers; more are working in shared flats with friends.[18] (Managers even complain about this!)[19] When working together is criminalised, predators can use the threat of arrest against workers, as we've seen throughout this book. In contrast, workers in New Zealand's small co-op workplaces are not vulnerable to violent men using the law against them in this way. As a worker in this set-up told the Prostitution Law Reform Committee, 'I feel more confident now I know I've got rights ... there's no fear now of being caught by police. It was difficult when I was younger. I felt like a criminal, and was less assertive.'[20] Petal, another private worker, says,

> I just think the biggest thing with the law change is ... emotional support for the girls to say, 'Yeah, you're not doing anything wrong ... you're only doing a job.' I think that's the biggest thing ... saying it's not illegal ... that's what I like about the law. It's supportive.[21]

New Zealand implemented some additional forms of regulation which – unlike German or Dutch laws – are designed with the benefit of sex workers in mind, rather than profiteering, control, or punishment. For example, one provision of the Prostitution Reform Act stipulates that if a sex worker wishes to leave the sex industry, they can access Social Security immediately, without facing the temporary penalty to which they would have been subject had they 'voluntarily' left another job.[22]

How did this come to be? In 1988, the New Zealand government started funding a newly formed sex worker led group: the New Zealand Collective of Prostitutes. The NZPC was funded as a health-promotion group; its founding basis was that sex workers should be able to 'take control of their own health programmes as much as possible in order to determine the direction those programmes should take'. The NZPC immediately identified the criminalisation of prostitution as a serious problem in the lives of sex workers and pressured the government to set up a committee to investigate decriminalisation.[23]

Throughout the 1990s, the NZPC worked on bringing their bill to Parliament; in 2000, MP Tim Barnett brought forward a proposal to decriminalise sex work. It passed in 2003, significantly helped by the intervention of MP Georgina Beyer, a Māori trans woman and former street-based sex worker. Beyer told Parliament, 'It would have been nice to know that ... I might have been able to approach the authorities and say: "I was raped, and, yes, I'm a prostitute, and, no, it was not right that I should have been raped." '[24]

The law was shaped by sex workers themselves. Beyond any one specific regulation, this was crucial – the extensive involvement of sex workers in putting together the law and the focus on the *safety of people who sell sex* are what distinguish decriminalisation from other legal models. Indeed, the text of the PRA describes its first priority as being to 'safeguard the human rights of sex workers'.[25] It is extremely unusual for legislation that deals with the sex industry to explicitly conceive of people who sell sex as having rights at all, other than the right to be rescued from being 'sold'.

Toppling Police Power

Decriminalisation, first and foremost, *displaces the police* as the de facto regulators of sex work. This is their role in systems where some or all aspects of the sex industry are criminalised – in other words, in every legal system discussed so far in this book. Decriminalisation rolls back a police officer's powers to make an unfair-but-lawful arrest and reduces their window of opportunity to bully, exploit, harass, extort, or assault a person with considerably less power.

In New Zealand, like everywhere else, the police would use their power over sex workers to humiliate. Shania, a street-based worker in New Zealand, says, 'Some would just be pricks and take you in and I think the worst thing was that you'd get taken in and then you'd have to go to court in the morning in your working gear ... And it was ... just like degrading.'[26]

What can decriminalisation do to address these harms? Bianca, a street-based sex worker, tells researchers, 'I didn't used to call the police, I would just call my friend ... But now it's changed ... the police are watching out for the safety of us which is quite good.'[27] Shannon, a street-based sex worker, describes a bad experience of reporting rape to the police prior to decriminalisation, saying, 'Well, that was shit', but adding that 'now that the law's changed it's different ... If it had been decriminalized back then, it would have been different.'[28] Dora, a street-based trans woman in New Zealand, says,

> You can work now. That made me feel safer; it made me feel better about the police. I used to hide from them before ... [especially after] being done for soliciting ... but I mean I feel much better about being on the street, just more legitimate, just more like 'yeah I'm allowed to be here'.[29]

This is reflected in the data: 65 per cent of street-based sex workers told researchers that they felt the police had improved as a result of the law, and about 70 per cent that they feel 'most or all' cops now look out for their safety.[30] This unusually positive sex worker–cop relationship made headlines around the world in 2014, when it was reported that a police officer had helped a woman get the money that she was owed by a client – by escorting the client to a cash machine. The police spokesperson told journalists, 'It sounds remarkable but it is a routine thing. Police would help any citizen having a disagreement whether they were a sex worker or working in a pizza shop.'[31]

It's important not to get carried away. The New Zealand model hasn't solved every problem. GAATW observe that, in not going far enough with decriminalising sex work, the New Zealand model fails to protect migrants:

> The prohibition of migrants engaging in sex work has created a contradictory context in which New Zealand–born sex workers enjoy the benefits of a work context that is characterised by openness and transparency, while migrant sex workers are essentially forced 'underground' and are vulnerable to exploitation and violence as a result.[32]

Migrants in New Zealand say that their criminalisation makes reporting crimes difficult, and they report precarious and exploitative working conditions.[33] Sex worker Amy explains how she has encountered this kind of pressure: 'One client will say ... they will think that you don't have a proper visa here and they will say ... give them a good service and if not, they will tell the police.'[34] Clients and employers alike are able to prey on their precarious status.

Healy, from the NZPC, says, 'I think it's important to remember that … the law facilitates the conditions that are required for trafficking by rendering the sex workers who are working as migrants illegal … the concern is very, very real.'[35]

In a recent survey of sex workers in New Zealand, 3 per cent had been raped by a client in the last year, and the majority of that 3 per cent had not reported it to the police. Street-based workers were more likely than indoor workers to be victimised, and significantly less likely to report.[36] This is unsurprising; street-based sex workers are both more likely than others to have mental health problems and more likely to use drugs.[37] In other words, they are more likely to have fewer resources and to be living within a nexus of stigmatised and still-criminalised experiences and communities. As with many nations, the shortcomings of New Zealand's criminal justice system mean that complainants who use drugs or are mentally ill are more likely to be disbelieved at the time of initial reporting and more likely to be knocked back (or to step away) from the system.[38] This is not specific to sex workers: the vast majority of survivors of sexual violence, both in New Zealand and around the world, do not report their experiences to the police. Survivors are well aware that the criminal justice system is more often a site of further trauma than a site of healing or justice.

Sex workers have many reasons to mistrust the police. Decriminalisation addresses *one* of those reasons. As street worker Sally tells researchers, 'I don't really relate well to [the police] … But I've never had a problem when I'm out [working]. They're really good. They're just like "are you alright?" and you know, they've never asked for my name.'[39] Fellow sex worker Hollie says, 'I still don't trust them. I mean a cop's a cop. But yeah, they try and talk to me and make sure I'm alright and I'm just like "yeah just leave me alone, I'm fine."'[40] Decriminalisation has given sex workers like Hollie and Sally the power to keep the police at arm's length. Pania also speaks to this theme, saying, 'They come round heaps but like they all know what I'm doing. They see me and they'll just blabber or something. And I'm like "well can you go away now. You're going to stop a client from coming". And they're all good about it.'[41]

The power to keep the police at arm's length is a power that criminalisation largely denies to sex workers and other over-policed populations all over the world. However, New Zealand sex workers appear to have and exercise this power to avoid police intrusion at least some of the time. No change in law can fundamentally alter the attitude of a police officer – and they will continue to symbolise intrusive violence to the poorest and most vulnerable – but decriminalising prostitution offences explicitly removes one of the tools in their arsenal. Police officers in decriminalised jurisdictions find that an avenue to exploit or bully is 'closed off' to them – a strategy far more effective and radical than trying to 'sensitize' machismo outlooks and siege mentalities.[42]

It is closing off avenues to abuse – by rolling back police power – that will reduce harms against sex workers. This must be implemented with a slew of other reforms that address the other vulnerabilities of over-policed populations, such as Indigenous sex workers, and sex workers of colour. Those who will continue to be treated as troublesome and disorderly – like drug users, queer youth, migrants, or homeless people – know that decriminalisation is *not enough by itself*. As Alex Vitale writes, 'Reforming police forces to make them better trained, more accountable, and less racist are all laudable goals. But they leave intact the basic institutional functions of the police, which have never really been about public safety or crime control.'[43] When people like drug users and sex workers are made vulnerable by the denial of their basic human rights, and when an officer can easily gain cash or sexual gratification from their compromised position, it is not enough to hope that those tasked with controlling their lives will simply be nice.

Feminist Scepticism

Debunking the misconception that *decriminalising* sex work is the same thing as *legalising* it is one of the biggest frustrations of sex worker advocacy. The two words are deceptively close in what they suggest, and many people use one in error when they mean to use the other. The thinking is understandable: Surely both terms simply mean something is legal? So it's worth going over the difference once more. *Decriminalisation* positions workers within the sex trades as primarily rights-holders who need additional support, while *legalisation* or *regulationism* (as seen in the previous chapter) positions prostitutes as unruly, alarming, and needing to be controlled through specific punitive measures. What flows from the perspective of decriminalisation is a system where the knowledge, safety, and rights of people who sell sex are prioritised – and, in order to do this, the regulations placed on the sex industry are shaped by sex workers themselves.

As well as genuine error, this 'mix-up' is often a useful bit of lexical sleight of hand. One anti-prostitution journalist, for example, writes, 'If you think decriminalisation will make prostitution safe, look at Germany's mega brothels' – an incoherent argument that smears the failings of the latter onto the former.[44] The New Zealand model is often dismissed out of hand, with opponents paradoxically arguing that giving *workers'* rights to people who sell sex will increase the exploitation of prostitutes.

New Zealand's approach to sex work stokes fears among anti-prostitution feminists. They often worry that if prostitution were decriminalised, job seekers would be forced into prostitution by job centres or at high-school careers fairs.[45] In reality, no such thing happens. New Zealand job centres do not display sex industry–related job ads, and forcing sex workers to start or stay in sex work – including under the threat of losing out on unemployment benefits – is banned.[46] The Prostitution Reform Act states that 'A person's benefit, or entitlement to a benefit, under the Social Security Act 1964 may not be cancelled or affected in any other way by his or her refusal to work, or to continue to work, as a sex worker.'[47]

This is not an unfamiliar system; in the UK, working in a strip club or on a webcam is completely legal, yet jobs in strip clubs or on webcams are not foisted onto job seekers or high-school students. The *current legal status* of porn and peep-shows does not result in office-job candidates being obliged to provide a lap-dance or naked selfies in a job interview.

Decriminalised prostitution, it is argued, would mean no sex workers could ever be protected from sexism and abuse in the workplace. The national director for the Nordic Model Australia Commission asks, 'What can police do if sexual harassment is part of your working conditions? You can report rape, but it's already a form of rape.'[48]

Recognising something as *a job* in some contexts and *sexual harassment* in others is something we, as feminists, collectively manage to do all the time. For example, it is already part of some people's jobs to give massages, but if you do an office job and your boss asks you for a massage, that is harassment. Such an occurrence is not a legitimate argument against allowing people to sell massages.

It is striking and painful that these concerns about sexual harassment are so back-to-front. Far from failing to grant such protections to sex workers, decriminalisation is the only measure that can start to make these workplaces protections *possible*. Far from making the concept legally meaningless, decriminalisation *extends* protections against workplace sexual harassment *to sex workers*. In some ways, the repeated construction of 'all sex work is rape' is reminiscent of sexist teenage boys 'joking' about whether the sexual assault of a prostitute constitutes rape or 'theft': both rely on the idea that, because you sell sex, it is intrinsically absurd to imagine that society might recognise harm to you as a real violation.

In fact, in 2014 a sex worker in a brothel in New Zealand took her manager to an employment tribunal for sexual harassment and won her case. Such a ruling would be unimaginable anywhere that sex workers' workplaces are criminalised. *There is no labour law in a criminalised workplace.* The tribunal ruling in the case commented, 'Sex workers are as much entitled to protection from sexual harassment as those working in other occupations ... Sex workers have the same human rights as other workers.'[49]

Some feminist reservations about decriminalisation seem at times to be a little out of touch with sex workers' lives. One campaigner, for example, worries that under the New Zealand model, we'd be obliged to pay taxes and that 'as a regular "worker" ... she could be pursued [for non-payment] by the tax authorities'.[50] Sex workers actually already are obliged to deal with taxes and tax penalties, whether their work is legal or illegal, including in the UK currently, and in the Nordic countries whose laws she is advocating.[51] To be treated as 'a regular worker' under decriminalisation might mean that sex workers have the opportunity to benefit from their contributions in the form of labour rights and workplace protections, benefits currently denied to them in Britain, Sweden and Norway.

Even if some fears are misplaced it is nonetheless crucial for us to examine decriminalisation with a rigorous eye. Will people who are struggling in the sex trade under decriminalisation get meaningful assistance to leave or otherwise change their situation? And what does 'meaningful assistance' look like?

In New Zealand, the single strongest initiative to help people leave sex work is that sex workers do not receive a 'voluntary unemployment' penalty upon quitting, and so can apply for benefits immediately.[52] Other than this (and that decriminalisation removes the obvious impediment of a criminal record for prostitution), it is unclear whether enough has been done to make provisions for people who want to transition into new work, aside from a handful of shelters run by religious groups, NGOs, or individuals.[53]

Lauren, a sex worker and activist who has worked in both the UK and New Zealand, says, 'I feel like it's difficult to separate [a shortage of funding for services] from a broader social context in New Zealand, where homelessness is extremely high, and domestic violence services for migrant women have been cut and years of neoliberal government has destroyed social welfare.'[54] As we saw in the example of Sweden in the previous chapter, inadequate provision in this area is not unique to New Zealand's sex work model. It could easily apply in the UK – where cuts to welfare and services are increasingly harsh.

Sex workers' needs are diverse in ways which aren't necessarily covered by generic 'exit' funding. In South Africa, for example, people in the sex trade identify intersecting health issues such as TB, HIV and mental illness as factors that impede their ability to leave sex work.[55] Indigenous sex workers of Canadian group Sex Workers United Against Violence note that services should reflect their specific needs as Indigenous people, such as funding to Indigenous communities for self-administered education and vocational training, and other programmes related to housing, health, income assistance and childcare that are based in Indigenous traditions.[56]

This form of specialised support often comes from within the community. Vancouver-based organiser Kerry Porth says 'sex work support organisations have been supporting women to exit sex work forever and we generally do that off the side of our desk and without there being any specific funding for it.'[57] This is not a burden that should be placed on sex workers and other communities – it is incumbent upon the government to fund non-judgmental support services that meet the needs of sex workers on their terms, rather than forcing solutions on them that weren't asked for, or stigmatising them as lazy, damaged, or sinful.

Some feminists are concerned that decriminalisation will make it harder to tackle exploitation and punish abusers. On the contrary: it is criminalisation which means that sex workers must hide from the police for fear of penalties such as arrest, eviction, or deportation.[58] Abusers know that sex workers cannot call on the state for help and are unlikely to be taken seriously in the occasional instances that we do. The criminalisation of prostitution drives violence against *all women*; criminalised sex workers become a 'training ground' where violent men can experiment with perpetrating violence, safe in the knowledge that their targets are unable to protect themselves or to get justice. Having 'practiced' on sex workers, such men often then move on to non–sex working women – a pattern we see in predators like Peter Sutcliffe and Adrian Bayley.

Many worry that if we allow the sex industry to exist without prohibition, we are condoning it and it will proliferate. This concern arguably reveals an unspoken belief that keeping prostitution dangerous – through making it illegal – acts as a useful downward pressure what might otherwise be an 'unchecked' tendency to sell sex. (Occasionally, this 'unspoken' belief is spoken: when sex workers met with the Irish justice minister to argue that criminalisation would make them less safe, the minister responded by observing that sex workers' increased vulnerability to violence would at least deter women from entering the trade.)[59]

It is worth noting that the number of sex workers in New Zealand has remained stable – the 'explosion' predicted in some quarters has not materialised.[60] There is no evidence that changes to criminal law – including its removal – have a significant impact on the numbers of people who sell sex. As sex worker Jenny tells researchers,

> I've worked illegally in other jobs, you know, I've worked under the table and that sort of thing. So … I guess I would say I probably would have done it [sex work] anyway. But, you know, I certainly felt that because it was legal … I felt more safer about it.[61]

Nonetheless, conversations in feminist spaces become a tug-of-war. One anti-prostitution feminist organisation comments, 'There are no advantages to sending the message to men that women and girls are commodities to be bought. The disadvantages to a society that sends this message, however, are severe and very difficult to reverse.'[62] At the other end of this argument lies the unheard voice of sex workers like Pania, who speaks to the actual result of punitive 'messaging': 'I've had clients who have come from countries where it's illegal to be a client, and they have been on edge, scared, and difficult to manage.'[63] Whose worries, then, are to be given more weight? The relatively abstract anxieties of non-prostitute women about 'messaging', or the everyday, practical needs of working class people who want their work to be safer? The latter choice is the essence of harm reduction.

Real, daily violence against sex workers happening all over the world *today* cannot be held up for comparison with a feminist forecast of a yet-to-happen future. Compare these concerns to the reality under prohibition, in which criminalising sex work has come *nowhere near* eradicating commercial sex, and violence is seen as a hazard of the job. The criminalisation of sex work and the 'messaging' flowing from it – that 'women's bodies are not for sale' – clearly has not prevented people from Stockholm to New York to Harare from selling sex. It should be obvious that the real message of criminalisation is that people who sell sex exist outside of safety, rights, or justice.

Still, one anti-prostitution writer grapples unsuccessfully with the concept of harm reduction,

> Will wearing a condom reduce the impact of rape? … If I 'consent' to letting a man penetrate me … but he doesn't give me chlamydia in the process, does that mean what happened to me is ok? That I

should feel good about it? That society should turn away? ... Why is it that they refuse to admit that the harm of prostitution cannot be dealt with through condoms and brothels?[64]

Those asking these questions would do well to consider posing them – with respect and compassion – to current sex workers who've survived sexual violence or who live with HIV. They, and not those pontificating in the abstract, are best placed to say whether condoms are immaterial *to them* during their continued time in the sex trade.

It is not a new idea to work on smaller measures to mitigate immediate harms, while at the same time working towards more radical solutions that target the root of the problem. Feminist campaigners protest for access to abortion while *at the same time* organising for better sex education, more money for mothers, and increased access to contraception. We fight tooth and nail for more domestic-violence shelters while *at the same time* working towards a world where domestic violence no longer occurs. We work towards a world without borders while *at the same time* organising against specific incursions by immigration enforcement into homes, schools, and hospitals.

This process is perhaps slower than many anti-prostitution feminists would like. For these commentators, nothing short of criminalisation – and the complete and rapid abolition of prostitution that is assumed to follow – is radical enough. But to decriminalise sex work is to treat as important the immediate, material safety of people who are selling sex. In that, decriminalisation is a deeply radical demand, far more so than throwing the world's poorest sex workers to the wolves in an attempt to annihilate the sex industry through increased policing.

Dudu Dlamini, a sex worker in South Africa, understands the far-reaching impact decriminalisation will have. Describing her fears as she prepares to advocate for decriminalisation in a trade union meeting, she recounts,

> I thought about all the bad things that are happening in the streets because of criminalisation. What if my daughter joins the sex industry and these bad things happen to her? If I don't say these things

to these people they won't support decriminalisation, and then what about my daughter?[65]

Decriminalising sex work will not solve all the injustices of the world: that is too huge a problem for any one legislative change. But it will make people who are selling sex, right now and tomorrow, safer while they are doing what they need to in order to survive. That is profoundly worthwhile. As Joyce, a sex worker in New Zealand, says, 'It changed the whole street, it's changed everything. So it was worth it.'[66]

Conclusion

The likelihood that your acts of resistance cannot stop the injustice does not exempt you from acting in what you sincerely and reflectively hold to be the best interests of your community.

– Susan Sontag[1]

Each of us must find our work and do it. Militancy no longer means guns at high noon, if it ever did. It means actively working for change, sometimes in the absence of any surety that change is coming.

– Audre Lorde[2]

In the autumn of 2016, the two of us and a colleague attended a feminist conference in Glasgow. A somewhat hostile but curious woman came over to speak with us. She ran an NGO, it turned out, that defended the rights of migrant women across Europe, and she wanted to talk to us about the men – the *punters*. Weren't they *disgusting*, she wanted to know. How could we disagree that they should be punished? We agreed that clients are often bad, but explained that punishing them produces harms for people who sell sex. We mentioned the evictions of sex workers in Nordic countries. Our interlocutor agreed that these evictions are real; women are thrown out of their houses in Scandinavia, yes. In fact, she told us, migrant women *come to her NGO* complaining that they have been thrown out of flats or hotels in Sweden, sometimes in the middle of the night. She continued, a note of derision entering her voice: 'When that happens, I just think to myself', she told us, mimicking her interactions with these evicted women, 'I just think, lucky you: at least you're not murdered'. She rolled her eyes at us.

We aren't asking you to love the sex industry. We certainly don't. We are asking that your disgust with the sex industry and with the men – the *punters* – doesn't overtake your ability to empathise with people who sell sex. A key struggle that sex workers face in feminist spaces is trying to move people past their sense of what prostitution *symbolises,* to grapple with what the criminalisation of prostitution *materially does* to people who sell sex. People in these spaces see abstractions like 'objectification' and 'sexualisation' as universally relatable everywoman concerns. When we point out that the policies which flow from such discussions often lead to sex workers being evicted or deported, we are seen as raising 'niche' issues – or as obtusely unable to understand the 'bigger picture'.[3] We need to push our sisters to grapple with the 'niche' questions. Nobody can build a better, more feminist world by treating sex workers' *current material needs* – for income, for safety from eviction, for safety from immigration enforcement – as trivial.

Both carceral and liberal forms of feminism are attractive because they offer seemingly easy answers to complex problems. Women's work is underpaid and undervalued? *Ask for that raise!* Sexual violence is endemic? *Fund more cops!* There's commercial sex online? *Pass legislation to kick sex workers off the internet!* Carceral feminism even styles itself as radical in doing so: radically uncompromising with male sexual entitlement, radically seeking to 'burn down' the sex industry.[4] Such radicalism evaporates on closer examination: *cops are not feminist.* The mainstream feminist movement is correct in identifying prostitution as a patriarchal institution; they conveniently miss that policing is, too. Attempting to eradicate commercial sex through policing does not tackle patriarchy; instead, it continues to produce harassment, arrest, prosecution, eviction, violence, and poverty for those who sell sex.

The Nordic model sweeps trafficking under the rug. Poverty and barriers to legal migration are what create vulnerability for migrants; arresting clients and sending undocumented people home on the next flight does nothing to remedy this. Although it purports to take away the power of abusers, no solution that comes in the form of increased power to the police can be a good substitute for putting power in the hands of sex workers themselves.

People in the sex trade should not be the *focus* of the anti-trafficking movement, but its *leaders.* Not even the staunchest anti-prostitution activist has a better incentive to tackle violence and exploitation in the sex industry than someone who's selling sex. A Global Alliance Against Traffic in Women notes that

> This divisiveness within the field has deprived global anti-trafficking efforts of a crucial ally, who could dramatically improve the outcomes of the anti-trafficking response through its valuable insider knowledge of the industry, the people involved in it, and the conditions of work.[5]

Prostitute activism is never given the foreground in the mainstream anti-trafficking movement, and some would consider the very idea absurd – but if they were given the chance, sex workers could capably lead by example.

'First, Do No Harm'[6]

In Myanmar, the AIDS Myanmar Association (AMA – *ama* is the Burmese word for 'big sister') sees poverty and financial disempowerment as a key driver of trafficking in the sex industry, so they provide training on financial management and assistance obtaining identity cards and opening a bank account. Founding member Kay Thi Win says,

> Our dream is of a sex-worker-led organisation: for the community, with the community and done by the community. AMA is a fully sex-worker-led organisation and we can make our own decisions based on need. We are standing by our independence from other organisations and we know best the problems and issues of our daily life as sex workers ... We believe that money is power.[7]

Members of the Durbar Mahila Samanwaya Committee (DMSC), a sex worker group in West Bengal, formed thirty-three small committees around the state, called self-regulatory boards (SRBs). Each committee has six sex workers, along with a local councillor and four other health- and labour-sector professionals. In the space of three years, more than two thousand people in the sex trade were screened by their local SRBs, with just under 10 per cent of them considered to be 'minors or unwilling adults'. They were offered assistance and support to leave their situation, including being accompanied to their home by another sex worker or housed in DMSC accommodation. Other sex workers screened were provided with counselling, health care, and the option to join peer-led community schemes designed to reduce sex workers' vulnerability. One of these is a bank run entirely for and by sex workers, which combats debt bondage by helping sex workers open accounts and save money.[8]

Bharati De of DMSC comments that mainstream anti-trafficking 'rescue' style interventions are

> simply too small in scale to be of any real use. There are organisations offering training to sex workers in stitching, sewing, candle-making and so on, with which they can make only around two to three thousand rupees per month, but a sex worker today, even without a family, needs a minimum of five thousand rupees to live in Kolkata.[9]

The feminist movement should be paying attention to groups like DMSC: they pose a significant threat to exploitative pimps. Only a few decades ago, the entirety of the sex industry in Sonagachi, a large red-light district in Kolkata, was controlled by mercenary gangs headed by *hadiya*, or madams. Through the power of collective bargaining and union meetings, DMSC has brought 80 per cent of Sonagachi's brothel bosses to heel: they now abide by a fairer fee and commission system.[10]

Indian sex worker group Veshya Anyay Mukti Parishad (VAMP) is coming up with similar solutions. They formed special taskforces called *Thanta Mukti Samithis* – (TMS) or Conflict Redress Committees – that intervene when a sex worker is being harassed or exploited in and out of the workplace. Global Alliance Against Traffic in Women observed that through the TMS process, a madam (brothel owner) raised a dispute with a pimp who tried to bring a minor to her workplace. The minor was reunited with her parents and given counselling and support in making a police referral. Meanwhile the pimp's details and description were shared among the TMS groups in neighbouring areas.

Thai group Empower also adopts a pragmatic approach to dealing with managers. Som, a migrant sex worker who attended their English language classes, eventually disclosed that her employer was restricting her movements, docking her wages, and had confiscated her passport.

She was scared to antagonise the employer by attempting to run away and leave her travel debt unpaid, as he knew where her family lived. She was also frightened of detainment or deportation, and refused to make a report or identify herself as a trafficking victim to the police. She actually wished to continue doing sex work and repaying her debt, but with more freedom and flexibility in her working conditions. She asked Empower for backup in negotiating this with her boss, and they successfully helped her establish a new agreement with him; the same repayment schedule, but working independently elsewhere.

There is a sense among carceral feminists that justice has not been served if there are no bad guys in jail, but a community-led approach means *putting sex workers first*. GAATW comments: 'The solutions are not always obvious or conventional; in some cases sex workers have to get creative in order to find the best, 'first, do no harm' solution to the concrete situation.'[11]

These practical and effective approaches are a world away from ill-conceived and abusive 'humanitarianism' sometimes forced onto sex workers in the global south. For example, sex workers in Cambodia and India are regularly subjected to 'raid and rescue' operations, in which women seized from brothels are assigned minimum wage jobs in garment factories.* Sex workers simply want to be asked what they think is best *for them*, rather than being forcibly rescued from the life they are trying to build for themselves. As the slogan of Cambodian sex worker group Women's Network for Unity states, 'Don't Talk to Me about Sewing Machines, Talk to Me about Workers' Rights'.[12]

No Throwaway People

Sex workers' rights cannot be disentangled from other rights movements. Human rights for all sex workers means tackling injustice across a broader spectrum than just prostitution law, and so

---

* One company, The International Princess Project, manufactures 'punjammies' – pajamas made by women who have been 'rescued' from brothels. They aim to 'create pathways to freedom for women escaping the ravages of sex slavery to achieve lives of hope and dignity'. See sudara.org/collections/punjammies.

decriminalisation is one step on a long route. For example, as we saw in chapter 4, the war on drugs is a sex-worker issue. If some brothel workers can take their boss to court for wage theft, but these same workers are still spending every penny of those wages on dangerous drugs that could be made cheap and safe, then our movement has much further to go.

Likewise, as chapter 3 made clear, borders are a sex worker issue. Our movement's work isn't finished if the police are letting some sex workers go about their business on the stroll but arresting and deporting their migrant colleagues. Stigma and discrimination in the wider health care system, too, are sex worker issues. It's going to take more than a sex worker friendly STD clinic to remedy the many other ways sex workers have been failed by racist, transphobic, and ableist medical gatekeeping.

For as long as people continue to navigate the margins by selling sex, all the social issues affecting them are sex workers' rights issues. As former sex worker Janet Mock writes, 'We will not be free until those most marginalized, most policed, most ridiculed, pushed out and judged are centered. There are no throwaway people.'[13]

These frontiers are key for sex worker activists because decriminalisation alone will not 'solve' the things that marginalise people and drive them into sex work. Decriminalising sex work will not suddenly make anyone less poor; sex work is an effective strategy for resisting poverty, but it doesn't address poverty systematically. Neither criminalising nor decriminalising the sex industry eradicates, for example, homelessness; the way to end homelessness is to get people into stable and affordable housing, with support that's appropriate to them.[14] What the removal of criminal law *can* do is help ensure that people are safer while they're doing what they need to do, right now, to survive.[15] Decriminalisation can also simply prevent life getting worse for sex workers, unlike all other models we have considered.

Decriminalisation needs to be implemented in tandem with other vital policies that remedy the precarity of marginalised sex workers. The idea that it would work by itself is a self-serving expression of the interests of privileged sex workers whose lives would be more or less fine if they had access to labour rights in the sex industry. For them, criminalisation is the *only* problem, so lifting that criminalisation is enough. Just as we remind non–sex working feminists that there is more to sex workers' struggle than bad clients, so too should the sex worker movement be aware that, for poor sex workers, for migrant sex workers, for disabled sex workers, and many more, it is not enough to overturn soliciting laws or brothel-keeping laws.

Our movement must centre the experiences and the activism of sex workers of colour, who bear the brunt of extreme interpersonal and state violence. The lives of these workers, particularly Black women, are often seen as disposable. The novelist and poet Aya de Leon writes, 'In an era where we in the US fight for the idea that Black Lives Matter, to be Black and female, African and a sex worker, is to inhabit a location of deepest neglect and disregard.'[16] Whether African, African-American, or members of the African and Caribbean diasporas, Black sex workers suffer from the violent alignment of racialised poverty, societal stigma, and abandonment and abuse at the hand of the police. This compounds the violence committed against them when perpetrators receive the signal that Black prostitutes are nobody's priority and can be brutalised without accountability. Black sex workers continue to be incarcerated, deported, and evicted simply for trying to survive.

Advocates for decriminalisation must take care not to over-emphasise the potential of small changes in policing. Decriminalising sex work will not magically end police profiling of Black people – all it can do is roll back police powers in specific ways and give sex workers some recourse when police over-step those powers. We should be wary of harsh bylaws that effectively re-criminalise sex workers, devolving power back to police officers by a different route. Where police still retain power over sex workers via routes other than prostitution law (for example, the prosecution of migrants or those in possession of drugs), they abuse it.[17]

Sex worker advocates need not feel defensive about this realistic view of decriminalisation. The limits of legal reform are not unique to sex work. Spousal-rape law reform has not ended rape in marriage. Nor has access to legal abortion achieved complete reproductive justice. These measures are just the necessary first steps on a longer route that all feminists should be travelling in collaboration.

Decriminalisation is necessary but not sufficient for sex worker justice, just as abortion access is crucial but not sufficient for reproductive justice.

Our position is not that the sex industry is valuable or desirable in itself. As feminists, we know the misogyny and violence we've experienced in the sex trade to be abhorrent. But the real end of sex work can only happen when marginalised people no longer have to sustain themselves through the sex industry; when it is no longer necessary for their survival.

To make sex work *unnecessary*, there is much work to do: winning rights for freedom of movement, labour rights, access to services and to work without threat of deportation, employment alternatives, better welfare provisions, cheaper housing, support services for single mothers, and so on. If everybody had the resources they needed, nobody would need to sell sex.

To be impatient with this goal is to deprioritise the physical and economic safety of sex workers while continuing to use them as cannon fodder in the fight against patriarchy. Hoping for instant abolition and harm eradication by knocking 'the problem' of prostitution on the head with criminalisation is in itself harmful. Instead, a strategy of harm reduction through decriminalisation would make sex work safer right now. If we are then able to end poverty and borders (and the litany of other ills discussed here), sex work might indeed whither away and effectively be abolished for all but the small number who genuinely love it.

'The Terrorism That Is Practiced by the Man and by Individual Men'[18]

Be wary of liberalism. It is not enough to consider yourself an ally of sex workers if your politics remain a mere defence of 'equality and respect' or the freedom 'to do with one's body as one wishes'.

Not that there is anything objectionable about ideas like this. In homes and workplaces, benign rhetoric about stigmatised and outcast groups being 'just like everyone else' can be an effective antidote to social ostracism. Representation is also a powerful political tool; a blockbuster movie with a relatable sex worker character could go a long way in fighting a cultural fondness for 'dead hooker' jokes. At any level, tackling stigma against sex workers is crucial work.

However, those who support sex workers' rights – and indeed, even some sex workers – often understand the struggle to be *only* about fighting stigma, better representation, achieving 'acceptance', and securing respect for what we do.

When Swedish sex worker and activist Jasmine, whom we discuss in chapter 2, was stabbed to death by the father of her children, her death triggered a protest outside the Swedish Embassy in London. Sex workers gathered to raise awareness about their opposition to the *sexköpslagen*, with signs saying 'Stigma Kills'. Stigma did, of course, kill her – her killer stigmatised her as worthless and disposable, as many women are stigmatised.

But this is only part of the picture. At the time of her death, Jasmine had been locked in an acrimonious dispute with her former partner to regain custody of her children, who had been removed from her and given to her abusive ex-partner on the grounds that she was an unfit mother. In the eyes of Swedish social workers, her job as an escort was evidence for this assessment. By giving the children to him, the state aggravated the situation, forcing Jasmine to continue to meet with him in order to see her children. It was during one these meetings that he fatally stabbed her.

It's not enough to locate the blame for Jasmine's death solely in the violence of her ex-partner or to dismiss it as unrelated to prostitution law, as some feminist commentators have.[19] He murdered her, but in a context where the state of Sweden ignored and tacitly condoned his history of violence. Jasmine's life and death show how misogyny and oppressive state mechanisms work in tandem.

Ending violence against women requires interrogating the full extent of how it operates. Everyone can understand a loaded gun and the damage it can cause. But who has the licence to carry the gun? Who can use it with impunity? When and why were they bestowed this power? These things are just as important as the murderous intentions of the person pulling the trigger. We must tackle gender-based violence at a human level *and* find a different strategy for upending the systems that underpin it – and some of these solutions will overlap. It is crucial to understand the symbiotic coexistence of these mechanisms and not divert all attention to one 'fix'.

Representation is a feminist issue, and campaigns to get women into boardrooms, into government cabinets, and onto banknotes are all very well. For some, the link from representation to stigma or respect is clear. The *symbol* of the woman-as-president may well help someone look more credible as the only woman on a board of directors.

But all this is ineffectual without a material analysis of working class lives. To only examine the way sex workers are *represented* in society – instead of the mechanisms of their oppression – is a politics of gesture. We could see sex workers fighting stigma by starring in Netflix shows, living in the White House – or even appearing on banknotes – but without real legislative and economic change, the most marginalised people will continue to hide from cop cars in the shadows, sleep on the streets, and languish in prison cells and detention centres.

'Power to Prostitute Women All Over the World – Power to All Women'[20]

At the beginning, we said this book would not be a personal memoir or a tale of empowerment. *Empowerment* is a word that comes up a lot in discussions of sex work. It is overused to the point of satire (often in media depictions of middle class sex workers), to talk about sexual rebellion, the thrill of sudden cash, or the so-called free choice of the individual to sell sex. These flippant conversations frame having sex for money as an inherently empowering thing. This liberal perspective – that one person's ability to profit off their own sexual objectification can magically overturn the status quo for all – leaves many feminist critics dubious.[*]

---

[*] 'I want real choices. I want to change the system within which those choices are made, not just use the language of choice to benefit or to comfort me ... I want collective empowerment, not temporary empowerment for only

We too are critical of glib descriptions of 'empowerment' or 'choice'. Whilst it is up to each sex worker to describe their own experiences (and knowing that such arguments are often a defensive response to stigma), we share the view of other feminists who observe that prostitution is generally contextualised by a *lack* of choices, not an abundance.

'Empowerment' is a red herring. We see it deployed as clickbait in headlines like 'Is Sex Work Empowering or Enslaving?', 'I Became an Escort to Empower Myself, but It Only Crushed My Soul', 'It Happened to Me: I Was an Escort for Eight Years, Believing It Would Empower Me, and It Didn't', or 'Sex Worker and Mother: Yes, I AM Empowered by My Job'.[21] These invocations of personal feeling distract from a far more complicated conversation – about colonialism, capitalism, and patriarchy.

Unfortunately for sex workers, the push to bring these structures back into focus often seems to come with a side order of bile. Critiques of 'choice feminism' almost inevitably escalate towards scathing judgment in which the work prostitutes do is not 'real work' and the legitimate economic arguments for their strategies are not only *not radical* but contemptible or traitorous. Journalist Meghan Murphy writes, 'Your "freedom" to make "choices" may well represent your feelings of personal empowerment in your own life, but in no way does this liberate anyone but you and, in fact, your "choice" may exist at the expense of another woman's oppression.'[22]

This type of statement is rarely applied to women's 'choice' to take jobs propping up the carceral state. One anti-prostitution feminist, for example, takes to the familiar confessional mode to offer up an essay which could easily have been titled, 'It Happened to Me: I Loved Jail, and You Will Too'. The essayist writes that her experiences, 'thankfully, led me to jail', adding, 'I never expected that jail would be my saving grace. Now I hope to make it the same for more victims like me.'[23] At the end of the essay, it is revealed that the author now works as a prosecutor. When sex workers write these kinds of personal essays – 'I Sold Foot Porn to Fund My Way through

College!' – they are inevitably told, 'It may have been okay for you, but do you really think your experience is representative? Think of the women harmed in this system.' If ever an essay was crying out for such a response, surely it is this glowing review of arrest and jail. However, mainstream feminism seems more comfortable asking these questions of cam-girls than of prosecutors.

Sex workers are subject to disproportionate scapegoating in this regard. One ostensibly feminist anti-prostitution organisation suggests that prostitution causes significant environmental damage, highlighting sex workers' use of medications (presumably oral contraceptives) and make-up.[24] By contrast, we do not see such widespread contempt for feminists who seek to navigate the patriarchal marriage contract as best they can. Nor should we. Not everyone has the resources to tear down the institution of marriage – an institution that is shaped by women's economic needs in much the same way that prostitution is.

Sex workers who do not appear in glossy magazines sometimes define the ability to migrate away from poverty, to say no to loan sharks, to go to night school, or to securely leave an abuser as 'empowerment'. Instead of wrangling over whether the individual triumphs of sex workers over adversity constitute 'real feminism', we should be asking a more useful question: What has taken power away from them? How can they reclaim it?

The most potent source of untapped power for sex workers is not sexual liberation, social rebellion, or even money, but solidarity. The sex worker community is expanding rapidly as people wake up to the potential of standing shoulder to shoulder. 'For three years I lived a divided life: the life of a woman and the life of a prostitute', says Barbara, co-leader of the sex worker church occupation in Lyon, France, that launched the modern sex worker movement. 'And one day, in 1975, I realised by talking to others, it could no longer go on'. When news of the Lyon occupation broke, sex workers all over France were inspired: over the following week, they occupied churches in Paris, Marseille, Grenoble, Saint-Étienne, and Montpellier. The idea that a prostitute being abused by the police one day could forcibly take over a church with dozens of friends the next was exhilarating and hopeful. 'None of us will go to prison', the protestors fearlessly proclaimed. 'The police will have to massacre us in the church.'[25]

In the same decade but half a world away, Brazilian prostitute Gabriela Leite was similarly inspired into action. After her friend was murdered by a policeman in 1978, she began speaking publicly about life on the streets.[26] She hitchhiked alone around Brazil to enact her vision of a movement of *putas revolucionárias*, persuading those she met in the streets and in brothels to get organised – to refuse to be brought to heel, to transform repression into rage, and to be the protagonists of their own stories.

Nobody will give us power: not the police, not our bosses, not our clients. Power is always won. We need to take what's owed to us, as activists like Gabriela and Barbara demonstrated four decades ago. They knew then what the movement knows now: that being deprived of the chance to speak is not voicelessness. Forty shouting sex workers protesting deportations outside a government building are easy to hear.[27] One hundred sex workers blockading traffic are easy to see.[28]

Sex workers have been made to listen; now it is our turn to speak. We are not waiting to be invited into the feminist movement. We have always been here. In 1977, Black Women for Wages for Housework stated that 'part of the work of being a prostitute is to be made an example of what it costs us to refuse the poverty the Man forces us to live in, to be a whip against other women'.[29] The threat of being 'treated like a whore' compels women to keep their distance from us; but the way a whore fights the power is of value to everyone.

The politics of prostitution should not be a feud between women but a collaboration. As much as we all do, sex workers want a better future – one where everyone gets their fair share of resources and where survivors can access healing and justice. We want a future where feminist revolt and resistance is uplifted by the brazen spirit of the prostitute who demands to be safe, to be paid, and to be heard. In the words of Black Women for Wages for Housework: 'When prostitutes win, all women win.'

Acknowledgements

We owe so much to our community – and such debts are incredibly joyful things to have and to acknowledge. So many people have taught us and supported us in so many ways both during the writing of this book, and in terms of forming our politics over (almost) the last decade. First thanks should perhaps go to Luca, who brought both of us into the community to begin with, and who does (and has done) a staggering amount of work, much of it unseen, to ensure that there is a sex worker community in the UK. Thank you to Jo Breeze (and to the new baby Breeze, who sat in with us – in foetus mode! – throughout much of the process) for putting in place a structure that enabled us to finish this project. It is not exaggeration to say we truly might never have completed this work if it were not for you, Jo.

Thank you to Frankie Mullin for your unwavering support, friendship, and insight; to Melissa Gira Grant for your encouragement, comments, and your inspirational work; to Chloë for so much, but particularly for your Magdalene laundries insights and your lasagne. Thank you to Charlotte Shane for your writing and sisterly love. Thank you to Niki, Laura, Cari, Sarah, and all the ECP women: your strength, community, and unwavering fight for sex workers are a beacon of love.

So many people (including many names we have already mentioned) read all or part of the draft manuscript and gave us comments. Thank you so much to everyone who did so; your insights, encouragement, and sometimes tough corrections helped us more than we can say. (Any errors that remain are, of course, our own.) Thank you to Emily Dall'Ora Warfield, to Zoé Samudzi, to Jenn Clamen and to PJ Starr. Thank you to Janet Eastham, Hamish Allen, Alison Phipps, Sarah Woolley, Meg-John Barker, Brit Schulte, Justin Hancock, Sarah Dorman, Sami, William and Natalie Huntley-Clarke, Clare Havell, and Hollis Robin. Thank you to Tom Peters and Tom Sissons, whose optimism and encouragement provided two shoves in the right direction.

Thank you to Ray Filar for your support and for the brilliant time we had with you in Wiltshire; thank you to Ash, for listening to three trips' worth of sex workers' rights chatter; thank you to everyone at SCOT-PEP – particularly Stew, Staci, Fiona, Raven, George, Jewel, Jamie, Lily, and Fran. Thank you to everyone at SWARM: to Ethie, Catty, Caoimhe, Yigit, Jordan, Vanessa, Priscilla, Travis, Jet Young, Grace, Fez, Aggie, Martha, Konsequent, Lauren, Daisy, Emma, Amber, Harley, and Nikita. Thank you to Dani Anderson (particularly for your delightful comments on the draft, which, as you know, we loved), Justin, Nine, Bridget Minamore, Aisling Gallagher, Marika Rose, Clark, Naomi Beecroft, and Nell. Thank you to Ruth Jacobs for your incredible comments on 'A Victorian Hangover'. Thank you to Lilith Brouwers for your invaluable help with 'A Charmed Circle'. Thank you to everyone who was on the Lackett Retreat – particularly Eleanor Newman-Beckett for your crucial role embodying our ideal reader. Thank you to April, Alice and Devon, for being there. Thank you to Jennifer Moore, whose gentle friendship and stickler-ish nature has undoubtedly made us better people and whose kind attention to this book has sharpened and clarified our work in so many ways. Thank you to Tash for your incredible help with the you-know-what.

Love and gratitude to Laura Lee, who tragically died while we were in the process of completing this work. Your unwavering and tireless advocacy for sex workers is an inspiration, and you remain deeply missed and often thought of.

Thank you to everyone whose writing, thinking, and work has contributed so much to our thinking and understanding. Thank you in this regard to Sarah Mann, to Charlotte Cooper, to Sofie Buckland, to Mariame Kaba, to Laura Agustín, to Peech, to Wendy Lyon, to Reni Eddo-Lodge (both for your work in general and for your gentle and timely suggestion that we could write a book), to Nic Mai, to Thierry Schaffauser, to Chi Adanna Mgbako, to Jay Levy, and to Julia O'Connell Davidson. Thank you to Carol Leigh, Gail Pheterson, and

Nickie Roberts. Thank you to Caty Simon and the entire *Tits & Sass* team: the work you do maintaining a space for in-depth, complex conversations is extraordinary. Profound thanks to the global sex workers' rights movement, which is organizing every day to transform the world for the better and to which we owe an immense debt.

Thank you to everyone at Verso, who have been unwaveringly supportive and encouraging. Particular thanks, of course, to Rosie Warren and Sarah Grey, who have been amazingly attentive, patient and kind editors. Thank you to the Open Society Foundations, whose decision to give us a grant for this project gave us the irreplaceable gift of time.

Our final thanks go to Dean and James, whose support – both material and emotional – has been truly incalculable. Thank you both so, so much.

Notes

Introduction

1 Millett, K. (1976) *The Prostitution Papers: A Quartet for Female Voice*, New York: Ballantine Books.

2 Green, V. (March 1977) 'We're not criminals': Prostitutes organize', *Spare Rib* 56, quoted in Kinnell, H. (2008) *Violence and Sex Work in Britain*, Oxford, UK: Routledge, 22.

3 Anonymous ('suzyhooker') (14 December 2017) 'Black Trans Sex Worker Leaders Reflect On December 17th', *Tits and Sass*, titsandsass.com.

4 Aimee, R., Kaiser, E. and Ray, A. (2015) 'A short history of *$pread*', in *$pread: The Best of the Magazine That Illuminated The Sex Industry and Started a Media Revolution*, New York: The Feminist Press, 20.

5 Otis, L.L. (1985) *Prostitution in Medieval Society: The History of an Urban Institution in Languedoc*, Chicago: University of Chicago Press, 61.

6 Roper, L. (Spring 1985) 'Discipline and Respectability: Prostitution and the Reformation in Augsburg', *History Workshop* 19, 3–28.

7 Agustín, L. (2012) 'Letter from the prostitute that didn't want saving, 1858', *The Naked Anthropologist*, lauraagustin.com.

8 Anderson, L. (25 January 2017) '100 Years Ago Today, Sex Workers Marched for Their Rights in San Francisco', *San Francisco Magazine*, modernluxury.com.

9 Luddy, M. (1992) 'An outcast community: The "wrens" of the curragh', *Women's History Review* 1:3, 341–55.

10 Mgbako, C.A. (2016) *To Live Freely in This World: Sex Worker Activism in Africa*, New York: NYU Press, 92.

11 White, L. (1990) *The Comforts of Home: Prostitution in Colonial Nairobi*, Chicago: University of Chicago Press, 206.

12 Mgbako, C.A., *To Live Freely*, 14.

13 Schlaffer, N. (23 October 2016) 'The Unsung Heroines of Stonewall: Marsha P. Johnson and Sylvia Rivera', *Femmes Fatales*, sites.psu.edu/womeninhistory; Yaeger, L. (19 August 2016) 'Before Stonewall: Remembering the Compton's Cafeteria Riot', *Vogue*, vogue.com.

14 Booth, M.L. (18 February 1976) 'New Tricks in the Labor Zone', *Harvard Crimson*, thecrimson.com.

15 Chateauvert, M. (2014) *Sex Workers Unite: A History of the Movement from Stonewall to SlutWalk*, Boston: Beacon Press, 47–82.

16 Ibid.

17 Prunier, G. (2015) 'The Ethiopian Revolution and the Derg Regime' in Prunier, G. and Ficquet, E. (eds) *Understanding Contemporary Ethiopia: Monarchy, Revolution and the Legacy of Meles Zenawi*, London: C. Hurst & Co, 209–32.

18 James, S. (2012) 'Hookers in the House of the Lord' in *Sex, Race and Class, the Perspective of Winning: A Selection of Writings 1952–2011*, Pontypool, Wales: The Merlin Press, 110–29.

19 Krajeski, J. (28 March 2014) 'Loud and Proud', *Slate*, slate.com.

20 Martin, L.R. (2012) '"All the Work We Do As Women": Feminist Manifestos on Prostitution and the State, 1977' in *LIES: A Journal of Materialist Feminism* 1, 217–34.

21 Reuters (25 October 2007) 'Prostitutes sew lips together in protest', *Reuters*, reuters.com.

22 Friedman-Rudovsky, J. (24 October 2007) 'Prostitutes Strike in Bolivia', *Time*, time.com.

23 Gall, G. (2016) *Sex Worker Unionization Global Developments Challenges and Possibilities*, London: Palgrave Macmillan.

24 Friedman-Rudovsky, 'Prostitutes Strike in Bolivia'.

25 Millett, *Prostitution Papers*; Agustín, L.M. (2007) *Sex at the Margins: Migration, Labour Markets and the Rescue Industry*, London: Zed Books (see especially chapter 4).

26 Millett, *Prostitution Papers*.

27 Gillis, J. (1981) *Youth and History: Tradition and Change in European Age Relations, 1770–Present*, Cambridge, MA: Academic Press, 166–7; Iriye, A. and Saunie, P. (eds) (2009) *The Palgrave Dictionary of Transnational History: From the Mid-19th Century to the Present Day*, Basingstoke, UK: Palgrave Macmillan, 45.

28 UCL Bloomsbury Project (2011) 'Society for the Prevention of Cruelty to Children – History', ucl.ac.uk/bloomsbury-project/institutions/nspcc.htm.

29 Vegan Feminist Network (13 March 2015) 'A Feminist Critique of "Service" Dogs', veganfeministnetwork.com; Vegan Feminist Network (1 February 2015) 'The Reality of Sex Trafficking in the U.S. and Women-Positive Alternatives to LUSH Cosmetics', veganfeministnetwork.com; Williams, J. (2 December 2016) 'Why is Pokemon Go like prostitution?' Nordic Model Now!, nordicmodelnow.org.

30 Phipps, A. (2017) 'Sex Wars Revisited: A Rhetorical Economy of Sex Industry Opposition', *Journal of International Women's Studies* 18:4, 306–20.

31   Raymond, J.G. (11 December 1995) 'Perspective on human rights: Pros-
     titution is rape that's paid for', *Los Angeles Times*; Barry, K.L. (1995)
     The Prostitution of Sexuality, New York: NYU Press, 70.

32   See Willis, E. (1979/1992) 'Lust horizons: Is the women's movement
     pro-sex?' in *No More Nice Girls: Countercultural Essays*, Minneapolis:
     University of Minnesota Press, 3–14.

33   Ferguson, A. (1984) 'Sex War: The Debate between Radical and Libertar-
     ian Feminists', *Signs* 10:1, 106–12; Chancer, L.S. (2000) 'Pornography to
     Sadomasochism: Reconciling Feminist Differences', *Annals of the Amer-
     ican Academy of Political and Social Science* 571, 77–88.

34   Leidholdt, D.(1993) 'Prostitution: A violation of women's human rights',
     Cardozo Women's Law Journal 1:1, 133–47.

35   Dworkin, A. (1993) 'Prostitution and Male Supremacy', *Michigan
     Journal of Gender and Law* 1:1, 1–12.

36   Leidholdt, D., 'Prostitution: a violation of women's human rights'.

37   Høigård, C. and Finstad, L. (1992) *Backstreets: Prostitution, Money,
     and Love*, Cambridge: Polity Press, 114–15.

38   Millett, *Prostitution Papers*.

39   Chateauvert, *Sex Workers Unite*.

40   Lockett, G., Lawson, M., Irie, J., Gold, G., B, Hima., Aarens, B. (1997)
     'Showing Up Fully; Women of Colour Discuss Sex Work' in Nagle, J.
     (ed.) *Whores and Other Feminists*, New York: Routledge, 209.

41   Mann, S. (2014) 'More Than Survival Strategies: Sex Workers' Unhappy
     Stories', Athabasca University, Alberta (MA Thesis).

42   Ray, A. (31 March 2013) 'Why the Sex Positive Movement is Bad for Sex
     Workers' Rights', Audacia Ray blog, audaciaray.tumblr.com.

43   Mullin, F. (11 February 2015) 'Sorry, UK Sex Work Protesters, There's
     No Such Thing as a "Pimp Lobby"', *Vice*, vice.com.

44   International Committee on the Rights of Sex Workers in Europe
     (March 2016) 'Feminism Needs Sex Workers, Sex Workers Need Fem-
     inism: Towards a Sex-Worker Inclusive Women's Rights Movement',
     Intersection briefing paper #2, sexworkeurope.org.

45   Flynn, J. (22 April 2016) 'The Church's Lingering Shadows on Sex Work
     in Ireland', *University Times*, universitytimes.ie.

46   Amnesty International (11 August 2015) 'Global movement votes to
     adopt policy to protect human rights of sex workers', amnesty.org.

47   Some examples: Alabama Whitman (@lunarfish1524) Twitter, 6:07am,
     23 October 2015; Liberation Language (30 January 2014) 'Amnesty
     International for Traffickers of Women', *Liberation Language*, liberation
     language.wordpress.com; Mix, J. (19 August 2015) 'On Prostitu-
     tion, the Left has Taken a Right-Wing Turn', Medium (@JonahMix),
     medium.com.

48   Mackay, F. (24 June 2013) 'Arguing against the industry of prostitution:

Beyond the abolitionist versus sex worker binary', *Feminist Current*, feministcurrent.com.

49 Turner, K.B., Giacopassi, D. and Vandiver, M. (2006) 'Ignoring the Past: Coverage of Slavery and Slave Patrols in Criminal Justice Texts', *Journal of Criminal Justice Education* 17:1, 181–95.

50 Whitehouse, D. (24 December 2014) 'Origins of the police', libcom.org.

51 Rushe, D. (1 March 2017) 'Police say they were "authorized by McDonald's" to arrest protesters, suit claims', *Guardian*, theguardian.com.

52 Hayter, T. (2004) *Open Borders: The Case Against Immigration Controls*, London: Pluto Press, 25.

53 Ibid., 36–43.

54 Luibhéid, E. (2002) *Entry Denied: Controlling Sexuality at the Border*, Minneapolis: University of Minnesota Press, 41.

55 Ibid.

56 Bernstein, E. (2007) 'The Sexual Politics of the "New Abolitionism"', *Differences* 18:3, 128–51. See also Bernstein, E. (2010) 'Militarized Humanitarianism Meets Carceral Feminism: The Politics of Sex, Rights, and Freedom in Contemporary Antitrafficking Campaigns', *Signs* 36:1, 45–71.

57 Bianco, M. (19 Decembet 2014) 'One Group Has a Higher Domestic Violence Rate Than Everyone Else – And It's Not the NFL', *Mic*, mic.com.

58 Laville, S. (14 June 2015) 'Woman strip-searched and left naked wins damages from Met police', *Guardian*, theguardian.com.

59 Packman, D. (5 April 2011) '2010 NPMSRP Police Misconduct Statistical Report', National Police Misconduct Reporting Project, policemisconduct.net.

60 Bloomer, N. (28 November 2017) 'Woman reports rape to police – and is arrested on immigration charges', Politics.co.uk.

61 Corvid, M. (2016) 'London's Romanian Sex Workers Are Worried That Brexit Would Screw Them', *Vice*, vice.com.

62 Eigendorf, J. and Neller, M. (2013) 'Nur eine Welt ohne Prostitution ist human' [Only a world without prostitution is humane], Welt, welt.de.

63 Bindel, J. (13 July 2016) 'Decriminalising the sex trade will not protect its workers from abuse', *Guardian*, theguradian.com.

64 Bindel, J. (2017) *The Pimping of Prostitution: Abolishing the Sex Work Myth*, London: Palgrave Macmillan.

65 MacKinnon, C.A. (2011) 'Trafficking, Prostitution, and Inequality', *Harvard Civil Rights–Civil Liberties Law Review* 46, 271–309.

66 Amnesty International (26 May 2016) 'The Human Cost of "Crushing" the Market: Criminalization of Sex Work in Norway', report, EUR/36/4024/2016, amnesty.org.

67 Sex Workers' Rights Advocacy Network (SWAN) (November 2009) 'Arrest the Violence: Human rights abuses against sex workers in central and eastern Europe and central Asia', Open Society Foundations, opensocietyfoundations.org.

68 Whitford, E., Gira Grant, M., and Xiaoqing, R. (15 December 2017) 'Family, Former Attorney of Queens Woman Who Fell to Her Death in Vice Sting Say She Was Sexually Assaulted, Pressured to Become an Informant', *The Appeal*, theappeal.org.

69 Ibid.

70 Hardy, K. (2010) '"If you shut up, they kill you": Sex Worker Resistance in Argentina' in Hardy, K., Kingston, S. and Sanders, T. (eds) *New Sociologies of Sex Work*, London: Routledge, 167–80.

71 Ray, S. (2 November 2016) 'Sex-workers' rights activist's death shrouded in mystery', *Times of India*, timesofindia.indiatimes.com.

72 Revista Forum (2018) 'Denúncia: Prostitutas que defendem o reconhecimento da profissão são assassinadas em Belém' [Complaint: Prostitutes who defend recognition of the profession are murdered in Belém], *Revista Forum*, revistaforum.com.br.

73 Havell, C., Lee, V. and Stevenson, L. (5 January 2013) 'The Honey Bringer: Stories from Sex Worker Freedom Festival', Sex Worker Open University, video, Vimeo (user: documentary x), vimeo.com/113934399.

74 Nation Team (9 June 2010) 'I still have 83 more women to kill', *Daily Nation*, nation.co.ke.

75 Haron, M. (20 September 2012) 'Sex Workers Protest Raw Footage in Thika', video, YouTube (user: Musa Haron), youtube.com/watch?v=g NImWNzPDHY.

76 Mgbako, *To Live Freely*, 195.

1. Sex

1 Corbin, A. (1990) *Women for Hire: Prostitution and Sexuality in France After 1850*, trans. A. Sheridan, Cambridge, MA: Harvard University Press, 53.

2 Corbin, A. (1986) 'Commercial Sexuality in Nineteenth-Century France: A System of Images and Regulations', *Representations* 14, 209–19.

3 Gira Grant, M. (2014) *Playing the Whore*, London: Verso Books.

4 Acton, W. (1870/1972) *Prostitution, Considered in Its Moral, Social and Sanitary Aspects*, Oxford: Routledge, 166.

5 Kraus, I. (3 December 2017) 'Can the vagina be a work tool?', Scientists For A World Without Prostitution, trauma-and-prostitution.eu.

6 Eveleth, R. (17 November 2014) 'Why No One Can Design a Better Speculum', *The Atlantic*, theatlantic.com.

7   Lombroso, C. and Ferrero, G. (1893/2004) *Criminal Woman, the Prostitute, and the Normal Woman*, Durham, NC: Duke University Press.

8   Zola, E. (1880) *Nana*, Paris: Charpentier.

9   Acton, *Prostitution, Considered*.

10 Schneider, M. (26 February 2015) 'There's No Medicine for Regret: Incredibly Misogynist Venereal Disease Posters from WWII', *Dangerous Minds*, dangerousminds.net.

11 Gira Grant, M. (22 March 2016) 'Who Birthed The Anti-Trans Bathroom Panic?', *Pacific Standard*, psmag.com.

12 Bersani, L. (Winter 1987) 'Is the Rectum a Grave?', *October* 43, 197–222.

13 Berg, S. (1 September 2015) 'Dead Rentboys tell no tales', *Feminist Current*, feministcurrent.com.

14 Doezema, J. (2010) *Sex Slaves and Discourse Masters: The Construction of Trafficking*, New York: Zed Books, 18.

15 Feminist Whore (14 December 2009) 'Anti-Sex-Trafficking Dude Calls Prostitutes "Nasty, Immoral" – Prostitute Not Shocked', *Feminist Whore*, feministwhore.wordpress.com.

16 Knight, I. (15 November 2009) 'I'm Belle de Jour', *The Times*, thetimes.co.uk.

17 Burton, A. (1994) *Burdens of History: British Feminists, Indian Women, and Imperial Culture*, Chapel Hill: University of North Carolina Press, 129.

18 Gira Grant, M. (14 March 2014) '"I Have a Right to My Own Body": How Project ROSE Tries to "Save" Sex Workers', *Rewire*, rewire.news.

19 Davis, O. (10 November 2016) 'Don't Be A Hero', *The New Inquiry*, thenewinquiry.com.

20 Finnegan, F. (2004) *Do Penance or Perish: Magdalen Asylums in Ireland*, Oxford: Oxford University Press.

21 Ryan, C. (25 May 2011) 'Irish Church's Forgotten Victims Take Case to U.N.', *New York Times*, nytimes.com.

22 McGarry, P. (25 June 2011) 'Laundry orders run sex workers' aid group', *The Irish Times*, irishtimes.com.

23 Good Shepherd Sisters Ireland (3 October 2013) 'Pre-Budget 2014 Submission Focus on Prostitution and Human Trafficking', Good Shepherd Sisters, goodshphersisters.com, 2.

24 Ryan, C. (5 July 2011) 'Penance for a Sorry Past', *Irish Examiner*, irishexaminer.com; O'Sullivan, N. (2 August 2013) 'Magdalene compensation snub is "rejection of Laundry women"', *Irish Post*, irishpost.com.

25 Ruhama (n.d., accessed June 26 2018) 'Turn Off the Red Light', campaign leaflet, ruhama.ie/advocacy-awareness-campaigns-and-media/campaigns/turn-off-the-red-light.

26 Scottish Coalition Against Commercial Sexual Exploitation (9 September

2011) 'There's no medicine for regret', reproduction of poster, Facebook (group: Scottish Coalition Against Commercial Sexual Exploitation), 9 September 2011; Ellen Grogan, quoted by FeministWhore (@FemWho), Twitter, 5:23am, 26 November 2015: 'We don't wanna criminalize sellers, but these ppl r "pimps" and should "rot in HIV infected pits"' #FEMINISM YAY.

27 Comment by ElisabethAlice (11 November 2010) 'How do you feel about prostitution?', Mumsnet.com/Talk/relationships/1080476-How-do-you-feel-about-prostitution.

28 Høigård, C. and Finstad, L. (1992) Backstreets: Prostitution, Money, and Love, Cambridge, UK: Polity Press.

29 Comment by Mary Smith at Murphy, M. (4 September 2013) 'Femen was founded and is controlled by a man. Exactly zero people are surprised', Feminist Current, feministcurrent.com.

30 Moore, J. (22 December 2013) 'NWC2013: write-up & some opinions', Uncharted Worlds, uncharted-worlds.org; Anonymous, quoted by @desiredxthings,Twitter, 12 August 2015: '@EavesCharity We are made into sub-human sexual goods, buying the prostituted is like buying a loaf of bread'; Caitlin Roper (@caitlin_roper), Twitter, 1:04pm, 12 August 2015: 'Difference between working at McDonalds and prostitution is in prostitution you're the meat #sexworkWA'; Object! (@ObjectUK) Twitter, 1:00pm, 18 May 2018: 'Does it strike you as odd that, particularly in regards to pornography, a dog has more rights than a woman? There are things one can do to a woman which would land one in prison if you did it to a dog'; see also the Campaign Against Sex Robots, at campaignagainstsexrobots.org.

31 Ditum, S. (1 December 2014) 'Why we shouldn't rebrand prostitution as "sex work"', New Statesman, newstatesman.com.

32 Glosswitch (@glosswitch) Twitter, 4:46pm, 14 October 2014: '@CCriado Perez @sarahditum You "absorb" the nuance in the jizz'; Lewis, H. (@helenlewis) Twitter, 5 May 2014: '@MFrancoisCerrah I did think that was not the most appropriate title! "Orifices for sale" was presumably vetoed by the TV Times'; Devlin, S. (@JerikoGenie) Twitter, 9 August 2015: '@LoriAdorable poppet. Leave the hair splitting to those of us who read the facts as opposed to sucking & fucking all day #ICM2015 @hrw'.

33 Doezema, J. (2010) Sex Slaves and Discourse Masters: The Construction of Trafficking, New York: Zed Books, 137–8.

34 Megarry, J. (20 April 2015) '#FreetheNipple or #FreeMaleDesire? Has social media really been good for feminism?' Feminist Current, feministcurrent.com; Freeman, H. (19 April 2016) 'From shopping to naked selfies: How "empowerment" lost its meaning', Guardian, theguardian.com.

35 Turner, J. (28 October 2017) 'Millennial women are too quick to shame men', *The Times*, thetimes.co.uk.

36 Cameron, D. (2014) 'Minding our language', troubleandstrife.org.

37 Fletcher, S., comment on Bodenner, C. (26 Feburary 2016) 'The Divide Over Prostitution on the Feminist Left', *The Atlantic*, theatlantic.com.

38 Kington, T. (11 April 2014) 'Nuns help rescue trafficked prostitutes in new police operation', *The Telegraph*, telegraph.co.uk.

39 Moore, A.E. (1 April 2015) 'From brothel to sweatshop? Questions on labour trafficking in Cambodia', *Open Democracy*, opendemocracy.net; Greig, A. (n.d., accessed June 26 2018) 'What Can I Do?', *Moral Revolution*, moralrevolution.com; see Escape to Peace, available at escapetopeace.org; see The Butterfly Project, available at butterflyprojectjewelry.org; Boffa, S. (2017) '7 Jewelry Brands Giving Hope To Survivors Of Human Trafficking', *The Good Trade*, thegoodtrade.com; Simply Liv & Co. (19 December 2016) '17 Brands That Fight Human Trafficking', simplylivandco.com.

40 One business describes itself as an 'EMPOWERMENT & High End Jewelry Company', Purity & Majesty, puritymajesty.com.

41 Ludlow, J. (2008) 'The Things We Cannot Say: Witnessing the Traumatization of Abortion in the United States', *WSQ: Women's Studies Quarterly* 36:1 and 2, 28–41.

42 Ibid., p. 30.

43 Strinkovsky, M. (2015) 'Like 95% of women, I don't regret my abortion – it was the happiest day of my life', *New Statesman*, newstatesman.com.

44 Sless, E. (23 November 2012) 'Sex worker & mother: "Yes, I AM empowered by my job"', *Mama Mia*, mamamia.com.au.

45 Comment by 'jemima101' on Mann, S. (10 May 2013) 'Unhappy Hooking, or Why I'm Giving Up On Being Positive', *Autocannibal*, autocannibalism.wordpress.com.

46 Roper, M. (2017) 'Advertisement "I prefer to orgasm and get paid": Brazilian lawyer dumped career at bar to become a PROSTITUTE (and now she makes more money)', *Daily Mail*, dailymail.co.uk.

47 Queen, C. (1997) 'Sex Radical Politics, Sex-Positive Feminist Thought, and Whore Stigma' in Nagle, J. (ed.) *Whores and Other Feminists*, New York: Routledge, 125–35.

48 Ibid.

49 Phipps, A. (31 August 2015) '"You're not representative": Identity politics in sex industry debates', *genders, bodies, politics*, genderate.wordpress.com.

50 Adorable, L. (30 March 2016) 'The Peculiar Political Economics of Pro-Domming', *Tits and Sass*, titsandsass.com.

51 Anon (suzyhooker) (19 February 2014) 'I Don't Care About Clients', *Tits and Sass*, titsandsass.com.

52 Hooker Hideout (accessed 23 May 2018), hookerhideout.tumblr.com.

53 Queen, *Sex Radical Politics*.

54 Murphy, M. (2015) 'The Sex Industry's Attack on Feminists', *Truthdig*, truthdig.com.

55 Sweeney, T. (2015) 'A play about sex work: "I want people to come out of the theatre angry"', *Irish Times*, irishtimes.com.

56 Bindel, J (@bindelj) Twitter, 6:06am, 12 December 2016.

57 Mann, S. (2014) 'More Than Survival Strategies: Sex Workers' Unhappy Stories', Athabasca University, Alberta (MA Thesis).

58 Sumaq, P. (2015) 'A Disgrace Reserved for Prostitutes: Complicity & the Beloved Community', *LIES: A journal of materialist feminism* 2, 11–24.

59 Ditum, S. (5 February 2015) 'If you think decriminalisation will make prostitution safe, look at Germany's mega brothels', *Guardian*, theguardian.com.

60 See Sporenda, F. (19 April 2016) 'Interview: Meghan Murphy on the liberal backlash against feminism', *Feminist Current*, feministcurrecnt .com.

61 Steinem, G (1995) 'Erotica and Pornography: A Clear and Present Difference' in Dwyer, S (ed.) *The Problem of Pornography*, Belmont, CA: Wadsworth.

62 Gira Grant, M. (2014) *Playing the Whore*, London: Verso Books.

2. Work

1 Brooks, S. (2007) 'An Interview with Gloria Lockett' in Oakley, A. (ed.) *Working Sex: Sex Workers Write About a Changing Industry*, Berkeley, CA: Seal Press.

2 Waugh, P. (7 March 2016) 'Jeremy Corbyn Tells His Critics To "Stop Sniping" As He Warns Parliamentary Labour Party Against Disunity', *Huffington Post*, huffingtonpost.com.

3 Banyard, K. (2016) 'It's not work, it's exploitation: Why we should never legalise prostitution', *Stylist*, stylist.co.uk; Stout, J. (17 December 2015) 'Decriminalisation of sex work backed by sex workers', *CommonSpace*, commonspace.cot.

4 Costa-Kostritsky, V. (20 January 2014) 'On Malmskillnadsgatan', *London Review of Books*, lrb.co.uk.

5 Given, P. (2014) comment directed at Laura Lee; Dechert, B. (2014) comment directed at Naomi Sayers openparliament.ca; Marina S. (@marstrina) Twitter, 5:29am, 18 February 2016: '@sarahditum like I always say: if it's their choice, what is the money for?'; Claire OT (@ claireOT) Twitter, 2:27pm, 31 March 2015: '@MrsWomannion do you think there are any sex workers/prostitutes who would do it for free, if

they weren't paid? @Elisablerb'.

6 See Internships, available at equalitynow.org.

7 See Volunteering, available at ruhama.ie; Cockroft, S. and Spillett, R. (19 January 2017) 'Oh the irony! Fight Against Slavery group advertises for "volunteer unpaid" staff to work a minimum of eight hours a week for FREE and "join the battle against worldwide poverty"', *Daily Mail*, dailymail.co.uk.

8 Guest Blogger (24 September 2014) 'FIL 2014 responds to SWOU', *The F-Word*, thefword.org.uk.

9 Mullin, F. (11 April 2017) 'In Full Sight: "The pimp lobby" at the Amnesty AGM', *Verso*, versobooks.com.

10 Babcock, W. quoted by Ha-Redeye, O. (10 August 2011) 'In Memorandum: Wendy Babcock (1979–2011)', *Law is Cool*, lawiscool.com.

11 Criado-Perez, C. (@ccriadoperez) Twitter, 2:39pm, 17 September 2016 '@hey Lee, ever thought of having multiple penises shoved up you as a career? It comes with great benefits like increased risk of ...'; Criado-Perez, C. (@ccriadoperez) Twitter, 2:44pm, 17 September 2016, 'well ... the longer you do it the more your earning potential decreases, but they say there's a fetish for everything!'

12 Harman, H. et al. (September 2013) 'The Commission on Older Women', interim report, *Labour*, available policyforum.labour.org.uk.

13 Smith, M., Satija, N. and Walters, E. (23 February 2017) 'How Texas' crusade against sex trafficking has left victims behind', *Reveal*, revealnews.org.

14 Gee, O. (23 July 2013) 'Selling sex doesn't make you an unfit parent', *The Local*, thelocal.se; Simon, C. (16 July 2013) 'The Bloody State Gave Him The Power: A Swedish Sex Worker's Murder', *Tits and Sass*, titsandsass.com.

15 Kumar, S. (1 December 2017) 'Playboy made sexual abuse ordinary', *Open Magazine*, openthemagazine.com.

16 Sex Workers' Rights Advocacy Network (May 2015) 'Failures of Justice: State and Non-State Violence Against Sex Workers and the Search for Safety and Redress', report available at nswp.org, 45.

17 Scambler, G. et al. (1990) 'Women prostitutes in the AIDS era', *Sociology of Health & Illness*, 12:3, 260–73.

18 Banyard, K. (2010) *The Equality Illusion: The Truth about Women and Men Today*, London: Faber and Faber, 146.

19 SCOT-PEP (n.d., accessed 27 June 2018) 'Assumptions used to discredit sex workers', *Scot-Pep*, report available scot-pep.org.uk.

20 Hester, M. and Westmarland, N. (July 2004) 'Tackling Street Prostitution: Towards an holistic approach', *Home Office Research, Development and Statistics Directorate*, available dro.dur.ac.uk.

21 Laite, J. (30 April 2014) '(Sexual) Labour Day', *Notches*, notchesblog.com.

22 Ibid.

23 Roberts, N. (1986) *The Front Line: Women in the Sex Industry Speak*, London: Grafton Books, 232–3.

24 Scambler, G. et al., 'Women prostitutes in the AIDS era'.

25 Mgbako, C.A. (2016) *To Live Freely in This World: Sex Worker Activism in Africa*, New York: NYU Press, 38.

26 Mai, N. (2009) 'Migrant Workers in the UK Sex Industry: First Findings', London Metropolitan University, available archive.londonmet.ac.uk.

27 Sumaq, P. (2015) 'A Disgrace Reserved for Prostitutes: Complicity & the Beloved Community', *LIES: A journal of materialist feminism*, 2, 11–24, 13–14, available at liesjournal.net.

28 'A Mother' (4 September 2017) 'Sex work is how I support my family', *The Spinoff*, thespinoff.co.nz.

29 Gorton, T. (27 February 2015) 'A quarter of the UK's homeless youth are LGBT', *Dazed*, dazeddigital.com.

30 Bindel, J. (26 August 2017) 'If women's rights are human rights, why do such organisations push for the decriminalisation of prostitution?', *Independent*, independent.co.uk.

31 Pye, K. (24 February 2017) 'Councillor John Tanner apologises for calling Oxford homeless "a disgrace"', *Cherwell*, cherwell.org.

32 Dr Langtry (@DrLangtry_girl) Twitter, 6:37pm, 18 November 2014: 'Nope. Giving up exploitative work isn't a sacrifice'.

33 Murphy, M. (@MeghanEMurphy) Twitter, 3:41am, 2 February 2018: 'I mean, I suppose we shouldn't try to stop the oil industry because people will lose jobs? It isn't suuuper progressive (or intelligent tbh) to defend harmful practices lest people lose jobs … We have capitalists and liberal politicians to do that'.

34 Mgbako, *To Live Freely*, 37.

35 New Syndicalist (4 July 2015) 'What does a union mean to you?', available at newsyndicalist.org.

36 Federici, S. (15 September 2010) 'Wages Against Housework', *Caring Labor: An Archive*, caringlabor.wordpress.com.

37 Friedman-Rudovsky, J. (24 October 2007) 'Prostitutes Strike in Bolivia', *Time*, content.time.com.

3. Borders

1 Anderson, B. and Andrijasevic, R. (2008) 'Sex, slaves and citizens: the politics of anti-trafficking', *Soundings* 40, 135–45, available at oro.open.ac.uk.

2 Crown Prosecution Service (2018, accessed 27 June 2018) 'Human Trafficking, Smuggling and Slavery', available cps.gov.uk.

3   Government Publishing Office (24 January 2000) 'Victims of Trafficking and Violence Protection Act of 2000', report available at gpo.gov.

4   Amnesty International (19 January 2016) 'Exposed: Child labour behind smart phone and electric car batteries', amnesty.org; Environmental Justice Foundation 'Combating Seafood Slavery: Tackling human rights abuses and slavery at sea', available ejfoundation.org, accessed 27 June 2018; National Domestic Workers Alliance, domesticworkers.org.

5   Moore, A.E. (8 April 2015) 'The American Rescue Industry: Toward an Anti-Trafficking Paramilitary', *Truthout*, truth-out.org; Moore, A.E. (27 January 2015) 'Special Report: Money and Lies in Anti-Human Trafficking NGOs', *Truthout*.

6   Moore, A.E. (11 January 2017) 'Rich in funds but short on facts: the high cost of human trafficking awareness campaigns', *openDemocracy*, opendemocracy.net.

7   Mama Cash/Red Umbrella Fund (2014) 'Funding for sex workers' rights: Opportunities for foundations to fund more and better', report available mamacash.org.

8   Melencio Herrera, A.A. (2004) 'Opening and Welcome Remarks', *Philja Judicial Journal* 6:1, 1–4, philja.judiciary.gov.ph.

9   Nolot, B. (2011) 'Nefarious: Merchant of Souls', available nefariousdocumentary.com; Bois, P. (20 December 2017) 'How This Catholic Church Helps Sex Trafficking Victims', *The Daily Wire*, dailywire.com; Farrell, L. (28 January 2015) 'Supercomputers expose the telltale signs of human traffickers', *Science Node*, sciencenode.org; Papadimitrakopoulos, G. (4 December 2015) 'Happy trafficking: How criminals profit from an iniquitous trade', *University of Cambridge*, cam.ac.uk.

10 Smith, M., Satija, N. and Walters, E. 'How Texas' crusade … '

11 Change.org Petition (2015) 'Pass legislation that would save lives and prevent human trafficking', *Change.org*; Sardina, C. (13 January 2017) 'Marketing mass hysteria: anti-trafficking awareness campaigns go rogue', *openDemocracy*, opendemocracy.net; 'Guest Post' (2015, accessed 28 June 2018) 'Sex Trafficking', *The Hope Line*, thehopeline.com.

12 Koyama, E. (16 July 2012) 'Gangs and sex trafficking: How the movement against "modern day slavery" targets descendants of slavery as its primary perpetrators', *Eminism*, eminism.org; Koyama, E. (1 September 2016) in response to Kiernan, J.S. 'Should Prostitution Be Legal?', *WalletHub*, wallethub.com.

13 Children at Risk (23 March 2017) 'Human Trafficking Bus Tour', *Children at Risk*, childrenatrisk.org.

14 The Drum (2017) 'The task force on human trafficking and prostitution: Meet the meat by M&S Saatchi Tel Aviv', *The Drum*, thedrum.com.

15 Shane, C. (27 July 2011) 'Top 10 Anti-Sex Trafficking Campaigns', *Tits*

and Sass, titsandsass.com.

16 *Saving Innocence*, savinginnocence.org; *Innocents at Risk*, innocent-satrisk.org; *Freedom 4 Innocence*, freedom4innocence.org; 'Protected Innocence Challenge', *Shared Hope International*, sharedhope.org; *Restore Innocence*, restoreinnocence.org; Harpster, M.T. (26 March 2014) 'Innocence for Sale: Domestic Minor Sex Trafficking', *FBI*, fbi.gov.

17 Suchland, J. (23 November 2015) 'The Missing "P" in U.S. Anti-Trafficking Law', *The Feminist Wire*, thefeministwire.com.

18 Doezma, J. (1998) 'Forced to Choose: Beyond the Voluntary v. Forced Prostitution Dichotomy', *Global Sex Workers: Rights, Resistance, and Redefinition*, New York: Routledge, 45.

19 Suchland, J., 'The Missing "P" in U.S. Anti-Trafficking Law'.

20 Freedom Challenge, 'Just the Facts', available thefreedomchallenge.com, accessed 28 June 2018.

21 Helmer, K. (11 July 2017) 'Hopkinsville on high alert for sex trafficking around next month's solar eclipse', WDRB, wdrb.com.

22 Earl, J. (30 March 2017) 'Mom's warning about "human trafficking" at IKEA goes viral; what you need to know', *CBS News*, cbsnews.com.

23 Pliley, J.R. (2014) *Policing Sexuality: The Mann Act and the Making of the FBI*, Cambridge, MA: Harvard University Press.

24 Exodus Cry (10 January 2018) 'Is Prostitution a Choice?', video, YouTube (user: Exodus Cry), youtube.com/watch?v=YFUa31WO_ho.

25 Hooton, C. (7 January 2015) 'Liam Neeson is here to remind frightened American parents that Taken isn't real', *Independent*, independent.co.uk.

26 Luddy, M. (2007) *Prostitution and Irish Society, 1800–1940*, Cambridge: Cambridge University Press, 166.

27 UK Independent Anti-Slavery Commissioner (2017, accessed 28 June 2018) 'Combating modern slavery experienced by Vietnamese nationals en route to, and within, the UK', *Anti Slavery Commissioner*, report available antislaverycommissioner.co.uk.

28 Walia, H. (2013) *Undoing Border Imperialism*, Chico, CA: AK Press, 40.

29 Murdock, H. (24 November 2015) 'From Syria to Europe: The Price They Pay', *VOA News*, voanews.com.

30 Carlsen, L. (24 November 2013) 'Under Nafta, Mexico Suffered, and the United States Felt Its Pain', *New York Times*, nytimes.com

31 Haddal, C.C. (2010) *'Border Security: The Role of the U.S. Border Patrol'*, Washington, D.C.: Congressional Research Service.

32 Majidi, N. and Dadu-Brown, S. (10 April 2017) 'Human smugglers roundtable: On border restrictions and movement', *openDemocracy*, opendemocracy.net.

33 Jones, R. (4 October 2016) 'Death in the sands: the horror of the

US-Mexico border', *The Guardian*, theguardian.com.

34 Moreno, C.J. (17 August 2012) 'Border Crossing Deaths More Common As Illegal Immigration Declines', *Huffington Post,* huffingtonpost.co.uk.

35 Roberts, B. et al. (2010, accessed 28 June 2018) 'An Analysis of Migrant Smuggling Costs Along the Southwest Border', *US Department of Homeland Security,* report available dhs.gov.

36 Martinez, S. (30 October 2014) 'Human trafficking: A parasite of prohibitionism?', *openDemocracy*, opendemocracy.net.

37 International Labour Organization (2015, accessed 28 June 2018) 'No Easy Exit: Migration Bans Affecting Women from Nepal', report available ilog.org.

38 Human Rights Watch (2013, accessed 28 June 2018) 'Rape Victims as Criminals: Illegal Abortion after Rape in Ecuador', report available hrw.org.

39 PICUM (2014, accessed 28 June 2018) 'On the European Commission Communication on an EU Strategic Framework on Health and Safety at Work 2014–2020', report available ilo.org.

40 France, B. (2016, accessed 28 June 2018) 'Labour Compliance to Exploitation and the Abuse In-Between', *Focus on Labour Exploitation (FLEX) and the Labour Exploitation Advisory Group (LEAG)*, report available labourexploitation.org.

41 Focus on Labour Exploitation (FLEX), Fairwork, and ADPARE (2016, accessed 28 June 2018) 'Pro-act: Improving the Identification and Support of Victims of Trafficking for Labour Exploitation in the EU', *LEAG*, report available labourexploitation.org,.

42 France, B., 'Labour Compliance to Exploitation and the Abuse In-Between'.

43 Kelly, N. and McNamara, M. (28 May 2016) 'A slave in Scotland: "I fell into a trap – and I couldn't get out"', *Guardian*, theguardian.com.

44 Wood, R. (13 March 2017) '"He was the master and we were his servants": The men kept as "slaves" in a remote Scottish hotel', *CNN*, cnn.com.

45 Hafiz, S. and Paarlberg, M. (2017, accessed 28 June 2018) 'The Human Trafficking Of Domestic Workers In The United States: Findings from the Beyond Survival Campaign', *National Domestic Workers Alliance*, report available domesticworkers.org.

46 Kalayaan, (4 July 2014) 'Producing Slaves: The tied Overseas Domestic Worker visa', available at kalayaan.org.uk.

47 Human Rights Watch (2014) 'Hidden Away Abuses Against Migrant Domestic Workers in the UK', *HRW*, hrw.org.

48 Marstrina, S. (@marstrina) Twitter, 1:48pm, 18 September 2016.

49 UK Government (2016, accessd 28 June 2018) 'Immigration Act 2016', available legislation.gov.uk.

50 Bridget Anderson, Bridget (2010) 'Migration, immigration controls and the fashioning of precarious workers', *Work, Employment and Society* 24:2, 300–17.

51 Mai, N. (2009, accessed 28 June 2018) 'Migrant Workers in the UK Sex Industry', *London Metropolitan University Institute for the Study of European Transformations*, report available scot-pep.org.uk.

52 Ibid., 20.

53 Ibid., 38.

54 Ibid., 40.

55 Ibid., 42.

56 Ibid., 22.

57 BBC (18 April 2018) 'German mass raids target forced prostitution gang', bbc.co.uk

58 Ditum, S. (@sarahditum) Twitter, 2:11pm, 18 April 2018.

59 Patatayoh, S. (19 April 2018) 'Thai sex workers in Germany may be charged with not having work permit', *Nation*, nationmultimedia.com.

60 Ibid.

61 Sharma, N. (30 March 2015) 'Anti-trafficking: whitewash for anti-immigration programmes', *openDemocracy*, opendemocracy.net.

62 Goldman, B. (2 February 2015), 'Photo Essay: Houston's Sex Trade in Nine Objects', *Houstonia Magazine*, houstoniamag.com.

63 Maynard, R. (19 September 2015) 'Black Sex Workers' Lives Matter: Appropriation of Black Suffering', *Truthout,* truthout.org.

64 Doezema, J. (2010) *Sex Slaves and Discourse Masters: The Construction of Trafficking*, New York: Zed Books, 49.

65 Abbott, K. (2007) *Sin in the Second City: Madams, Ministers, Playboys, and the Battle for America's Soul*, New York: Random House, 48.

66 Luddy, M. (2007) *Prostitution and Irish Society, 1800–1940*, Cambridge: Cambridge University Press, 163.

67 Doezema, *Sex Slaves*, 89; Weiner, E. (2008) 'The Long, Colorful History of the Mann Act', *NPR*, npr.org.

68 Lammasniemi, L. (2017, accessed 28 June 2018) 'Anti-White Slavery Legislation and its Legacies in England', report available at antitraffickingreview.org.

69 Dasgupta, A. (20 April 2016) 'Trafficking Briefing', *English Collective of Prostitutes*, prostitutescollective.net.

70 Pringle, B. (20 June 2016) 'Breaking Point', *Political Advertising UK*, politicaladvertising.co.uk.

71 Walshe, G. (@garvanwalshe) Twitter, 7:01pm, 26 February 2017: 'I was in 2005 Tory campaign – we worked assiduously to ramp up anti immigrant feeling. And from Brown on nobody challenged lies that immigrants took jobs, were here on benefits etc'.

72 Champion, S. (10 August 2017) 'British Pakistani men ARE raping

and exploiting white girls … and it's time we faced up to it', *The Sun*, thesun.co.uk.

73 Jones, R. (2016) *Violent Borders: Refugees and the Right to Move*, London: Verso Books.

74 Action of Churches Together in Scotland (2017) '"More Slaves Today than at any Time in Human History" Exchanging Scottish and International Perspectives on Human Trafficking', *Eventbrite*, eventbrite.com; MacShane, D. (2 January 2006) 'Prosecute "massage parlour" rapists', *The Telegraph*, telegraph.co.uk.

75 Renzi, M. (22 April 2015) 'Matteo Renzi: Helping the Migrants Is Everyone's Duty', *New York Times*, nytimes.com.

76 CBC News (14 November 2006) 'Modern human trafficking worse than slave trade: Vatican', *CBC*, cbc.ca.

77 Townsend, M. (14 May 2011) 'Trafficking victims lured to the UK: Locked up and raped at £30 a time', *Guardian*, theguardian.com.

78 Nolot, 'Nefarious: Merchant of Souls'.

79 See Greene, J. and Mason McAward, J. (n.d., accessed 28 June 2018) 'The Thirteenth Amendment', *Constitution Center*, report available at constitutioncenter.org.

80 Prisoner Support (1 April 2016) 'Announcement of Nationally Coordinated Prisoner Work stoppage for Sept 9, 2016', *Support Prison Resistance*, supportprisonresistance.noblogs.org.

81 Lu, T. (30 March 2011) 'Michelle Alexander: More Black Men in Prison Than Were Enslaved in 1850', *Color Lines*, colorlines.com.

82 Doward, J. (25 September 2016) 'From Jane Austen to Beatrice and Eugenie … the long reach of UK slave-owning families', *Guardian*, theguardian.com.

83 Kingsley, P. (7 January 2015) 'Trading in souls: Inside the world of the people smugglers', *Guardian*, theguardian.com.

84 Travis, A. (11 July 2017) 'EU-UK naval mission on people-smuggling led to more deaths, report says', *Guardian*, theguardian.com.

85 Balmer, C. (7 July 2017) 'Italy's Renzi urges end to "do gooder" mentality on migrant influx', *Reuters*, reuters.com.

86 Charlemagne (2018) 'How Italy's interior minister tackles illegal migration', *The Economist*, economist.com; Médecins Sans Frontières (19 September 2017) 'Libya: Arbitrary detention of refugees, asylum-seekers and migrants must stop', *MSF*, msf.org.uk.

87 Maynard, R. (2017) *Policing Black Lives: State Violence in Canada from Slavery to the Present*, Fernwood Publishing.

88 The Yorkshire Post (8 June 2017) 'Could you spot a pop-up brothel?', *Yorkshire Post*, yorkshirepost.co.uk.

89 Burns, T. (n.d., accessed 28 June 2018) 'People in Alaska's Sex Trade: Their Lived Experiences And Policy Recommendations', *Sex Trafficking*

in Alaska, report available at sextraffickingalaska.com.

90 Healy, A. (31 October 2016) 'Four women plead guilty to operating Galway brothel', *The Irish Times*, irishtimes.com.

91 Ibid.

92 CBC News (8 May 2015) 'Massage parlour, body rub investigation leads to 11 deportations', *CBC*, cbc.ca.

93 Lam, E., 'Behind the Rescue', report, *Butterfly* (Asian and migrant sex workers support network), available at nswp.org/sites/nswp.org/files/behind_the_rescue_june_2_butterfly.pdf.

94 Mullan, F. (27 October 2016) 'Are the Soho Brothel Raids Really About Saving Sex Workers?', *Vice*, vice.com.

95 Proctor, I. (21 October 2016) 'Brothel shut down and prostitutes spoken to during human trafficking crackdown', *Bolton News*, boltonnews.co.uk.

96 The Irish News (3 August 2016) 'Jail for asylum seekers arrested in suspected trafficking racket', *The Irish News,* irishnews.com.

97 Dottridge, M. (26 September 2016) 'How did we get the Modern Slavery Act?', *openDemocracy*, opendemocracy.net.

98 BBC (24 August 2017) 'Suspected trafficking victims turned back at Glasgow Airport', *BBC*, bbc.co.uk.

99 Ibid.

100 United States Citizenship and Immigration Services (2013,) 'Immigration and Nationality Act', report available at uscis.gov.

101 US Department of Homeland Security (DHS) (2017) 'Fact Sheet: Executive Order: Border Security and Immigration Enforcement Improvements', report available at dhs.gov; DHS and Customs and Border Protection (2012) 'Job Advert: Paralegal Specialist Position-JFK Airport', available at nyceda.org.

102 UN General Assembly Resolution 55/25 (2000) 'Protocol to Prevent, Suppress and Punish Trafficking in Persons Especially Women and Children, Supplementing the United Nations Convention against Transnational Organized Crime', *Office of the High Commissioner for Human Rights*, report available at ohchr.org.

103 Dotteridge, M. (2007) 'Introduction' in Global Alliance Against Traffic in Women (GAATW) 'Collateral Damage: The Impact of Anti-Trafficking Measures on Human Rights around the World', report available at gaatw.org, 1–27.

104 UN General Assembly Resolution 55/25, 'Protocol to Prevent, Suppress and Punish Trafficking in Persons Especially Women and Children, Supplementing the United Nations Convention against Transnational Organized Crime'.

105 UN General Assembly Resolution 55/25, 'Protocol to Prevent, Suppress and Punish Trafficking in Persons Especially Women and Children,

Supplementing the United Nations Convention against Transnational Organized Crime'.

106　Murdoch, S. (15 May 2017) 'Anti-Immigrant Far Right Takes to the Seas', *Hope Not Hate*, hopenothate.org.

107　Hopkins, K. (@KTHopkins) Twitter, 17 July 2017: 'Good to meet Team C-Star @DefendEuropeID in Sicily. Young people, 8 nations, crowd-funded, shining a light on NGO people traffickers in Med'.

108　Wintour, P. (27 Februayr 2017) 'NGO rescues off Libya encourage traffickers, says EU borders chief', *Guardian*, theguardian.com.

109　Townsend, M. (11 November 2017) 'Trafficking laws target refugee aid workers in EU', *Guardian*, theguardian.com.

110　White, P. (@unbreakablepenn) Twitter, 12:24am, 9 March 2016: '@Lavender_Blume Take in refugee women & kids – leave the nasty men home'.

111　Eigendorf, J. and Neller, M. (4 November 2013) 'Nur eine Welt ohne Prostitution ist human', *Welt*, welt.de.

112　Poschardt, U. (15 January 2016) 'Kalaschnikows, Sprenggürtel und jetzt die sexuelle Gewalt', *Welt*, welt.de.

113　Green, L.H. (@LinHelenGreen) Twitter, 7:06am, 3 July 2017: '@paul masonnews Should be deported if no right to be in the country. Such women are being trafficked into country. Do you support that?'.

114　Associated Press (23 February 2017) 'Trump vows to fight "epidemic" of human trafficking', *Associated Press*, apnews.com.

115　May, T. (30 July 2016) 'My Government will lead the way in defeating modern slavery', *The Telegraph*, telegraph.co.uk.

116　The Migrant Sex Workers Project, (n.d., accessed 28 June 2018) 'Report on Migrant Sex Workers Justice and the Trouble with "Anti-Trafficking": Research, Activism, Art', report available at migrantsexworkers.com.

4. A Victorian Hangover

1　Northern Ireland, which criminalised the purchase of sex in 2015, will be discussed in Chapter 6: The People's Home. Like other countries that have implemented the Swedish Model of sex work law, Northern Ireland previously would have been accurately described as having a system of 'Partial Criminalisation'. In practice, much is the same as is covered in this chapter, with the addition of penalties for clients.

2　Kevan, P. (12 December 2006) '"Dead" prostitute's TV interview: I have to work, I need the money', *Metro*, metro.co.uk.

3　Alleyne, R. (14 December 2006) 'She was intelligent, pretty. But the drugs gave her a death wish', *The Telegraph*, telegraph.co.uk.

4   BBC (21 February 2008) 'Wright guilty of Suffolk murders', *BBC News*, news.bbc.co.uk.

5   BBC (5 July 2016) 'Daria Pionko death: Lewis Pierre jailed for murder', *BBC*, bbc.co.uk.

6   Perraudin, F. (4 July 2016) 'Man found guilty of murdering sex worker in Leeds', *Guardian*, theguardian.com.

7   Ditum, S. (13 January 2016) 'The death of Daria Pionko shows there is no "safe" way to manage prostitution', *New Statesman*, newstatesman.com.

8   Richie, B.E. (2012) *Arrested Justice: Black Women, Violence, and America's Prison Nation*, New York: NYU Press, chapter 3.

9   Seaward, T. (16 January 2018) 'Wiltshire Police's Mike Veale criticised over 'drunken prostitute' comments', *Swindon Advertiser*, swindon advertiser.co.uk.

10 Woods, V. (23 February 2008) 'Ipswich victims drug addicts, not "sex workers"', *The Telegraph*, telegraph.co.uk.

11 Littlejohn, R. (18 December 2006) 'Spare us the "People's Prostitute" routine', *Daily Mail*, dailymail.co.uk.

12 Sanders, T. and Sehmbi, V. (2015) 'Evaluation of the Leeds Street Sex Working Managed Area', *University of Leeds*, report available at nswp.org.

13 Agustín, L.M. (2007) *Sex at the Margins: Migration, Labour Markets and the Rescue Industry*, London: Zed Books, chapter 4.

14 Yorkshire Evening Post (22 August 2017) 'Sex in the city: Leeds residents on life near "legal" red light zone', *Yorkshire Evening Post*, yorkshire eveningpost.co.uk.

15 Kinnell, H. (2008) *Violence and sex work in Britain*, Cullompton: Willan Publishing.

16 Cohen, N. (3 April 2000) 'When self-help is not enough', *New Statesman*, newstatesman.com.

17 Sexual Offences Act 2003, s. 52(1), available at legislation.gov.uk, accessed 28 June 2018; English Collective of Prostitutes 'Prostitution: What you need to know', available at prostitutescollective.net, accessed 28 June 2018; Sexual Offences Act 2003, Explanatory note on section 52, available legislation.gov.uk, accessed 28 June 2018.

18 We witnessed this in court.

19 Crown Prosecution Service, 'Prostitution and Exploitation of Prostitution', available cps.gov.uk, accessed 28 June 2018.

20 Bowcott, O. (16 January 2012) 'Call for change in law to protect prostitutes from violent crime', *The Guardian*, theguardian.com.

21 Smith, M. (13 June 2012) 'Educating Rhoda', *A Glasgow Sex Worker*, glasgowsexworker.wordpress.com.

22 Mullin, F. (2017) 'In Full Sight: 'The pimp lobby' at the Amnesty AGM'.

23 Addley, E. (21 February 2008) 'Steve Wright's victims', *The Guardian*, theguardian.com.

24 Jeal and Salisbury (op. cit.); Smith, F.M. and Marshall L.A. (2007) 'Barriers to effective drug addiction treatment for women involved in street-level prostitution: A qualitative investigation', *Criminal Behaviour and Mental Health*, 17(3): 163–170.

25 INPUD (op. cit.),19 – 21.

26 Dugan. E (31 January 2014) 'Jack the Ripper copycat murders spark call for sex worker protection', *The Independent*, independent.co.uk.

27 Lopez, G. (12 June 2017) 'The case for prescription heroin', *Vox*, vox.com; Strang, J. et al. (2015) 'Heroin on trial: Systematic review and meta-analysis of randomised trials of diamorphine-prescribing as treatment for refractory heroin addiction', *The British Journal of Psychiatry*, 207(1): 5–14.

28 Evening Telegraph (20 February 2018) 'Dundee's drug epidemic laid bare to nation on Channel 4 News', eveningtelegraph.co.uk.

29 Mann, J. (5 October 2014) 'British drugs survey 2014: Drug use is rising in the UK – but we're not addicted', *The Guardian*, theguardian.co.uk.

30 Eastwood, N., Shiner, M. and Bear, D. (2013) 'The Numbers in Black And White: Ethnic Disparities In The Policing And Prosecution Of Drug Offences In England And Wales', *Release*, available release.org.uk, accessed 28 June 2018.

31 Block, J. F. (1 March 2013) 'Racism's Hidden History in the War on Drugs', *Huffington Post*, huffingtonpost.com.

32 Eastwood, N., Shiner, M. and Bear, D. (2013) op. cit; Halperin, A. (29 January 2018) 'Marijuana: Is it time to stop using a word with racist roots?', *The Guardian*, theguardian.com.

33 Release (2017) 'Sex Workers and the Law', available release.org.uk, accessed 28 June 2018.

34 Although even after 1982, street-based sex workers were sent to prison for non-payment of soliciting fines. Of 213 street-based sex workers interviewed by researchers in Birmingham in the late 1980s, 90 per cent had been prosecuted or received a caution for soliciting in the last twelve months, and 45 per cent had been prosecuted *more than twenty times*. See; Kinnell, H. (2008) *'Violence and sex work in Britain'*, Cullompton: Willan Publishing. 96.

35 NIA (2017) '"I'm no criminal": Examining the impact of prostitution-specific criminal records on women seeking to exit prostitution', *NIA*, report available niaendingviolence.org.uk, accessed 28 June 2018.

36 Smith, L. (25 May 2005) 'Asbos "are bringing back jail for prostitutes"', *The Guardian*, theguardian.com.

37 The 2009 Act, section 16. Report available legislation.gov.uk, accessed 28 June 2018.

38 Fawcett Society (22 November 2006) 'Theresa May in her Fawcett "This is what a feminist looks like" t-shirt', *Flickr*, flickr.com.

39 NIA, 'I'm no criminal', op. cit.

40 "… the great scourges of contemporary Britain: aggressive all-female gangs of embittered, hormonal, drunken teenagers; gym-slip mums who choose to get pregnant as a career option; pasty-faced, lard-gutted slappers who'll drop their knickers in the blink of an eye."
    Delingpole, J. quoted in Jones, O. (2011) *'Chavs: The Demonization of the Working Class'*, London: Verso, 128.

41 Fishwick, B. (26 June 2015) 'Sex-for-cash Asbo woman dodges prison', *The Portsmouth News*, portsmouth.co.uk.

42 Sandhu, N. (20 January 2017) 'Prostitute jailed after breaching ASBO 10 times in three weeks to visit 90-year-old 'sugar daddy', *Mirror Online*, mirror.co.uk.

43 Sexton, D. (4 August 1984) 'Another Yorkshire' Spectator', *The Spectator*, archive.spectator.co.uk.

44 BBC (11 July 2013) 'Luton prostitution: Police out to clean up Hightown', *BBC News*, bbc.co.uk.

45 Rodriguez, M. (18 February 2016) 'Police Make Big Busts In Effort To Clean Miami Streets', *CBS Miami*, miami.cbslocal.com.

46 Jacobs, R. (21 February 2014) 'Kent Police 'Safe Exit' Scheme Claiming to Help Women in Prostitution Instead Caused Them Harm', *Huffington Post*, huffingtonpost.co.uk.

47 Private correspondence with Ruth.

48 Both of these are orders that police officers are able to make at their own discretion, without obtaining a court order. Section 21 (and Schedule 2) of the Policing and Crime Act 2009 allows a senior officer to order premises to be closed if they suspect prostitution offences are occurring there; typically a court order is needed to reopen it again; see the Anti-social Behaviour, Crime and Policing Act 2014, available legislation. gov.uk, accessed 28 June 2018. Section 35 allows any uniformed officer to order someone to leave a particular area for up to 48 hours; 2009 Scotland Housing Act: immorality clause, available legislation.gov.uk, accessed 28 June 2018.

49 Mullin, F. (3 November 2016) 'Immigration Officers Are Targeting Sex Workers in the UK's Only "Legal Red Light District"', *Vice*, vice.com.

50 Ibid.

51 Ibid.

52 Mann, S. (27 June 2014) 'Mariana Popa murder: Timeline of a sex worker's killing', *Ilford Recorder*, ilfordrecorder.co.uk.

53 Taylor, D. & Townsend, M. (19 January 2014) 'Mariana Popa was killed working as a prostitute. Are the police to blame?', *The Guardian*, theguardian.com.

54 Ibid.

55 Redbridge MPS (@MPSRedbridge) Twitter, 4:43am, 17 April 2016: '#LoxfordSNT and #RedbridgeCommunityPoliceTeam issued 11 prostitute cautions on Ilford Lane tonight #Yousaidwedid'.

56 Knowles, R. (21 January 2014) 'Sex worker stabbed to death after launch of Operation Clearlight in Ilford', *East London and West Essex Guardian*, guardian-series.co.uk.

57 Ibid.

58 Vonow, B. (24 January 2017) 'Jack the Ripper-obsessed killer stabbed mum-of-two to death and scrawled 'JACK' over her naked body', *The Sun*, thesun.co.uk.

59 Clej, M. (16 October 2014) 'Israeli woman's murderer is jailed for 25 years', *Jewish News*, jewishnews.timesofisrael.com.

60 Bennett, C. (21 February 2016) 'Criminalise the sex buyers, not the prostitutes', *The Guardian*, theguardian.com.

61 Arla Propertymark (23 September 2016) '30 years since Suzy Lamplugh disappeared, what's changed?', *Arla*, arla.co.uk; 'Personal Safety', *Suzy Lamplugh* Trust available suzylamplugh.org, accessed 28 June 2018.

62 Royal College of Nursing (4 October 2016) 'Personal safety when working alone: Guidance for members working in health and social care', *Royal College of Nursing*, rcn.org.uk; British Association of Social Workers (2009) 'Keeping Safe in the Workplace – A Guide for Social Work Practitioners' *UNISONScotland*, available basw.co.uk, accessed 28 June 2018.

63 Unison (2009) 'Working Alone: A health and safety guide on lone working for safety representatives', report available unison.org, accessed 28 June 2018.

64 Doward, J. (25 April 2010) 'Police boost funds from assets taken in raids on prostitutes', *Guardian*, theguardian.com.

65 Urquhart, J. (2015) 'Prostitution Law Reform (Scotland) Bill: A proposal for a Bill to decriminalise activities associated with the buying and selling of sexual services and to strengthen the laws against coercion in the sex industry', *Scottish Parliament*, available parliament.scot, accessed 28 June 2018.

66 Patterson, S. (5 January 2017) 'Murder Trial Claim: Aberdeen hooker Jessica McGraa phoned lover to tell him a man she was with refused to leave on the day she was killed', *The Scottish Sun*, thescottishsun.co.uk.

67 Loweth, J. (21 November 2013) 'Police were greeted at Bradford brothel by half-naked woman', *Telegraph & Argus*, thetelegraphandargus.co.uk.

68 Ibid.

69 Guttridge, R. (23 August 2017) 'Suspected Smethwick brothel shut down by police', *Express & Star*, expressandstar.com.

70 Swindon North Police (4:20am, 30 June 2017) Facebook: 'adultworks'

is an obvious misspelling of 'Adultwork', the name of one of the main UK platforms for advertising sex work online.

71 Haworth, T. (30 June 2017) 'Romanian sex workers to be deported following immigration offences', *Swindon Advertiser*, swindonadvertiser.co.uk.

72 Swindon North Police, op. cit.

73 Bowcott, O. (3 August 2017) 'Police accused of threatening sex workers rather than pursuing brothel thieves', *The Guardian*, theguardian.com.

74 CPS 'Prostitution and Exploitation of Prostitution', report available at cps.gov.uk, accessed 28 June 2018.

75 Mullin, F. (6 April 2016) 'Sex Workers Reveal What Cops Took from Them During Police Raids', *Broadly*, broadly.vice.com.

76 Doward, J., 'Police boost funds from assets taken in raids on prostitutes'.

77 The Economist (19 January 2017) 'Police in Britain want to keep more of the loot they confiscate', *Economist*, economist.com.

78 Mullin, F., 'Sex Workers Reveal What Cops Took from Them During Police Raids'.

79 Greater London Authority (2016) 'Written Answers to Questions Not Answered at Mayor's Question Time on 16 November 2016', report available at london.gov.uk, accessed 28 June 2018.

80 Mullin, F., 'Sex Workers Reveal What Cops Took from Them During Police Raids'.

81 Hodgson, N. (15 January 2012) 'Why prostitutes are living in a "climate of fear"', *New Statesman*, newstatesman.com.

82 BBC (26 July 2017) 'Lifesaving bid woman guilty of Bournemouth brothel charge', *BBC News*, bbc.co.uk.

83 Aitkenhead, D. (26 August 2016) '"I've done really bad things": The undercover cop who abandoned the war on drugs', *Guardian*, theguardian.com.

84 Bindel, J. (2017) *The Pimping of Prostitution: Abolishing the Sex Work Myth*, London: Palgrave, chapter 8.

85 Marina S (@marstrina) Twitter, 4:54pm, 7 June 2015: '@SoranaBanana decriminalised SW *is* the status quo in the UK. If that harms SWs, then how will extending it be better? #lylsc15'.

86 Hirsch, A. (8 February 2016) 'Police Could Stop Raids On Suspected Brothels', *Sky News*, news.sky.com.

87 Aleem, Z. (13 March 2015) '16 Years Since Decriminalizing Prostitution, Here's What's Happening in Sweden', *Mic*, mic.com; Ditum, S. (5 February 2015) 'If you think decriminalisation will make prostitution safe, look at Germany's mega brothels', *New Statesman*, newstatesman. com. This systematic confusion is discussed by Mullin, F. (19 October 2015) 'The difference between decriminalisation and legalisation of sex work', *New Statesman*, newstatesman.com; Witnessed by the authors,

Amnesty UK AGM, Nottingham, April 2017.

88 All-Party Parliamentary Group on Prostitution and the Global Sex Trade: Shifting the Burden (2014), report, available at appgprostitution. files.wordpress.com, accessed 28 June 2018; Ingala Smith, K. (2015) 'Standing up for All Women: Statement in response to London Young Labour Summer Conference Motion 8', *Karen Ingala Smith*, kareninga-lasmith.com; Zero Tolerance (2012) 'Take action now – Consultation on prostitution laws closing soon', report available at zerotolerance.org.uk, accessed 28 June 2018.

89 Godman, T. (2010) 'Criminalisation of the Purchase and Sale of Sex (Scotland) Bill', *Scottish Parliament*, report available at parliament.scot, accessed 28 June 2018; Kettles, L. (9 September 2016) 'Women are not for sale – women campaign against prostitution', *Third Force News*, thirdforcenews.org.uk.

90 Comment by 'bounce' on Murphy, M. (4 September 2013) 'Femen was founded and is controlled by a man. Exactly zero people are surprised', *Feminist Current*, feministcurrent.com.

91 Nordic Model Now! (6 April 2017) 'How to Spot an Illegal Brothel', *Nordic Model Now!*, nordicmodelnow.org.

92 Topping, A. (15 July 2013) 'Tough or tolerant? Scotland turns up heat on prostitution debate', *Guardian*, theguardian.com.

93 Proctor, I., 'Brothel shut down and prostitutes spoken to during human trafficking crackdown'.

94 Private correspondence.

95 SWARM (2 July 2017) 'Call To Action: Release The Women! No Arrests, No Deportations!', *Sex Worker Advocacy and Resistance Movement*, swarmcollective.org; Seaward, T. (6 July 2017) 'Campaigners hit out after immigration brothel raids', *Swindon Advertiser*, swindon advertiser.co.uk.

96 Marina S (@marstrina) Twitter, 2:31pm, 3 July 2017: 'From the local press report it's ambiguous whether these women were working in the brothels or operating them ... The lovely catch-all 'sex worker', of course, allows the pimps to hide amongst the prostituted people.'

97 Tweet since deleted but confirmed to the authors by Alison.

5. Prison Nation

1 Gira Grant, M. (22 November 2016) 'The NYPD Arrests Women for Who They Are and Where They Go – Now They're Fighting Back',

Village Voice, villagevoice.com.

2   Bell, B. (26 April 2013) 'Prostitution led by growth of area gambling, police say', *WJLA*, wjla.com.

3   Walsh, J. (12 February 2017) 'Sex-trafficking victims fight their way out of "the life" to help others', *East Valley Tribune*, eastvalleytribune.com.

4   Gira Grant, M., 'The NYPD Arrests Women for Who They Are and Where They Go – Now They're Fighting Back'.

5   Support Ho(s)e (2017) 'No Bad Whores: Year One', available support hosechi.tumblr.com, accessed 28 June 2018.

6   NBC News (1 December 2014) 'Obama Requests $263 Million for Police Body Cameras, Training', *NBC News*, nbcnews.com.

7   Richie, B.E. (2012) *Arrested Justice: Black Women, Violence, and America's Prison Nation*, New York: NYU Press.

8   SCOT-PEP (2013) 'I felt so bad, so violated.' op. cit; Andrews, K. (7 August 2015) 'Stop and search is a disgrace across the UK – not just in our cities', *Guardian*, theguardian.com.

9   Davis, A.Y. (2003) *Are Prisons Obsolete?* New York: Seven Stories Press, 16–18.

10 Schenwar, M. (11 November 2014) 'Prisons Are Destroying Communities and Making All of Us Less Safe', *The Nation*, thenation.com.

11 Ibid.

12 American Civil Liberties Union (ACLU) (2014) 'War Comes Home: The Excessive Militarization of American Policing', available aclu.org, accessed 28 June 2018.

13 Filkins, D. (13 May 2016) '"Do Not Resist" and the Crisis of Police Militarization', *New Yorker*, newyorker.com.

14 McCoy, A.W. (2009) *Policing America's Empire: The United States, the Philippines, and the Rise of the Surveillance State*, Madison, WI: University of Wisconsin Press; Bell, E. (2013) 'Normalising the exceptional: British colonial policing cultures come home', *Mémoire(s), identité(s), marginalité(s) dans le monde occidental contemporain* 10, available journals.openedition.org.

15 Economist (20 March 2014) 'Cops or soldiers?', *Economist*, economist.com.

16 Ritchie, A.J. (2017) *Invisible No More: Police Violence Against Black Women and Women of Color*, Boston, MA: Beacon Press, 146.

17 Ibid., 149.

18 Gira Grant, M. (18 July 2017) 'ICE is Using Prostitution Diversion Courts to Stalk Immigrants', *Village Voice*, villagevoice.com.

19 Gira Grant, G. (22 November 2016) 'Interactive Map: See Where the NYPD Arrests Women Who Are Black, Latina, Trans, and/or Wearing Jeans', *Village Voice*, villagevoice.com.

20 Ritchie, A., *Invisible No More*, 146.

21　Law, V. (8 October 2017) 'How $40 Can Land You in Prison for Seven Years and on the Sex Offender Registry for Life', *Truthout*, truthout.org.

22　Ibid.

23　Gruber, A., Cohen, A.J. & Mogulescu, K. (2016) 'Penal Welfare and the New Human Trafficking Intervention Courts', *Florida Law Review* 68:5, 1333–402.

24　O'Hara, M.E. (14 August 2015) 'Sex workers want to talk to you about parenting', *The Daily Dot*, dailydot.com; Curtis, M.A., Garlington, S. & Schottenfeld, L.S. (2013) 'Alcohol, Drug, and Criminal History Restrictions in Public Housing', *Cityscape*, 15:3, 37–52, available huduser.gov, accessed 28 June 2018.

25　Fernandez, F.L. (2016) 'Hands Up: A Systematized Review Of Policing Sex Workers In The U.S.', *Public Health Theses*, 1085, available elischolar. library.yale.edu, accessed 28 June 2018.

26　See Morrell (SB 381), Act No. 882, of the Louisiana legal code: 'The unnatural carnal copulation by a human being with another of the same sex or opposite sex or with an animal ... (and) the solicitation by a human being of another with the intent to engage in any unnatural carnal copulation for compensation.'

27　McTighe, L. & Haywood, D. (2017) '"There Is NO Justice in Louisiana": Crimes against Nature and the Spirit of Black Feminist Resistance', *Souls* 19:3, 261–85.

28　Prison Legal News (15 September 2005) 'Florida Bans Sex Offenders from Hurricane Shelters', *Prison Legal News*, prisonlegalnews.org.

29　Law, V., 'How $40 Can Land You in Prison for Seven Years and on the Sex Offender Registry for Life'.

30　Open Society Foundations (2012) 'Criminalizing Condoms: How Policing Practices Put Sex Workers and HIV Services at Risk in Kenya, Namibia, Russia, South Africa, the United States, and Zimbabwe', report available opensocietyfoundations.gov, accessed 28 June 2018; Open Society Foundations (13 July 2012) 'Condoms as Evidence', video, YouTube (user: Open Society Foundations), youtube.com/watch?v= boM6keZNIUM.

31　Human Rights Watch (2012) 'Sex Workers at Risk: Condoms as Evidence of Prostitution in Four US Cities', report available hrw.org, accessed 28 June 2018.

32　Ritchie, *Invisible No More*, 151.

33　Ibid., 153.

34　Chiu, J. (8 November 2010) 'Craigslist, Sex Work, and The End of "Innocence?": Why Our Efforts to Address Sex Work Are Misguided', *Rewire News*, rewire.news; Levin, S. (10 January 2017) 'Backpage's halt of adult classifieds will endanger sex workers, advocates warn', *Guardian*, theguardian.com; Simon, C. (10 November 2017) 'The Eros Raid

Means None of Us Are Safe', *Tits and Sass*, titsandsass.com.

35 CBS News (2 August 2017) 'Ex-CEO of male escort service website sentenced to prison', *CBS News*, cbsnews.com.

36 NSWP (27 June 2014) 'Sex Worker Website Seized in Anti-Trafficking Sweep; No Trafficking Charges Entered', *NSWP*, nswp.org.

37 Smith, M. (@pastachips) Twitter, 12:46pm, 24 March 2018.

38 Du, S. (16 May 2018) 'How Congress' attempt to rescue sex workers threatens their safety instead', *City Pages*, citypages.com.

39 Simon, C. (25 April 2018) 'On Backpage', *Tits and Sass*, titsandsass.com.

40 Mgbako, C.A. (2016) *To Live Freely in This World: Sex Worker Activism in Africa*, New York: NYU Press, 47.

41 Angel Torres, C. & Paz, N. (2012) 'Bad Encounter Line Report', *Young Women's Empowerment Project*, report available ywepchicago.files. wordpress.com, accessed 28 June 2018.

42 Ibid.

43 Boots, M.T. (7 May 2017) 'Bills to ban police sexual contact with prostitutes they investigate met with opposition', *Anchorage Daily News*, adn.com.

44 O'Connor, M. (8 October 2017) 'Henrico jail strikes deal with Chesterfield after female inmate population more than doubles', *Richmond Times-Dispatch*, richmond.com.

45 Metcalf, A. (11 June 2017) 'Human Trafficking Cases Rise in Montgomery County', *Bethesda Magazine*, bethesdamagazine.com.

46 Hersh, L. (2013) 'Sex Trafficking Investigations and Prosecutions' in Goodman, J.L. & Leidholdt, D.A. (eds.) 'Lawyer's Manual On Human Trafficking: Pursuing Justice For Victims'. Supreme Court of the State of New York, report available nycourts.gov, accessed 28 June 2018.

47 Biedka, C. (4 January 2018) 'Eight arrested in Frazer prostitution, human trafficking investigation', *Trib Live*, triblive.com.

48 Ditmore, M. (2009) 'The Use of Raids to Fight Trafficking in Persons', Sex Workers Project, report available sexworkersproject.org, accessed 28 June 2018.

49 Ibid.

50 Gruber, A. et al. 'Penal Welfare and the New Human Trafficking Intervention Courts'.

51 Ibid.

52 Dank, M. et al. (2015) 'Locked In: Interactions with the Criminal Justice and Child Welfare Systems for LGBTQ Youth, YMSM, and YWSW Who Engage in Survival Sex', *Urban Institute*, report available urban.org, accessed 28 June 2018.

53 Red Umbrella Project NYC (RedUP NYC) (2014) 'Criminal, Victim, or Worker? The Effects of New York's Human Trafficking Intervention Courts on Adults Charged with Prostitution-Related Offences', available

redumbrellaproject.org, accessed 28 June 2018.

54 Ibid.

55 Gira Grant, M., 'ICE is Using Prostitution Diversion Courts to Stalk Immigrants'.

56 Crabapple, M. (7 January 2015) 'Special Prostitution Courts and the Myth of 'Rescuing' Sex Workers', *Vice*, vice.com.

57 Gruber, A., et al. 'Penal Welfare and the New Human Trafficking Intervention Courts'.

58 Ibid., 1376.

59 RedUP NYC, 'Criminal, Victim, or Worker?', 8.

60 Torres, J. (22 September 2015) 'How New York City's Treatment of Sex Workers Continues to Harm Us', *Rewire News*, rewire.news.

61 RedUP NYC, 'Criminal, Victim, or Worker?', 25.

62 Mgbako, C.A., *To Live Freely in This World*, 55.

63 Lusher, A. (28 March 2017) 'Werewolf murderer tells police: "I may be one of Russia's worst serial killers, but I was a good husband"', *Independent,* independent.co.uk.

64 Daily Express (11 January 2017) 'Russia's worst serial killer claimed 81 FEMALE VICTIMS as he hates women drinking alone', *Express*, express.co.uk.

65 Mgbako, C.A., *To Live Freely in This World*, 55.

66 Ibid.

67 Arnott, J. & Crago, A. (2009) 'Rights Not Rescue: A Report on Female, Male, and Trans Sex Workers' Human Rights in Botswana, Namibia, and South Africa', Open Society Institute, report available opensociety foundations.org, accessed 28 June 2018.

68 Ibid.

69 SAFLII (20 April 2009) *'The Sex Worker Education and Advocacy Taskforce v Minister of Safety and Security and Others* (3378/07) [2009] ZAWCHC 64; 2009 (6) SA 513 (WCC)', report available saflii.org, accessed 28 June 2018.

70 Crockett, E. & Garcia, M. (21 January 2016) 'Ex-cop Daniel Holtzclaw was just sentenced to 263 years in prison for raping black women', *Vox*, vox.com.

71 Diaz, J. et al. (2016) 'How the Daniel Holtzclaw Jury Decided to Send the Ex-Oklahoma City Police Officer to Prison for 263 Years', *ABC News*, abcnews.go.com.

72 Guardian Staff (27 November 2017) 'Cyntoia Brown: Celebrities call for release of sex-trafficking victim', *Guardian*, theguardian.com.

73 Kaba, M. & Schulte, B. (6 December 2017) 'Not A Cardboard Cut Out: Cyntoia Brown and the Framing of a Victim', *The Appeal*, theappeal.org.

74 Jacobs, L. (19 February 2018) 'Tennessee Court Provides Explanation

For Cyntoia Brown's Imprisonment', *Vibe*, vibe.com.

75 *Survived and Punished*, survivedandpunished.org

76 Solutions Not Punishment Collaborative (SNaP Co) (2016) "The Most Dangerous Thing Out Here Is The Police', *SNaP Co.*, dev.rjactioncenter.org, accessed 28 June 2018.

77 Ibid.

78 Lussenhop, J. (18 April 2016) 'Clinton crime bill: Why is it so controversial?', *BBC News*, bbc.com.

79 Gearan, A. & Phillip, A. (25 February 2016) 'Clinton regrets 1996 remark on 'super-predators' after encounter with activist', *Washington Post*.

80 Frank, T. (15 April 2016) 'Bill Clinton's crime bill destroyed lives, and there's no point denying it', *Guardian*, theguardian.com.

81 Ritchie, *Invisible No More*, 196.

82 Henderson, T. (4 June 2015) 'Black Domestic Violence Survivors Are Criminalized From All Directions', *Truthout*, truthout.org.

83 Ibid.

84 Ibid., 191.

85 Prison Culture (24 August 2011) 'The Trial(s) of Tiawanda Moore', *Prison Culture*, usprisonculture.com.

86 Rubin, S. (17 June 2011) 'To Serve and Protect – And Sexually Assault?' *Ms.* magazine Blog, msmagazine.com.

87 Chicago Taskforce on Violence Against Girls & Young Women (24 August 2011) 'Now that Tiawanda Moore is free, what lessons can we learn?', chitaskforce.wordpress.com.

88 Feminist Newswire (12 September 2014) 'Violence Against Women Act Turns 20', Feminist Majority Foundation, feminist.org.

89 Legal Momentum 'History of the Violence Against Women Act', legalmomentum.org.

90 White, P. (5 October 2015) 'A thank you note to "carceral"/"sex-negative" feminists', *Feminist Current*, feministcurrent.com.

91 Marcotte, A. (25 February 2014) 'Prosecutors Arrest Alleged Rape Victim to Make Her Cooperate in Their Case. They Made the Right Call', *Slate,* slate.com.

92 Grant, J.M. et al. (2011) 'Injustice at Every Turn: A Report of the National Transgender Discrimination Survey', *Washington: National Center for Transgender Equality and National Gay and Lesbian Task Force*, report available endtransdiscrimination. org, accessed 28 June 2018; Brydum, S. (2014) 'Arizona Activist Found Guilty of "Walking While Trans"', *Advocate*, advocate.com.

93 Crabapple, M. (2014) 'Project ROSE Is Arresting Sex Workers in Arizona to Save Their Souls', *Vice*, vice.com.

94 NSWP (9 October 2017) 'Ugandan Sex Workers Arrested at

Crisis Meeting Over Murders of Sex Workers', *NSWP*, nswp.org.

95   Kuchu Times (10 August 2017) 'Sex Workers On The Rampant Murders Of Women', *Kuchu Times*, kuchutimes.com.

96   NSWP, 'Ugandan Sex Workers Arrested at Crisis Meeting Over Murders of Sex Workers'.

97   Ditmore, M.H. & Allman, D. (2013) 'An analysis of the implementation of PEPFAR's anti-prostitution pledge and its implications for successful HIV prevention among organizations working with sex workers', *Journal of the International AIDS Society* 16:1.

98   The Red Umbrella Diaries (26 July 2012) 'Sex Worker Activists Disrupt Special Session on US Congress and HIV', video, YouTube (user: The Red Umbrella Diaries), youtube.com/watch?feature=player_ embedded&v=110E941QntY.

99   Anderson-Minshall, J. and Mendus, E. R. (2016) 'Discrimination is literally killing trans women: Outlaw was just the latest', *Plus*, hivplusmag.com.

100 Mgbako, C.A., *To Live Freely in This World*, 5.

101 African Sex Workers Alliance (ASWA) 'Members', available aswaalliance.org, accessed 28 June 2018.

102 Warner, G. (30 August 2016) 'When The U.S. Backs Gay And Lesbian Rights In Africa, Is There A Backlash?', *NPR*, npr.org.

103 Ao, B. (21 May 2016) 'Battling a double dose of discrimination', *IOL*, iol.co.za.

104 Mgbako, C.A., *To Live Freely in This World*, 144.

105 Ekaterina (26 May 2017) 'Silver Rose has joined the 1st of May march', Sex Workers' Rights Advocacy Network (SWAN), swannet.org.

106 Ekaterina (1 May 2016) 'Silver Rose: A long way to success', SWAN, swannet.org.

107 Okoth, J. (2 February 2012) 'Kenya: Bunge la Mwananchi movement and its challenges', *Pambazuka News*, ambazuka.org.

108 Simon, C. (13 November 2018) 'Columnist Caty Simon: Spend money on treatment, not cameras', *Daily Hampshire Gazette*, gazettenet.com.

109 Robin D. (29 February 2016) 'Activist Spotlight: Bonnie On Violence And Endurance', *Tits and Sass*, titsandsass.com.

110 Lysistrata Mutual Care Collective & Fund 'Emergency Fund', *Lysistrata*, lysistratamccf.org.

111 Frishman, S. (7 September 2017) 'The End of The Life: Leaving Sex Work Because Of Progressive Illness', *Tits and Sass*, titsandsass.com.

112 NSWP (2016) 'Silver Rose (Russia)', *NSWP*, nswp.org.

113 Laura McTighe & Deon Haywood (16 January 2018) '"There Is NO Justice in Louisiana": Crimes against Nature and the Spirit of Black Feminist Resistance', *Souls* 19:3, 261–285.

114 Carmon, I. (5 September 2013) 'I am not a sex offender', Women with

a Vision, wwav.no.org.

115 On its list of 'success stories', one large anti-prostitution organisation in the US lists almost exclusively measures to further criminalise clients and 'rescues' of women selling sex; see Demand Abolition 'Category: Success Stories', available demandabolition.org, accessed 28 June 2018.

6. The People's Home

1 MacKinnon, C.A. (2011) 'Trafficking, Prostitution, and Inequality', *Harvard Civil Rights – Civil Liberties Law Review*, 46, 271–309, 301.

2 Dworkin, A. (1993) 'Prostitution and Male Supremacy', *Michigan Journal of Gender and Law* 1:1, available repository.law.umich.edu, accessed 28 June 2018.

3 Crouch, D. (17 February 2017) 'Is Sweden's feminist agenda working?', *BBC News*, bbc.co.uk; Agencies (4 February 2017) 'Is the Swedish deputy PM trolling Trump with this all-female photo?', *Guardian*, theguardian.com.

4 Jones, A. (28 January 2016) 'After I Lived in Norway, America Felt Backward. Here's Why', *The Nation*, thenation.com; Gjersø, J.F. (9 June 2017) 'Jeremy Corbyn – a mainstream [Scandinavian] social democrat', *openDemocracy*, opendemocracy.net.

5 For example, Bindel, J., *The Pimping of Prostitution*.

6 Levy, J. (2017) *The War on People who Use Drugs: The Harms of Sweden's Aim for a Drug-Free Society*, London: Routledge; The Local Sweden (22 August 2013) 'Structural racism "still a problem" in Sweden', *The Local*, thelocal.se; Momodou, J. (18 April 2012) 'Sweden: the country where racism is just a joke', *Guardian*, theguardian.com.

7 Neuman, C.E. (2010) *Sexual Crime: A Reference Handbook*, Santa Barbara, CA: ABC-CLIO, LLC, 154.

8 Grant, R. (2013) 'Proposed Criminalisation of the Purchase of Sex (Scotland) Bill (2): Summary of Consultation Responses', Scottish Parliament, s. 187, report available parliament.scot, accessed 28 June 2018.

9 Some of the strategies used by street sex workers in the UK are discussed by Sanders, T. (2001) 'Female street sex workers, sexual violence, and protection strategies', *Journal of Sexual Aggression*, 7:1, 5–18.

10 Fouche, G. (27 April 2014) 'View from the streets: New Nordic sex laws are making prostitutes feel less safe', *Independent*, independent.co.uk.

11 Levy, J. (2015) *Criminalising the Purchase of Sex: Lessons from Sweden*, Oxford: Routledge, 121.

12 Krüsi A, et al. (2014) 'Criminalisation of clients: Reproducing vulnerabilities for violence and poor health among street-based sex workers

in Canada – a qualitative study' *BMJ Open*, 4: e005191, available bmjopen.bmj.com, accessed 28 June 2018.

13 Socialstyrelsen (2008) 'Prostitution in Sweden 2007', 48, available socialstyrelsen.se, accessed 28 June 2018.

14 Norwegian Ministry of Justice and the Police (2004) 'Purchasing Sexual Services in Sweden and the Netherlands: Legal Regulation and Experiences', 19, available regjeringen.no, accessed 28 June 2018.

15 Ibid., 13, 19–20.

16 Levy, *Criminalising the Purchase of Sex*, 121.

17 Norwegian Ministry of Justice and the Police, 'Purchasing Sexual Services in Sweden and the Netherlands: Legal Regulation and Experiences', 13.

18 Sanders, T. (2005) *Sex Work: A Risky Business*, Cullompton: Willan Publishing, chapter 4.

19 Levy, *Criminalising the Purchase of Sex*, 189

20 Gallagher, C. (4 September 2017) "Dramatic rise' in attacks on sex workers since law change', *The Irish Times*, irishtimes.com.

21 Gentleman, A. (5 February 2016) 'Sex worker and activist Laura Lee: 'It's now far more difficult to stay safe', *Guardian,* theguardian.com.

22 Rasmussen, I. et al. (2014) 'Evaluation of Norwegian legislation criminalising the buying of sexual services (English summary)', Norwegian Government, report available rm.coe.int, accessed 28 June 2018.

23 Lyon, W. (2014) 'Client Criminalisation and Sex Workers' Right to Health', *Hibernian Law Journal*, 13, 58–97, 69.

24 Ibid., 70.

25 Rasmussen, et al., 'Evaluation of Norwegian legislation criminalising the buying of sexual services (English summary)'.

26 Costa-Kostritsky, V. (20 January 2014) 'On Malmskillnadsgatan', *LRB Blog*, lrb.co.uk.

27 Banyard, K. (2010) *The Equality Illusion: The Truth about Women and Men Today,* London: Faber and Faber, 136.

28 See Amnesty International (2016) 'Q&A: Policy to Protect the Human Rights of Sex Workers', available amnesty.org, accessed 28 June 2018.

29 The Women's Support Project (2018), available womenssupportproject. co.uk, accessed 28 June 2018.

30 Nordic Model Now (2017), slideshow, available nordicmodelnow.files. wordpress.com, accessed 28 June 2018.

31 Brown, A. (22 January 2018) '"I never looked back" Women's Aid worker opens up about own domestic abuse horror to highlight why organisation is still vital', *Daily Record,* dailyrecord.co.uk.

32 Farley, M. (2017) 'Book Review: *Shadow's Law, The True Story of a Swedish Detective Inspector Fighting Prostitution* by Simon Häggström', *Dignity: A Journal on Sexual Exploitation and Violence* 2:2, article 5.

33 Nordic Model Now!, slideshow.

34 Heiberg, T. (2011) 'Exploring Prostituted Women's Experiences of a South African Exit Intervention: An Interpretative Phenomenological Analysis', University of Cape Town (Thesis), available knowledgeco-op .uct.ac.za, accessed 28 June 2018.

35 Glass, A., 'Fact: Women often struggle to leave prostitution'; Nordic Model Now!, slideshow.

36 Parliament of Sweden (2005) 'Makt att forma samhället och sitt eget liv-jämställdhetspolitiken mot nya mål [Power to shape society and its own life – Equality policy towards new goals]', available riksdagen.se, accessed 28 June 2018.

37 Sköld Jansson, C. et al. (2004) 'Nationellt resurscentrum för prostitue-rade [National Resource Center for Prostitutes], Motion 2004/05:S3068', Swedish Parliament, available riksdagen.se, accessed 28 June 2018.

38 VG Nyheter [VG News] (2017) 'Mann fikk lavere straff fordi voldtek-tsofrene var prostituerte [Man got lower punishment because rape victims were prostitutes]', available vg.no, accessed 28 June 2018.

39 Ashton, C. (30 September 2010) 'Could Sweden's prostitution laws work in the UK?' BBC News, bbc.com.

40 Levy, Criminalising the Purchase of Sex, 189.

41 Ibid.

42 Sex Professionals of Canada (2013) 'STOP the Arrests!!! SSM – One year and still fighting with love and RAGE', SPOC, available spoc.ca, accessed 28 June 2018.

43 Levy, Criminalising the Purchase of Sex, 144, 148, 190–1.

44 Ibid., 150.

45 Ibid., 166.

46 Minihan, M. (2 September 2014) 'Minister 'shocked' by reports of direct provision prostitution', The Irish Times, irishtimes.com.

47 Lyon, W. (6 December 2014) 'On Frances Fitzgerald's bill to criminalise clients', Feminist Ire, feministire.com.

48 Irish Reception and Integration Agency 'Direct Provision', report available ria.gov.ie, accessed 28 June 2018.

49 Banyard, K. (22 August 2017) 'Legalise prostitution? We are being asked to accept industrialised sexual exploitation', Guardian, theguardian.com.

50 Debbonaire, T. (@ThangamMP) Twitter, 10:20am, 27 September 2016.

51 Cox, S. (13 April 2017) 'What's Current: 937 johns, zero prostituted women arrested in France since adoption of Nordic model', Feminist Current, feministcurrent.com.

52 Lyon, W. (17 April 2017) 'Sex work in France, one year on', Feminist Ire, feministire.com.

53 Coyne, E. (3 February 2017) 'Bill makes sex workers "poorer and

unsafe"', *The Times*, thetimes.co.uk.

54 Amnesty International (2016) 'The Human Cost Of "Crushing" The Market: Criminalization Of Sex Work In Norway', s. 3.13, *Amnesty USA*, available amnestyusa.org, accessed 28 June 2018.

55 Ibid.

56 Ibid.

57 Ibid.

58 Gira Grant, M. (26 May 2016) 'Amnesty International Calls for an End to the 'Nordic Model' of Criminalizing Sex Workers', *The Nation,* thenation.com.

59 Benoit, C., et al. 'Lack of Confidence in Police Creates a "Blue Ceiling" for Sex Workers' Safety'. *Canadian Public Policy* 42:4, 456–68.

60 From private correspondence.

61 Amnesty International, *The Human Cost.*

62 Butcher, M. (4 August 2012) 'Police Bust Prostitutes Using Airbnb Apartment in Stockholm', *Tech Crunch*, techcrunch.com.

63 McNamee, M.S. (5 November 2015) 'First man arrested under new prostitution laws in the North', thejournal.ie.

64 Radio Kerry News (3 July 2017) 'Two Romanian women admit involvement in Tralee brothel', radiokerry.ie.

65 Ryan, K. (@KarinDianeRyan) Twitter, 2:27pm, 29 September 2016: '.@Davidontour1 @ThangamMP "working together for safety" is code for running brothel/pimping. Pimps call themselves SWs so that's convenient'.

66 Moran, R. (19 September 2015) 'My lessons in prostitution: How I learned the myth of the high-class hooker', *Salon*, salon.com.

67 Moran, R. (@RachelRMoran) Twitter, 10:34am, 9 April 2018; SWARM (@SexWorkHive) Twitter, 11:19am, 8 April 2018.

68 Deegan, G. (9 May 2018) 'Husband and wife hooker team selling sex from Irish home avoid jail', *Irish Mirror*, irishmirror.ie.

69 Nugent, R. (7 August 2017) 'Sex worker (73) was trying to pay for son's kidney transplant operation', *Independent.IE*, independent.ie.

70 Swedish Penal Code (1962: 700, amended 2017: 1136), ch. 6, s. 12, available riksdagen.se, accessed 28 June 2018.

71 Amnesty International, *The Human Cost.*

72 Ibid.

73 Ibid.

74 Ibid.

75 Ibid.

76 Ibid., section 3.9.

77 Ibid., section 3.10.

78 Ibid.

79 Ibid., section 3.4.

80 Lam, E., 'Behind the Rescue'.

81 Ibid.

82 Amnesty International, *The Human Cost*.

83 Ibid.

84 Siddique, H. & Rawlinson, K. (28 November 2017) 'Rape victim arrested on immigration charges after going to police', *Guardian*, theguardian.com.

85 Swedish National Police Board (2011) 'Trafficking in human beings for sexual and other purposes', 13–14, report available feminismandhuman rights.files.wordpress.com, accessed 28 June 2018.

86 Jahnsen, S.O. (2007) 'Women who cross borders – Black magic? A Critical Discourse Analysis of the Norwegian newspaper coverage of Nigerian women in prostitution in Norway', *University of Bergen* (Masters Thesis), available citeseerx.ist.psu.edu, accessed 28 June 2018.

87 Amnesty International, *The Human Cost*.

88 European Women's Lobby (2014) '18 myths on prostitution', report available womenlobby.org, accessed 28 June 2018; APT Ireland (2014) 'Prostitution And Sex Trafficking: Abuse Of Power, Abuse Of Vulnerability', available education.dublindiocese.ie, accessed 28 June 2018.

89 Bindel, *Pimping of Prostitution*.

90 Lam, E., 'Behind the Rescue'.

91 Norwegian Ministry of Justice and the Police, *Purchasing Sexual Services in Sweden and the Netherlands*.

92 Ibid., 13.

93 Swedish Parliament (2002) 'Statens offentliga utredningar [Government Public Investigations] 2002:69' s. 8.3.1.1, available riksdagen.se, accessed 28 June 2018.

94 Goldberg, M. (30 July 2014) 'Should Buying Sex Be Illegal?', *The Nation*, thenation.com.

95 Levy, *Criminalising the Purchase of Sex*; Skarhed, A. (2010) 'Evaluation of the prohibition of the purchase of sexual services (English Summary)', Government Offices of Sweden, 36, available government. se, accessed 28 June 2018.

96 Raymond, J.G. (2013) *Not a Choice, Not a Job: Exposing the Myths about Prostitution and the Global Sex Trade,* Washington, D.C.: Potomac Books, 72.

97 Swedish National Police Board, *Trafficking in human beings*.

98 Parliament of Sweden (2001) 'Riksdagens snabbprotokoll [quick protocol] 2001/02:78', available at riksdagen.se.

99 Banyard, K. (2016) *Pimp State: Sex, Money and the Future of Equality*, London: Faber and Faber, 198.

100 Levy, *Criminalising the Purchase of Sex*, Introduction.

101 Ibid., 5. See also Baldwin, P. (2005) *Disease and Democracy: The*

Industrialized World Faces AIDS, Berkeley: Univeristy of California Press, 242.

102 Levy, *Criminalising the Purchase of Sex*, 6–7.

103 Ibid., 7.

104 Ahlander, J. (27 March 2017) 'Sweden to offer compensation for transgender sterilizations', *Reuters*, reuters.com.

105 Transform (2014) 'Drug policy in Sweden: A repressive approach that increases harm', tdpf.org.uk.

106 Ederyd, C. (2016) 'Sweden's Battle Against Drugs and Prejudice', *Vice*, vice.com.

107 Object (2015) 'Prostitution – The Facts', object.org.uk; Woodward, S. (2016) 'Calls for Australia to adopt 'Nordic Model' on prostitution', *SBS News*, sbs.com.au.

108 Murphy, M. (28 November 2014) Comment on Berg, S. (2014) 'From Norway to New Zealand, pro-prostitution research is its own worst enemy', *Feminist Current*, feministcurrent.com.

109 Banyard, *Pimp State*.

110 Bindel, J. (n.d.) Contribution to 'Prostitution and Gender Inequality', SPACE International, spaceintl.org.

111 Nordic Model Now (@nordicmodelnow) Twitter, 3:57am, 27 May 2016: 'The Nordic model works and should keep on keeping on. https://t.co/SrIAGZFzZb'.

112 deVisser, L. (2013) 'Interview with MP Joy Smith – Human Trafficking and Prostitution', ARPA Canada, arpacanada.ca.

113 Pablo, C. (2014) 'New prostitution law leaves sex workers "invisible and anonymous"', advocate says', *Straight*, straight.com.

114 MacKay, P. (11 June 2014) 'Debate on Protection of Communities and Exploited Persons Act', openparliament.ca.

115 Macartney, C. (2015) 'Canada begins implementing transformational prostitution laws', *Christian Week*, christianweek.org.

116 McIntyre, C. (13 May 2015) 'Migrant sex workers caught up in Ottawa sting facing deportation, further exploitation: activists', *National Post*, nationalpost.com.

117 Banyard, *Pimp State*, 194.

118 Kuosmanen, J. (2010) 'Attitudes and perceptions about legislation prohibiting the purchase of sexual services in Sweden', *European Journal of Social Work* 14:2, 247–63.

119 Fullinwider, R.K. (n.d., accesses 28 June 2018) 'The Swedish Model – Abolitionist Nirvana? Part 3', *The New Prostitution Wars*, Essay 8, newprostitutionwars.net.

120 Ahlstrand, T. (2010) 'The Swedish example', presentation at the The Third Swedish-Dutch Conference on Gender Equality: Trafficking in Human Beings and Prostitution.

121   Levy, *Criminalising the Purchase of Sex*, 63.

122   Kristof, N.D. (23 January 2006) '"Sex Work" versus "Prostitution"', *New York Times*, kristof.blogs.nytimes.com.

123   For a discussion of one example, see Buckland, S. (2012) 'Call things by their proper names: A Reply to the Anti Porn Men Project', Zetkin.net.

124   Häggström, S. (2016) 'Shadow's Law: The True Story of a Swedish Detective Inspector Fighting Prostitution', Stockholm: Bullet Point Publishing; Häggström, S. (n.d.) Contribution to 'Prostitution and Gender Inequality', SPACE International, spaceintl.org.

125   Shane, C. (@CharoShane) Twitter, 10:34am, 7 June 2018: 'Men like CH, who are hardcore into sex worker rescue and determined to code all prostitution as rape, are so obviously getting a huge thrill from imagining sexually violated female bodies, helpless women ravaged by dozens of dicks, etc.'

126   Smith, J. (2013) 'Why the game's up for Sweden's sex trade', *Independent*, independent.co.uk.

127   Ekberg, G. (2008) 'Abolishing Prostitution: The Swedish solution', *Rain and Thunder*, available at catwinternational.org, 41.

128   Smith, J. (2016) 'Pimp State: Sex, Money and the Future of Equality by Kat Banyard – Review', *Guardian*, theguardian.com; Nordic Model Now! (2017), slideshow handout, available at nordicmodelnow.files .wordpress.com/2017/05/nmn-slideshow-handout-v1b.pdf.

129   Goodhart, D. (27 March 2013) 'Why the left is wrong about immigration', *Guardian*, theguardian.com.

7. Charmed Circle

1   Global Network of Sex Work Projects (NSWP) (2016) 'Mandatory Registration and Condom Use Proposed in Germany', nswp.org.

2   Mackay, F. (2015) *Radical Feminism: Feminist Activism in Movement*, New York: Palgrave Macmillan, 209–27.

3   Grimley, N. (2015) 'Amnesty International row: Should prostitution be decriminalised?', *BBC News*, bbc.com; Shanahan, C. (2015) 'Amnesty prostitution vote rebuked', *Irish Examiner*, irishexaminer.com.

4   See, for example, Richards, D.A. (1982) *Sex, Drugs, Death, and the Law: An Essay on Human Rights and Overcriminalization*, Totowa, NJ: Rowman and Littlefield, 133.

5   White, L. (1990) *The Comforts of Home: Prostitution in Colonial Nairobi*, Chicago: University of Chicago Press, 3.

6   Daalder, A.L. (2015) 'Prostitutie in Nederland anno 2014', Netherlands Ministry of Safety and Justice, available at rijksoverheid.nl, 17–18.

7   See Hydra Berlin (2016) 'Information Pamphlet about the "Prostitutes Protection Law"', available at hydra-berlin.de; and Herter, A. & Fem, E. (2017) 'Professed Protection, Pointless Provisions – Overview of the German Prostitutes Protection Act', International Committee on the Rights of Sex Workers in Europe (ICRSE), available at sexworkeurope.org.

8   Delgado, K. (2016) 'Stacey Dooley's Sex in Strange Places is a shocking look at Turkey's sexual underworld', *Radio Times*, radiotimes.com.

9   Koster, K. (6 December 2017) 'Legal in Theory: Germany's Sex Trade Laws and Why They Have Nothing to Do With Amnesty Sex Work Proposal', *Huffington Post*, huffingtonpost.com.

10 Scarlet Alliance (2014) 'The Principles for Model Sex Work Legislation', scarlettalliance.org.au.

11 Mansfield, B. (2014) 'Nevada's Brothels: Legalization Serves The Man', *Tits and Sass*, titsandsass.com.

12 Anna, F. (12 March 2015) 'How to start in window prostitution in Amsterdam?', Behind the Red Light District, behindtheredlightdistrict. blogspot.co.uk.

13 Tucker, G.M. (2012) 'The Invisible Challenge to HIV/AIDS Prevention: Clandestine Prostitution in Senegal', *Journal of International Women's Studies* 13:1, 19–31.

14 NSWP (2017) 'Greek Sex Workers Organise Conference and Demand Law Reform', nswp.org.

15 Hydra Berlin, 'Information Pamphlet about the "Prostitutes Protection Law"'.

16 Wagenaar, H., Altink, S. & Amesberger, H. (2013) 'Final Report of the International Comparative Study of Prostitution Policy: Austria and the Netherlands', Platform31, kks.verdus.nl/upload/documents/P31_prostitution_policy_report.pdf.

17 Quoted in Norwegian Ministry of Justice and the Police (8 October 2004) 'Purchasing Sexual Services in Sweden and the Netherlands: Legal Regulation and Experiences', report, regjeringen.no, 34.

18 Passion, M. (25 August 2008) 'Cautionary words from a brothel survivor: But still a sex worker activist', Personal blog, marikopassion. wordpress.com.

19 Walker, A. (2016) 'Women's Experiences Of Different Legislative Models', *SPACE International*, spaceintl.org.

20 From private conversation.

21 Herter, A. & Fem, E. (2017) 'Professed Protection, Pointless Provisions – Overview of the German Prostitutes Protection Act', International Committee on the Rights of Sex Workers in Europe (ICRSE), sexwork europe.org.

22 Ibid.

262 NOTES FROM PAGES 181 TO 186

23 Scarlet Alliance and the Australian Federation of AIDS Organisations (1999) 'Unjust and Counter-Productive The Failure of Governments to Protect Sex Workers from Discrimination', report, scarletalliance.org.au, 14.

24 Hydra Berlin, 'Information Pamphlet about the "Prostitutes Protection Law"'.

25 Spooner, R. (2015) 'Adrian Bayley trials: Street sex workers still reluctant to report crimes', *The Age*, theage.com.au.

26 Perkins R. (1991) 'Working girls: Prostitutes, their life and social control', *Australian studies in law, crime and justice*, Canberra: Australian Institute of Criminology, chapter 2.

27 Gira Grant, M. (2009) 'Resisting the Sex Panic: Sex Workers Struggle for Evidence-Based Regulation in Nevada', *Rewire*, rewire.news.

28 Ibid.

29 Global Network of Sex Work Projects (NSWP) (2016) 'Mandatory Registration and Condom Use Proposed in Germany', nswp.org.

30 Open Society Foundations (2012) 'Laws and Policies Affecting Sex Work: A Reference Brief', nswp.org.

31 Australasian Society for HIV, Viral Hepatitis and Sexual Health Medicine (n.d.) 'Sex Work', hivlegal.ashm.org.au.

32 Scarlet Alliance, Australian Sex Workers Association (2011) 'Mandatory or compulsory testing of sex workers for HIV and/or sexually transmissible infections in the Australian context', *Australian Parliament*, parliament.act.gov.au.

33 Gira Grant, M., 'Resisting the Sex Panic: Sex Workers Struggle for Evidence-Based Regulation in Nevada'.

34 Mansfield, B., 'Nevada's Brothels: Legalization Serves The Man'.

35 Wagenaar, H. & Altink, S. (2012) 'Prostitution as Morality Politics or Why It Is Exceedingly Difficult To Design and Sustain Effective Prostitution Policy', *Sexuality Research and Social Policy* 9, 279.

36 Gira Grant, M., 'Resisting the Sex Panic: Sex Workers Struggle for Evidence-Based Regulation in Nevada'; Heineman, Jenny, Rachel MacFarlane, and Barbara G. Brents (2012) 'Sex Industry and Sex Workers in Nevada' in Dmitri N. Shalin (ed.) *The Social Health of Nevada: Leading Indicators and Quality of Life in the Silver State*, Las Vegas, NV: UNLV Center for Democratic Culture.

37 Lehman, M. (2013) 'Sex Workers Protest Against Alice Schwarzer's Panel Discussion about Prostitution in Berlin', International Committee on the Rights of Sex Workers in Europe (ICRSE), sexworkeurope.org.

38 Hydra Berlin, 'Information Pamphlet about the "Prostitutes Protection Law"'.

39 Schon, M. (2016) 'Legalization has turned Germany into the "Bordello of Europe" and we should be ashamed', *Feminist Current*, feministcurrent.com.

40 Pearson, M. (2015) 'Inside one of Germany's "flat rate" brothels: What it's like working at the King George Club'. News.com.au.

41 van Rossum, F. (2015) 'Sex workers in the Netherlands are making history', Research Project Korea, researchprojectkorea.wordpress.com.

42 Smith, P. (2014) 'East London Strippers Collective Is Standing Up for Strippers' Rights', *Vice*, vice.com.

43 McLennan, W. (4 February 2015) '"676 hours less of objectification of women": Councillor's delight as Spearmint Rhino's opening hours are cut', *Camden New Journal*.

44 Dolinsek, S. (2016) 'Sex workers fight against compulsory registration and identification in Germany', *openDemocracy*, opendemocracy.net; Bindel, J. (2016) 'Women's Experiences Of Different Legislative Models', *SPACE International*, spaceintl.org.

45 Banyard, K. (2016) *Pimp State: Sex, Money and the Future of Equality*, London: Faber and Faber, 182.

8. No Silver Bullet

1 The *Fa'afafine* are a third gender community of Samoa and surrounding Polynesian islands. Described by Japanese-Samoan artist Yuki Kihara as 'a liminal gender that encapsulates both a male and a female gender', the concept cannot be easily mapped onto the Western gender binary. The word itself translates to 'in the manner of a woman.' See Stevens, P. (2011) 'Bite 59: Shigeyuki Kihara – Fa'afafine: In the Manner of A Woman, 2004–5', realitybitesartblog.blogspot.com.

2 New Zealand Prostitutes' Collective (2012) 'Celebrating 25 Amazing Years', available at nzpc.org.nz.

3 De Santis, M. (2014) 'Sweden's Prostitution Solution: Why Hasn't Anyone Tried This Before?', Women's Justice Center, esnoticia.co.

4 Amnesty International (2015) 'Global movement votes to adopt policy to protect human rights of sex workers', amnesty.org; Human Rights Watch (2014) 'World Report 2014', 47; UNAIDS (2002) 'Sex Work and HIV/AIDS: UNAIDS Technical Update'; World Health Organisation Department of HIV/AIDS (2012) 'Prevention and Treatment of HIV and other sexually transmitted infections for sex workers in low-and middle-income countries: Recommendations for a public health approach'.

5 New Zealand Prostitutes' Collective, quoted in Global Network of Sex Work Projects (NSWP) (2014) 'Sex Work And The Law: Understanding Legal Frameworks and the Struggle for Sex Work Law Reforms', nswp.org.

6 McClure, T. (2017) 'A Racist System: Māori and Pacific Kiwis Talk About the Police', *Vice*, vice.com.

7   Livingston, T. and Dennett, K. (2017) 'Auckland's infamous K Road: NZ's first serial killer's hunting ground', *Stuff*, stuff.co.nz; Sherwood, S. and Ensor, B. (2016) 'Christchurch sex workers staying off the streets after death of Renee Duckmanton', *Stuff*, stuff.co.nz.

8   GAATW (2018) 'Sex Workers Organising for Change: Self-representation, community mobilisation, and working conditions', gaatw.org, 105.

9   Hati, C., Healy, C. and Wi-Hongi, A. (2017) 'It's work, it's working: The integration of sex workers and sex work in Aotearoa/New Zealand', wsanz.org.nz.

10 Armstrong, L. (2011) 'Managing risks of violence in decriminalised street-based sex work: A feminist (sex workers' rights) perspective', Victoria University of Wellington (PhD Thesis), available at core.ac.uk/download/pdf/41338266.pdf.

11 Armstrong, L. (2014) 'Screening clients in a decriminalised street-based sex industry: Insights into the experiences of New Zealand sex workers', *Australian & New Zealand Journal of Criminology*, 47:2, 207–22.

12 Abel, G., Fitzgerald, L. and Brunton, C. (2007) 'The impact of the Prostitution Reform Act on the health and safety practices of sex workers: Report to the Prostitution Law Review Committee', report, University of Otago, otago.ac.nz, 139.

13 Woodcock, J. (2017) 'As a call centre worker I saw how employees are stripped of their rights', *Guardian*, theguardian.com.

14 GAATW, 'Sex Workers Organising for Change', 104.

15 Stanley, T. (@timothy_stanley), Twitter, 3:19am, 13 April 2016. '@rmc ahill hmm. I don't like it. Suggests there's a union, pension fund etc'.

16 Abel, G. (2010) 'Decriminalisation: A Harm Minimisation and Human Rights Approach to Regulating Sex Work', University of Otago, Christchurch (PhD Thesis), available at prostitutionresearch.info/pdfs_all/GillianAbelPhDNewZealand.pdf, 233.

17 Abel et. al., 'The impact of the Prostitution Reform Act on the health and safety practices of sex workers: Report to the Prostitution Law Review Committee', 118–19.

18 Abel, G., Fitzgerald, L. and Brunton, C. (2009) 'The impact of decriminalisation on the number of sex workers in New Zealand', *Journal of Social Policy* 8:3, 515–31; Miller, C. (2017) 'Northland brothel bringing sex out of the shadows', *New Zealand Herald*, nzherald.co.nz.

19 New Zealand Ministry of Justice (2008) 'Report Of The Prostitution Law Review Committee On The Operation Of The Prostitution Reform Act 2003', report available at prostitutescollective.net, 38.

20 Mossman, E. and Mayhew, P. (2007) 'Key Informant Interviews Review of the Prostitution Reform Act 2003', New Zealand Ministry of Justice, chezstella.org/docs/NZ-KeyInformantInterviews.pdf.

21 Abel, G., et al., 'The impact of the Prostitution Reform Act on the health

and safety practices of sex workers'.

22 Prostitution Reform Act 2003, s. 18, New Zealand Legislation, available at legislation.govt.nz.

23 New Zealand Prostitutes Collective (2018) 'History', nzpc.org.nz/history.

24 Jordan, J. (2011) 'Sex work – Legislation and decriminalisation', Te Ara – the Encyclopedia of New Zealand, teara.govt.nz.

25 Prostitution Reform Act 2003, s. 3, New Zealand Legislation, available at legislation.govt.nz.

26 Armstrong, L. (2017) 'From Law Enforcement to Protection? Interactions Between Sex Workers and Police in a Decriminalized Street-based Sex Industry', *The British Journal of Criminology* 57:3, 570–88.

27 Ibid.

28 Ibid.

29 Abel, G., Fitzgerald, L. and Brunton, C., Abel, G., et al., 'The impact of the Prostitution Reform Act on the health and safety practices of sex workers', 140.

30 Ibid., p. 163

31 Wynn, K. (13 July 2014) 'Police help short-changed sex worker', *New Zealand Herald*, nzherald.co.nz.

32 GAATW, 'Sex Workers Organising for Change', 96.

33 Ibid.

34 Ibid.

35 Ibid., 89.

36 Abel et al., 'The impact of the Prostitution Reform Act on the health and safety practices of sex workers', 120.

37 Roguski, M. (28 March 2013) 'Occupational Health and Safety of Migrant Sex Workers in New Zealand', report, New Zealand Prostitutes' Collective, nswp.org.

38 Triggs, S. et al. (Septembet 2009) 'Responding to sexual violence: Attrition in the New Zealand criminal justice system', report, New Zealand Ministry of Women's Affairs, women.govt.nz.

39 Abel et al., 'The impact of the Prostitution Reform Act on the health and safety practices of sex workers', 165.

40 Armstrong, L. (2017) 'From Law Enforcement to Protection? Interactions Between Sex Workers and Police in a Decriminalized Street-based Sex Industry', *The British Journal of Criminology* 57:3, 570–88.

41 Ibid.

42 Woods, 'Ipswich victims drug addicts, not "sex workers"', 13.

43 Vitale, A.S. (2017) 'Police and the Liberal Fantasy', *Jacobin* jacobinmag.com.

44 Ditum, S. (5 February 2015) 'If you think decriminalisation will make prostitution safe, look at Germany's mega brothels', *New Statesman*, newstatesman.com.

45 Banyard, *Pimp State*.

46 TVNZ (1 July 2011) 'WINZ won't promote sex jobs', tekarere, tvnz.co.nz.

47 Prostitution Reform Act 2003, s. 18, New Zealand Legislation, available at legislation.govt.nz.

48 New Zealand Herald (8 April 2016) 'Former prostitutes call for ban to industry', *New Zealand Herald*, nzherald.co.nz.

49 Harris, M. (2014) 'Sex Workers Equally Protected from Sexual Harassment as Other Workers – Says New Zealand Case', Oxford Human Rights Hub blog, ohrh.law.ox.ac.uk.

50 Banyard, K., *Pimp State*, 64.

51 Local (2011) 'Norway a "pimp" for my prostitute client: lawyer', *The Local*, thelocal.no.

52 Prostitution Reform Act 2003, s. 18, New Zealand Legislation, available at legislation.govt.nz.

53 International Labour Organization (2007) 'Direct Request for information from the Government of New Zealand', Direct Request (CEACR), adopted 2007, published 97th ILC session (2008), available at ilo.org.

54 Private correspondence.

55 Learmonth, D., Hakala, S. and Keller, M. (2015) '"I can't carry on like this": barriers to exiting the street-based sex trade in South Africa', *Health Psychology and Behavioral Medicine* 3:1, 348–65.

56 Canadian Alliance for Sex Work Law Reform, (October 2016) 'Joint Submission for Canada's Review before the UN Committee on the Elimination of All Forms of Discrimination Against Women, 65th Session', nswp.org

57 GAATW, 'Sex Workers Organising for Change', 29.

58 Lam, E., 'Behind the Rescue'.

59 McGrath, M. (2015) 'Sex worker Kate McGrew (36): "I feel that once we stop seeing sex work as a social ill we'll start to see sex workers as humans"', *Independent*, independent.ie.

60 Abel, G., Fitzgerald, L. and Brunton, C. (2009) 'The impact of decriminalisation on the number of sex workers in New Zealand', *Journal of Social Policy* 8:3, 515–31.

61 Abel, et al., 'The impact of the Prostitution Reform Act on the health and safety practices of sex workers', 84.

62 Moran, R. (2015) 'SPACE International's response to consultation for Prostitution Law Reform (Scotland) Bill 2015', womenssupportproject. co.uk/userfiles/file/space%20international%20response.pdf.

63 New Zealand Prostitutes Collective (NZPC) (2015) 'Decriminalisation of Sex Work in New Zealand: Impact on Maori', available at sexworklaw.co.nz.

64 Murphy, M. (2015) 'Male progressives who support harm reduction

need a lesson in feminism and in radicalism', *Rabble*, rabble.ca.

65 Mgbako, C.A. (2016) *To Live Freely in This World: Sex Worker Activism in Africa*, New York: NYU Press, 40.

66 Abel, G. (2014) 'A decade of decriminalization: Sex work "down under" but not underground', *Criminology and Criminal Justice* 14:5, 580–92.

Conclusion

1   Sontag, S. (2003) 'Of Courage and Resistance', *The Nation*, thenation.com.

2   Lorde, A. (1982) "Learning from the 60s" in *Sister Outsider: Essays and Speeche*, Berkeley, CA: Crossing Press, 134–44.

3   Smith, J. (2016) 'The Duel: Should it be illegal to pay for sex?' *Prospect*, prospectmagazine.co.uk.

4   Jeni, H. (12 October 2017) 'Burning Down The Sex Trade', Medium (@GappyTales), medium.com.

5   GAATW, 'Sex Workers Organising for Change', 9.

6   Ibid., 36.

7   Ibid., 28.

8   Jana, S. et al. (2014) 'Combating human trafficking in the sex trade: Can sex workers do it better?' *Journal of Public Health* 36:4, 622–8.

9   NSWP, 'Sex Work And The Law', 11.

10 Ibid., 13.

11 GAATW, 'Sex Workers Organising for Change', 36.

12 Global Network of Sex Work Projects (NSWP) (October 2014) 'Sex Workers Demonstrate Economic and Social Empowerment. Regional Report: Asia and the Pacific', report, nswp.org, 15–16.

13 Mock, J. (17 January 2017) 'On the Women's March '"Guiding Vision" and its inclusion of Sex Workers', *Janet Mock on Tumblr*, janetmock.tumblr.com.

14 Of course, criminalising commercial sex does push some *into* homelessness – as evicted sex workers in Norway can testify.

15 Speech by the MP who proposed the PRA. Barnett, T. (25 June 2003) 'Prostitution Reform Bill — Procedure, Third Reading', New Zealand Parliament, parliament.nz.

16 de Leon, A. (October 2015) 'Black Sex Workers' Lives Matter', *For Harriet*, forharriet.com.

17 This is illustrated by the case of New South Wales in the late 1980s, where sex work was decriminalised on paper, but police continued to arrest sex workers at similar or even higher rates than in adjacent criminalised jurisdictions. Perkins R. (1991) 'Working girls: Prostitutes, their life and social control', in *Australian studies in law, crime and justice,*

Canberra: Australian Institute of Criminology, chapter 2, available at aic.gov.au.

18 Black Women for Wages for Housework (1977) 'Money for Prostitutes is Money for Black Women', *LIES: A journal of materialist feminism*, available at liesjournal.net.

19 Bindel, J. (2017) *The Pimping of Prostitution: Abolishing the Sex Work Myth*, London: Palgrave Macmillan, chapter 2.

20 English Collective of Prostitutes (ECP) (1977) 'Supporting Statement by the English Collective of Prostitutes', *LIES: A journal of materialist feminism*, available at liesjournal.net.

21 Ravishly (2014) 'Is Sex Work Empowering Or Enslaving? 12 Experts Weigh In', *Huffington Post*, huffingtonpost.com; Rebel Circus (2017) 'I Became An Escort To Empower Myself, But It Only Crushed My Soul', *Rebel Circus*, rebelcircus.com; Femme Fatale (2015) 'IT HAPPENED TO ME: I Was an Escort for Eight Years, Believing It Would Empower Me, and It Didn't', *xo jane*, xojane.com; Sless, E. (2012) 'Sex worker & mother: "Yes, I AM empowered by my job"', *Mamma M!a*, mamamia.com.

22 Murphy, M. (2011) 'The trouble with choosing your choice', *Feminist Current*, feministcurrent.com.

23 Hatcher, M. (2017) '76% of all inmates end up back in jail within 5 years. Here's how I broke the cycle', *Vox*, vox.com.

24 Object! (@objectUK), Twitter, 5:39am, 3 March 2018.

25 Aroney, E. and Beressi, J. (16 September 2015) 'La Revolte des Prostituees [The Prostitutes' Revolt]', RTBF (Brussels) and Radio France Culture, video, Vimeo (user: In The Dark), vimeo.com/139457788, English transcript at: religiondocbox.com/Atheism_and_Agnosticism/ 75007623-La-revolte-des-prostituees-produced-by-eurydice-aroney-for-rtbf-brussels-and-radio-france-culture.html.

26 Leite, G.S. (1996) 'The prostitute movement in Brazil: Culture and religiosity', *International Review of Mission* 85:338, 417–26.

27 Sex Worker Advocacy and Resistance Movement (SWARM) (15 May 2017) 'Shut Down Yarls Wood', SWARM, swarmcollective.org.

28 Davidson, T. (14 June 2014) 'Toronto sex workers protest new prostitution legislation', *Toronto Sun*, torontosun.com.

29 Black Women for Wages for Housework, 'Money for Prostitutes is Money for Black Women'.

Index